Defiant Brides

Mrs. Margaret (Peggy) Shippen Arnold   *Mrs. Henry Knox*

Defiant Brides

The Untold Story
of Two Revolutionary-Era
Women and the Radical
Men They Married

NANCY RUBIN STUART

BEACON PRESS, BOSTON

Beacon Press
Boston, Massachusetts
www.beacon.org

Beacon Press books
are published under the auspices of
the Unitarian Universalist Association of Congregations.

21 20 19   8 7 6 5 4 3

This book is printed on acid-free paper that meets the uncoated paper
ANSI/NISO specifications for permanence as revised in 1992.

Text design and composition by Kim Arney

Spelling and punctuation modernizations appear in certain quotations
to enhance readability.

Library of Congress Cataloging-in-Publication Data

Rubin Stuart, Nancy.
    Defiant brides : the untold story of two revolutionary-era women and the radical
men they married / Nancy Rubin Stuart.
        p. cm.
    Includes bibliographical references and index.
    ISBN 978-0-8070-3326-5 (paperback : alk. paper)
1. Arnold, Margaret Shippen, 1760-1804. 2. Knox, Lucy Flucker, 1760-1824.
3. Arnold, Benedict, 1741–1801. 4. Knox, Henry, 1750-1806. 5. United States—
History—Revolution, 1775-1783—Biography. I. Title.
    E278.A72R83 2012
    973.3092'52—dc23

                                                    2012027734

A NOTE ON CURRENCY

TO UNDERSTAND CURRENCY VALUES of late-eighteenth-century Colonial America and Great Britain in contemporary terms, I offer the following rough conversion methods: to convert late-eighteenth-century American dollars to contemporary American dollars, multiply the figure by 25; to convert late-eighteenth-century British pounds, multiply the figure by 150. For the former conversion, I relied upon the website *Measuring Worth* and for the latter on *Pounds Sterling to Dollars: Historical Conversion of Currency*, maintained by Eric Nye of the University of Wyoming. Both conversions are approximations since monetary values changed during the years described in *Defiant Brides*.

NRS

CONTENTS

LOVE STORIES FROM EIGHTEENTH-CENTURY America are rare and often fragmented. Fortunately enough of the correspondence of Lucy Flucker Knox (1760–1824) and Margaret (Peggy) Shippen Arnold (1760–1804) has been preserved to trace their controversial marriages and dramatic lives.

Born four years apart to wealthy parents in pre–Revolutionary Boston and Philadelphia, Lucy and Peggy were intelligent, well-educated girls. As each developed into an attractive teenager in the mid-1770s, the political ferment of the American Revolution reached the boiling point. In the midst of that turmoil, both might have married men of their privileged class and led docile, if historically invisible, lives.

Thankfully that did not happen. As the title of this double biography, *Defiant Brides: The Untold Story of Two Revolutionary-Era Women and the Radical Men They Married*, implies both teenagers bucked social convention. One married radical patriot and poor bookseller Henry Knox in 1774; the other wed the then-military hero Benedict Arnold in 1779. Coupled with the young women's fateful marriages was their feistiness. Under different circumstances, Lucy and Peggy might have become friends.

For generations, the books devoted to the Founding Fathers and the Revolution's military leaders have dismissed both women as mere footnotes to history, either as laughable or trivial helpmates married to Knox and Arnold. A close examination of their lives tells quite a different story, revealing Lucy and Peggy as remarkably resilient women who intimately witnessed and participated in the Revolution's turbulent course. The same spirit that impelled the annually pregnant Lucy to follow Henry Knox through the Revolution's army camps also drove her mirror opposite, Peggy, to support Arnold's betrayal of America and subsequently troubled life in England and the loyal colonies in North America later known as Canada.

Superficially Lucy's patriotism seems as commendable as Peggy's treason is condemnable. Yet that is not quite fair. For all our glorification of its origins, the Revolution was not universally supported by the American colonists. An estimated one-third of those living in America's thirteen states in the years following the Battle of Lexington and Concord doubted the wisdom of independence from the mother country. Some citizens remained Loyalists. Others, unnerved by the economic hardships of the war, hedged, declaring themselves neutralists. It was thus natural that as an enamored eighteen-year-old bride, Lucy would side with her husband, Henry Knox, to support the American Revolution. It was equally understandable that the teenaged Peggy Shippen would sympathize with her politically disappointed bridegroom, Benedict Arnold, to betray America to the British.

That twinned blend of youthful defiance and dedication to their men, though a hallmark of adolescent passion in any age, drew me to research the lives of Lucy Flucker Knox and Peggy Shippen Arnold in the context of the American Revolution. At first I suspected that the two women must have met. Arnold, after all, had gallantly escorted Lucy and her toddler from New Haven in late spring 1778 to join her husband in Valley Forge. Eight months later, Henry Knox rode to Philadelphia to meet with Congress. From there he enthusiastically wrote his brother about Arnold's engagement to the wealthy, beautiful, and accomplished Peggy Shippen. Lucy, however, had not accompanied him; then in the last weeks of pregnancy, she had remained in the Knoxes' temporary home near the Middlebrook army camp. As their lives diverged, the two women had no other occasion to meet, although they knew about each other through their husbands. Nor have letters between Lucy and Peggy subsequently been discovered.

Defiant Brides, nevertheless, traces Lucy and Peggy's initially parallel lives, from those as smitten newlyweds to mature wives and mothers. While researching this book I found several frustrating gaps in each of set of their correspondences. Lucy rarely wrote to anyone other than her husband, and then only when separated from him during the war. Today, most of her letters are preserved in archives, especially at the Gilder Lehrman Institute and the Massachusetts Historical Society.

Peggy's correspondence from her youth and the early years of her marriage was lost, a consequence of Shippen's decision to destroy it to protect her from accusations as Arnold's co-conspirator. Fortunately, the Shippen family began saving Peggy's letters after the September 1783 Peace of Paris, which formalized the British surrender. Today the Historical Society of Pennsylvania retains Peggy's correspondence from the last twenty-one years of her life. Many of those letters also appear in Lewis Burd Walker's 1900–1902 series in the *Pennsylvania Magazine of History and Biography.*

During the Revolution, Lucy and Peggy stood on opposite sides of the political schism, one as a staunch patriot, the second as a spy; one in shabby homespun, the other in silken English gowns; one in a log hut, the second in a luxurious townhouse; unwitting counterparts who lived dramatically different lives in the service of connubial love.

As women, their personal evolutions also stand in sharp relief. Subsequent to the Revolution, the exiled Peggy endured hisses and taunts as a suspected accomplice to Arnold's treason; crossed the Atlantic three times; excused her husband's public, often fractious enmities with peers and business associates; and, after his 1801 death, resolutely paid off his debts. During those same years, Lucy's devotion to Knox, her legendary hospitality, the deaths of ten of her children, and her obsession with cards transformed her into a superficially formidable, but ultimately sympathetic, character.

Their attitudes towards their husbands were equally contrasted. Although lamenting her separations from Knox during the war, Lucy refused to be intimidated by his promotions as General George Washington's chief of artillery and brigadier-general of the Continental army. In one of her letters, written during the siege of New York in 1777, she insisted upon having an equal voice in their marriage. Bluntly, she wrote that Knox must not "consider yourself as commander in chief of your own house, but be convinced . . . that there is such a thing as equal command."[1]

In contrast was Peggy's solicitous attitude towards Arnold—"the General," as she referred to him. During the tense days preceding a July 1792 duel in London between the contentious Arnold and the feckless Earl of Lauderdale, the frightened Peggy practiced restraint. To do so, as she later wrote her father, Judge Edward Shippen, in Philadelphia, had required "all my fortitude . . . [to] prevent [me from] . . . sinking under it, which would unman him [Arnold] and prevent his acting himself."[2]

Their marital styles were as significant as their political sensibilities. As the following pages reveal, Lucy, for all her patriotism and personal losses, was a temperamental, often difficult mate; Peggy, a shrewd accomplice to Arnold's treason, endured emotional and financial hardships with genteel restraint. It was my hope that their pairing in *Defiant Brides* would transcend the coincidence of their "defiant" marriages to reveal how lapses in one of them inadvertently highlighted admirable traits in the other.

Is treason or betrayal of others forgivable if the rest of that person's life seems admirable? Do sacrifices for patriotism—or for any other pro-social cause—excuse selfishness or insensitivities towards a loved one? To make such judgments must be left to you.

My goal was to capture the lives of Lucy Flucker Knox and Peggy Shippen Arnold beyond their iconic portraits as patriot and traitor, respectively, and depict them as human beings, as vulnerable, fallible, and praiseworthy as we are today.

PART I

Defiant Brides

1

"The Handsomest Woman in America"

DAWN BROKE GRAY OVER Philadelphia on May 18, 1778, nearly ninth months after thousands of scarlet-coated British soldiers occupied the once-patriotic Revolutionary stronghold. Added to the morning's gloom was the surprise arrival of a committee of scowling Quaker women at Edward Shippen's townhouse on Society Hill. Dressed in somber dresses and bonnets, the Friends minced no words: Judge Shippen must forbid his daughters from appearing that afternoon at the British gala known as the "Mischianza."

Warily, the balding forty-eight-year-old attorney listened to the Quakers' rant about the costumes his teenage daughters would wear—low-cut beaded and bangled gowns, their heads covered in feathered turbans suggestive of a Turkish harem. Those outfits hardly befit the daughters of the distinguished Judge Shippen, the women railed. Their appearance in such risqué outfits would taint the family name, prominent for four generations in Philadelphia society, finance, and politics.

Edward Shippen listened politely, steeled against their lecture, knowing that the Quakers had scolded other parents of daughters selected for the Mischianza. Nor did their warnings about his reputation threaten the judge. The truth was that he had little to lose. Three years earlier, during the first tumultuous months of the Revolution, Philadelphia's radical patriots had eradicated Pennsylvania's Crown-appointed ruling body, the Provincial Council, upon whose upper legislature he sat. Then, on September 26, 1777, the government changed again. That day, General William Howe and his troops marched into the city. Nobody resisted. Within a matter of hours, the British occupied Philadelphia's public buildings, its officers quartered in some of its finest homes while other, more raucous red-coated men gathered in the city streets and squeezed into its taverns.

From Edward Shippen's perspective, predicting the war's outcome seemed as dangerous as the lightning rod invented by his former Junto Club associate, Benjamin Franklin. Given the new political climate, the judge pandered to Philadelphia's latest rulers by inviting them to the drawing room in his home on South Fourth Street. There the officers met the Shippens' pretty daughters and soon invited them to English-style dinners, balls, and plays. After the first dreary years of the war, that seemed only fair. The Shippens' three teenagers, Peggy, Mary, and Sally, had been cheated out of Philadelphia's glittering social life just as they were coming of age.

Had the judge's youngest, seventeen-year-old Peggy, overheard the Quakers' lecture on May 18, she would have scoffed. Since early winter, the petite, gray-eyed blonde had gloried in her role as the toast of the British officers. To her delight, the dashing Captain John André often escorted her to dinners, promenades, and plays. Once, in a teasing flirtation, the trim, dark-haired gallant presented her with a lock of his hair encased in a gold locket.

Another of Peggy's social triumphs was a special invitation from A. S. Hammond, captain of the British flagship, the *H.M. S. Roebuck*, whose men piped Peggy aboard that vessel for dinner and a ball with other well-born young women. So lovely and demure was the Philadelphia belle that Hammond later admitted he and his fellow officers "were all in love with her."[1] Others, like Captain Francis Lord Rawson of the British army, insisted that Peggy was "the handsomest woman" in America.[2] Heady with admiration, Peggy was consequently thrilled when she learned that André—the self-appointed organizer of British galas—had selected her, the youngest of Philadelphia's beauties, for the Mischianza, to be held in honor of General Howe's imminent departure for London.

Ironically, the politics behind that event meant little to the Quakers who confronted Judge Shippen that May morning, for they prided themselves on neutrality. The Friends' apolitical stance had disgusted the patriots, especially those who had served on the second Continental Congress. Among them was Massachusetts delegate John Adams who, in 1777, acidly wrote his wife, Abigail, that the Quakers were "as dull as beetles. From these neither good is to be expected nor evil apprehended. They are a kind of neutral tribe, or race of the insipid."[3]

How seriously Peggy considered the political fallout from her flirtations remains a matter of historical debate. Subsequently, scholars have pointed to the Shippen family's reaction to her behavior as a clue to her loyalties. Why else would the family have destroyed all her letters written during the war? The few descriptions of Peggy from friends and relatives in that era do not reveal which side she favored in the Revolution—the patriots or the Loyalists. At seventeen, that conflict may have seemed less relevant to Peggy than her desire for good times. Those who knew her in 1777 and 1778 simply describe her as an accomplished Philadelphia belle, skilled in needlework, music, drawing, and dancing, and fond of stylish clothes. But beneath those gauzy symbols of feminine charm lurked a sensible young woman. "There was nothing of frivolity either in her dress, demeanor or conduct," recalled a family friend, "and though deservedly admired, she had too much good sense to be vain."[4] Subsequent to the Revolution, the Shippens saved Peggy's letters supporting the opinion that she was intelligent, well-informed, and pragmatic.

A few traces of Peggy's youthful personality are also preserved in sketches by John André. Most famous is one her of that captures her china-doll beauty as she smiled coyly in her Mischianza costume.

By early 1778, Peggy; her sisters, Mary and Sally; and friends like Becky Franks, Peggy Chew, and Becky Redman attended dances hosted by British officers at Philadelphia's exclusive City Tavern, Assembly balls, and plays at André's newly built Southwark Theatre. In winter the belles frolicked with scarlet-coated officers at skating parties and sleigh rides along the Delaware; in spring they appeared on the arms of their British beaux for outings, cricket matches, and horse races.

Little harm would come from allowing their daughters to participate, Judge Shippen and his wife, Margaret Francis, had decided. At the least it provided the girls with diversion, a reward for the dull months they had spent with their parents in the countryside when militant patriots had ruled Philadelphia from 1775 through summer 1777. At best, their daughters' popularity, especially Peggy's, served as social insurance for the judge's family in the event that the British won the Revolution.

Nor were the Shippens alone in their thinking. After the British occupation, while Philadelphia's remaining patriots fumed about flirtations between Colonial women and British officers, one resident rose to the defense of the young women. "Proper allowances," she insisted, must be made for those "in the bloom of life and spirits, after being so long deprived of the gaieties and amusements."[5] Why should Philadelphia's young beauties deny themselves pleasure because of politics—especially since females had no control over the war's outcome? Indeed, by January 1778, the wife of Tory James Allen reported that the city's social life had resumed. "Everything is gay & happy," she wrote her husband, "& it is like to prove a frolicking winter."[6]

Sometimes those frolics bordered on the frenetic. "You can have no idea of the life of continual amusement I live in," Becky Franks, Peggy's witty friend, gloated to Nancy Paca, the wife of a Maryland delegate to the Continental Congress who had fled to York, Pennsylvania. "I scarce have a moment to myself. I have stole this while everybody is retired to dress for dinner. I am but just come from under Mr. J. Black's hands, and most elegantly, as I dressed for a ball this evening at Smith's where we have one every Thursday. You would not know the [ball]room 'tis so much improved."[7]

Not only had the British refurbished the City Tavern and established English-style eating clubs, gaming casinos and theaters, but they had also sparked interest in the latest European clothes and hairstyles. Stylish dress suddenly became an imperative for Philadelphia's young women, an expensive endeavor demanding gossamer gowns and the two-feet-high hairdos then fashionable in England and France. "I mentioned to you the enormous head-dresses of the ladies here," the disapproving New Englander, Thomas Pickering, wrote his wife that spring. "The more I see, the more I am displeased with them. 'Tis surprising how they fix such loads of trumpery [false hair] on their polls."[8]

By late summer, rumors about the approach of the British had prompted thousands of frightened patriots to flee Philadelphia. "Carriages are constantly passing, and the inhabitants going away," Elizabeth Drinker, a Quaker, noted in her diary on September 11, 1777.[9] On the eve of the Continental Congress's flight to York, John Adams wrote Abigail that "more than half of the inhabitants have removed into the country."[10] Even those city residents who stubbornly remained in their homes, observed druggist Christopher Marshall, were "in confusion, of all ranks, sending all their goods out of town into the country."[11]

Finally, on September 26, 1777, at around 10 a.m., Howe's nine thousand soldiers had marched into Philadelphia. "Thus was this large city surrendered to the English without the least opposition whatever, or even firing a single gun," Quaker Sally Logan noted in her diary with awe.[12] Subsequent to the peaceful surrender of Philadelphia (then North America's largest city with forty thousand residents) Howe's soldiers had transformed it into a miniature London, its once-quiet taverns, shops, and inns converted into boisterous places to drink, gamble, flirt, and fornicate. To the war-weary redcoats and their German mercenary peers, the Hessians, Philadelphia was a place to let off steam, a reprieve from war during the long months of winter. "The only hardships I endure are, being obliged to sleep in my bed, to sit down to a very good dinner every day, to take a gentle ride for appetite's sake or to exercise my horses, to gossip in Philadelphia to consider something fashionable to make me irresistible this winter," John André gleefully wrote his sister Louisa in England that November.[13]

Nor did the British fear an American attack. That autumn, George Washington's Second Continental Dragoons had bitterly battled Howe's men in New Jersey until a snowstorm ended the threat. By mid-December British spies reported that the enemy had trudged twenty-five miles northwest of Philadelphia, its soldiers, ill, ragged, starved, and shoeless, leaving bloody footprints in the snow en route to a hilly hamlet called Valley Forge.

Why, then, mused the indolent General Howe, should he bother risking the lives of his troops?

Privately, critics whispered that Howe's fondness for high living—heavy drinking, revelry, and long hours with his beautiful, blonde mistress Elizabeth Loring, the wife of an obliging Boston Loyalist—set a bad example for his soldiers. A popular ditty reflected his dissolute image:

Sir, William, he, snug as flea
Lay all this time a-snoring
Nor dreamed of harm, as he lay warm
In bed with Mrs. _____ [14]

By early winter 1778, an atmosphere of frivolity and licentiousness dominated the once-dour Quaker City of Brotherly Love. Rumor had it that the costly imported silks and satins many young women suddenly sported were purchased "at the expense of their virtue" for "it is agreed on all hands that the British played the devil with the girls."[15] Sarah Logan, whose Quaker family had fled to Germantown, also reported in her diary "very bad accounts of the licentiousness of the English officers in deluding young girls."[16] Not everyone fell victim; especially the city's most affluent young women, whose mothers had stockpiled imported fabrics years earlier.

Still, few women could avoid noticing the bawdy behavior of the British. Becky Franks once confided such an incident to the Shippen sisters. After several officers courteously greeted her on the street, they walked down the road a few steps and entered the home of the notorious Mrs. McKoy, a woman "well known to the gentlemen." Outraged, Becky added, "And don't you think Grif and Laow had the impudence to go in while I was looking right at them. I never was so angry in my life. I never think of it, but I feel my face glow with rage."[17]

Far more disturbing to John André than his peers' sexual exploits was General Howe's decision to return to England. Regardless of his personal decadence, Howe had triumphed at the battles of Long Island, Brandywine Creek, and Germantown, and had earned admiration from his men.

"I do not believe there is upon record an instance of a Commander in Chief having so universally endeared himself to those under his command; or . . . who received such signal and flattering proof of their love," André wrote a friend in England. To demonstrate their devotion, they decided to "give [Howe] as splendid an entertainment as the shortness of the time and our present situation, would allow."[18] To accomplish that André and twenty-two other officers contributed over £3,000 for what that gallant dubbed the "Mischianza," an Italian term meaning a medley or "composition of several parts."

By the afternoon of the appointed day, May 18, the sun broke through the clouds as if in honor of André's "splendid entertainment." Philadelphia was decked out to commemorate the celebration. Ships, docked at the wharves of the Delaware flew colorful maritime flags. Banners and bunting embellished riverside homes and buildings. At four o'clock throngs of spectators gazed from the shore at the British regatta at full mast, festooned with bunting, flags, and streamers as it tacked towards patriot Joseph Wharton's abandoned estate to the strains of "God Save the King" wafting from a barge.

At the center of the regatta sailed the battleship *Hussar*, its flags flying in honor of General Howe, who was accompanied by his brooding replacement, Sir Henry Clinton. Trailing the *Hussar* was the *Cornwallis* carrying sixty-year-old General Wilhelm von Knyphausen, commander of the Hessians. At the vessels' approach to Walnut Grove, seventeen-gun salutes from the *Vigilant* and *Cornwallis* boomed across Wharton's sweeping lawn. By 6 p.m. the Mischianza's 423 guests, among them Philadelphia's neutralists and Loyalists, crossed the lawn to a playing field.

There, colorful, medieval-style tents stood in front of rows of risers, before which sat two groups of seven women in gauzy Turkish dress, representing the Saracens conquered by the crusaders in Palestine centuries before. Among them, according to André's published account, was Peggy Shippen, one of the fourteen women chosen who "excel in wit, beauty and every accomplishment, those of the *whole World*" (italics in original).[19]

A flourish of trumpets announced the start of the joust between two groups of knights. The first, announced by the clatter of gray horses, carried the seven "Knights of the Blended Rose," clothed in red and white silk. They were immediately followed by seven "Knights of the Burning Mountain," clad in black and orange. Clanging lances and clashing swords shattered the air through four rounds of the tournament, culminating in a match between the knights' two leaders. Suddenly the Marshall of the Field appeared, declaring the tournament a tie and the beauty of the ladies a draw. As the dusty field cleared, the Turkish women paraded into the Wharton mansion, where knights bent in homage to them before admiring crowds. Afterwards, the knights, ladies, and hundreds of guests entered a ballroom embellished with artificial flowers that glowed in the reflected light from eighty-five tall mirrors and countless candles.

"The ball was opened by the Knights and their ladies; and the dances continued till ten o'clock," André recalled in his report in London's *Gentleman's Magazine*.[20] After fireworks, and a supper, a ball recommenced, lasting until dawn.

More than two centuries since that night, Peggy's attendance at the Mischianza has intrigued scholars. Seemingly trivial compared to the horrors of war, Peggy's appearance has been posited as one more bit of evidence that she helped betray the American cause. Historians who doubted her presence cite a truncated account of the Mischianza that André penned for his sweetheart, Peggy Chew, which tactfully omitted a mention of her social rival, Peggy Shippen. Other scholars, however, point to Peggy Shippen's presence at the gala as described in André's long letter of May 23 to a British friend, which subsequently appeared in *Gentleman's Magazine*. It read: "Peggy— M. Shippen—had been paired with the sixth Knight of the Blended Rose, "Lieut. Sloper, in honour of Mlls. M. Shippen—Squire, Lieutenant Brown—Device, a Heart and Sword; Motto, Honour and the Fair."[21]

Another explanation for Peggy's presence was the likely consequence if Judge Shippen had forbidden her attendance at the Mischianza. Had he done so, family lore insists Peggy would have wept and howled, refusing food and drink until, utterly exhausted, she took to her bed for days. Whenever refused, Peggy reverted to that sort of behavior. High-strung, spirited and wily, Peggy, according to a family friend, consequently managed to get her way, both as the youngest of the Shippen girls and the "darling of the family circle."[22]

In spite of her willfulness, Peggy became Edward's favorite, perhaps as that friend suggested, because she always "made his comfort her leading thought."[23] From girlhood, Peggy had commanded the judge's attentions. Not only had he shared the writings of Pope, Defoe, Addison, Steele, and other commentators with her, but he also encouraged her to read newspapers and political tracts. As his intellectually gifted daughter matured, the judge taught Peggy about foreign trade, investments, accounting, and bookkeeping. Later, Peggy also observed Judge Shippen fuming over Thomas Paine's 1776 *Common Sense*, which called for independence from Great Britain.

Shrewdly, Peggy's father reminded her that when it came to politics, remaining silent was safer than arousing public scorn for one's opinions. By late 1776, the patriots suspected Judge Shippen of being a Loyalist. To avoid persecution, he moved his family out of Philadelphia to an obscure farm in Amwell, New Jersey. There, in lieu of formal teas with doting elders, tittering matrons, and fawning beaux, the Shippen daughters—teenagers Mary, Sarah, and Peggy, and their twenty-year-old sister Elizabeth, or Betsy—learned about cows, chickens, and crops. Late that year, when the Shippens briefly returned to Philadelphia, Pennsylvania's patriotic authorities, the militant Supreme Executive Council, accused Judge Shippen of being a spy. Placed on parole and forbidden to live more than six miles from Philadelphia, Peggy's father again hustled his family out of town, this time to nearby Schuylkill Falls. "The scarcity and advance price of every necessary of life makes it extremely difficult for those who have large families, and no share in the present measures to carry through . . . nothing but the strictest frugality will enable us to do it," the unemployed judge wrote his own father from Schuylkill Falls. There, fortunately, "the wants of our nature are easily supplied, and the rest is but folly and care."[24]

Not, however, according to his teenage daughters, who sorely missed the "folly" of Philadelphia's social life. Fearing that their former lifestyle was ruined, the Shippens' eldest daughter, Betsy, wrote her cousin Sarah Yeates in June 1777, "I sincerely . . . [hope] the good times to return, but we must make ourselves as happy as we can till that is the case. . . . I am determined not to suffer myself to be low spirited, as I think it probable we shall have many frights before the summer is over."[25]

By September 26, one of those "frights" would be Howe's invasion of Philadelphia. Worried that the British would plunder his vacated townhouse, Judge Shippen immediately brought his wife and children back to the city. Self-protection rather than political loyalties now became Edward Shippen's priority, leading him to hobnob with the British. Peggy, Sally, and Mary were thrilled. Little did it matter that the redcoats had slaughtered hundreds of Americans on the Brandywine, in Paoli, and in nearby Germantown. To the teenage Shippen girls, the social whirl created by Howe's young, handsome, and urbane British officers was a perfect antidote to the dull months they had spent in the country.

Who, after all, was to say, what was the "right side" of the war, especially after the turmoil, the food shortages, and scarcity of luxuries? Perhaps it would be best for the colonies to return to British rule—or so the girls often overheard their father debate with his Loyalists friends, the Chews, Franks, and Galloways. Like other Revolutionary-era families, the Shippens were politically divided. Peggy's uncle, Dr. William Shippen, was director general of Military Hospitals for the Revolutionary army and spent that winter at Valley Forge. Dr. Shippen's cousin, Mary Willing, and her husband, Colonel William Byrd, or Burd, were also patriots. So, too were Dr. Shippen's brothers-in-law, Richard Henry Lee and Francis Lightfoot Lee, signers of the Declaration of Independence. One of their cousins, Captain Henry "Lighthorse" Lee, became a hero of the Continental army.

Earlier friendships with men who later supported the Revolution further obscured the judge's true political stance. On September 28, 1774, he had hosted George Washington for dinner. Peggy, then fourteen years old, had attended and was fascinated by the dignified Virginian. Decades later, learning about Washington's December 1799 death, she wrote her sister Betsy, "Nobody in America could revere his character more than I did."[26]

Nor would Washington forget his earlier friendship with the Shippens. During the winter of 1776, Peggy's brother Edward V., or Neddy, rashly joined the British army and was captured by the patriots. Ultimately, Washington declared that Judge Shippen's son had "taken no commission nor done any act that showed him inimical [and] very kindly discharged him."[27]

British officers, too, sometimes inadvertently forged friendships with the enemy. Among these was Peggy's friend John André. On November 2, 1775, during General Richard Montgomery's conquest of Fort Saint John, which protected British-held Montreal, twenty-five-year-old André was captured at Lake Champlain and slated to be transported south to Pennsylvania. One stormy December night, the patriots ordered André into a tiny cabin he was to share with one of their peers. His gregarious, rotund companion was Henry Knox, traveling incognito on his way to Fort Ticonderoga. Finding much in common the two young men spent the night talking and regretfully parted the next morning. Only later did André and Knox realize each other's political affiliation, never suspecting they would meet again under very different circumstances.

By May 1778, that same charismatic André had been released from captivity and had become the chief organizer of British entertainments in Philadelphia. A fierce soldier on the battlefield, the lean twenty-eight year old also inspired admiration from fellow officers because of his fine character, creativity, and wit, a man as comfortable behind a musket as he was dancing a minuet. According to one American observer, the Geneva-educated André "conversed freely on the belles lettres: music, painting, and poetry."[28] Although novelists later interpreted his gift to Peggy of a gold locket containing strands of his hair as proof of a romantic attachment, contemporary historians believe André was simply a friend. His widely acknowledged sweetheart was a pretty brunette, Peggy Chew, daughter of another prominent but decidedly Loyalist judge, Benjamin Chew.

As her courtly beau, André penned love poems to Peggy Chew but with equal verve also wrote ditties about and sketched portraits of others in their social circle. On one occasion he created fashionable silhouettes of himself and Philadelphia belle Becky Redman. On another he drew a slightly caricatured portrait of Peggy Shippen with high-rolled hair and wearing her Mischianza turban and costume.

← →

The committee of Quakers who visited Judge Shippen on May 18 were not the only ones who disapproved of the Mischianza. In England, the *London Chronicle* complained that the time, effort, and money spent upon those festivities were "nauseous."[29] To an aging British major, the Mischianza was a "piece of tomfoolery."[30] Several months after Howe's return to London, a jeering pamphlet appeared entitled "Strictures Upon the Philadelphia Meschianza [*sic*], or the Triumph of Leaving America Unconquered." In Philadelphia, Elizabeth Drinker, famously scrawled in her diary, "This day may be remembered by man for the scenes of folly and vanity. . . . How insensible do these people appear, while our land is so greatly desolated and death and sore destruction has overtaken and impends over so many."[31] To eighteenth-century historian Charles Stedman the festivities for General Howe "rivaled the magnificent exhibitions of that vain-glorious monarch and conqueror, Louis XIV of France."[32]

During the Mischianza, the Continental army also sneered at the festivities. While guests at Wharton's estate enjoyed a midnight dinner, the British fortifications near Germantown suddenly exploded into flames. Under cover of night, the Marquis de Lafayette and his men had poured kettles of whale oil onto the British barriers, ignited them, and then deftly slipped away.

Stunned, Howe had ordered his officers to the burning fortifications, simultaneously assuring nervous guests that the racket emanated from the gala's fireworks. Regardless of that embarrassment, André's subsequent letter to the *Gentleman's Magazine* defended the Mischianza as a monumental symbol of the army's allegiance to Howe. The event, he insisted, was "one of the most splendid entertainments, I believe, ever given by an army to their General. But what must be most grateful to Sir W. Howe is the spirit and motives from which it was given."[33]

Implicitly, André had orchestrated the Mischianza as a rebuke to Lord George Germain, secretary of state for North America, who had ignored Howe's repeated requests for reinforcements. Without them, Howe had threatened, he would resign. They never arrived. After months of waiting, the disgusted general departed for London on May 24 to defend his role in the American campaign, leaving his querulous subordinate, Sir Henry Clinton, in his place.

For weeks before Howe's departure, Philadelphians wondered about the future of the British in their city. On May 6, as they woke to the thunder of cannons from the direction of Valley Forge, their anxieties increased. That evening, fireworks blazed through the sky from the patriots' army camp as Washington's men celebrated the French alliance of early 1778. Exuberantly, the *Pennsylvania Packet* reported that "the martial appearances of the troops conspired to exhibit a magnificent scene of joy, worthy of great occasion."[34]

Within another week Philadelphia buzzed about the actions of their British rulers. "There is some movement in the army which we do not understand. The heavy cannon are ordered on board the Ships, and some other things look very mysterious," Elizabeth Drinker noted on May 13.[35] By early June, rumors abounded that the redcoats were preparing to evacuate Philadelphia. Still, the British lingered. "I sincerely wish'd it might be true, but was afraid to flatter myself," sixteen-year-old Sally Wister, a Quaker living in nearby Germantown, confided to her journal. "I had heard it so often that I was quite faithless."[36]

On June 7, Peggy's uncle, Dr. William Shippen, wrote his fourteen-year-old daughter Nancy, "The enemy are preparing to leave Philadelphia and 'tis thought here they will go tomorrow."[37]

The delay had to do with General Clinton's uncertainty about his order by George III to send five thousand men to defend the West Indies against the French. "As my army would be much weakened by these detachments, I was commanded to evacuate Philadelphia and proceed by sea with the remaining troops and stores to New York," General Clinton explained in his subsequent narrative on his North American campaigns.[38] By dawn on June 18, 1778, Clinton and nine thousand British soldiers had evacuated Philadelphia. With them fled thousands of Loyalists.

New waves of disappointment swept over Peggy and her sisters. From bitter experience, they knew that the officers of the Continental army were unlikely to be as "witty or charming" as the British had been.[39] Already the rumor mills churned out news that the city would be governed by General Benedict Arnold, a hero of the Continental army, whose bravery during the 1777 Battle of Saratoga Springs had contributed to General John Burgoyne's defeat.

On May 20, the crippled general arrived at Valley Forge in a carriage. Surrounded by cheering soldiers, Arnold, the swarthy, blue-eyed "Eagle of Saratoga," stiffly climbed out of the coach and stood unsteadily on his feet, leaning on a crutch.

Less public was the arrival of the woman he had escorted from New Haven, an attractive, high-colored brunette, Lucy Flucker Knox, and her toddler. Rushing to her side was Henry Knox, Washington's young chief of artillery, who folded his wife into his fleshy arms. The couple "appear to be extravagantly fond of each other, and I think are perfectly happy," their friend Nathanael Green wrote in apparent envy.[40]

Temporarily at least, thoughts of war were dispelled by those of love. Before long, that timeless knot would entwine General Arnold and "the handsomest woman" in America in a union whose intrigues remain controversial.

2

"The Best and Tenderest of Friends"

FROM THAT MOMENT IN late August 1773 when sixteen-year-old Lucy Flucker first saw Henry Knox, she was smitten. The tall, "uncommonly good-looking officer" was drilling on horseback with the Boston Grenadier Corps, a local militia.[1] Adding to Lucy's curiosity was a black silk cloth wrapped around the officer's left hand. "Lieutenant Knox appeared with a wound handsomely bandaged with a scarf which, of course, excited the sympathy of all the ladies," recalled a fellow militiaman. That scarf concealed a raw red scar from a recent gun accident that had blown away Knox's two smallest fingers.

Intrigued, Lucy visited Knox at his bookstore in Cornhill, Boston's printing district, whose streets echoed with the clatter of churning presses. Within two years of its 1771 establishment, Knox's New London Bookstore became a popular meeting place, attracting clients like engraver Paul Revere, Rhode Island blacksmith Nathanael Greene, and attorney John Adams. One reason for its attraction, Adams recalled, was Knox's "pleasing manners and inquisitive turn of mind"—an opinion that others confirmed throughout Knox's life.[2] Another admirer, the French major general Francois Jean Beauvoir, Marquis de Chastellux, described Knox as "a man of understanding, a well formed man, gay, sincere and honest. It is impossible to know, without esteeming him, or to see without loving him."[3]

Lucy sensed that from the start. Warming to his congenial personality and erudite knowledge, the bookish teenager immediately fell in love. Knox was equally enamored with the spirited and stunning brunette. Often, he

Henry Knox

was so distracted by Lucy's snapping dark eyes, high color, and voluptuous curves that he fumbled making change for his clients. By late winter, the couple had decided to wed.

"Every particle of heat seems to be eradicated from the head or else entirely absorbed, in the widely ranging fire emitted from the heart," Knox penned on March 7. "To tell you how much I long to see you would be impossible—do my good girl let me hear from you some way or other." Although Lucy's parents disapproved, the twenty-four-year-old bookseller persisted in his courtship. "What news?" he asked. "Have you spoken to your father or he to you upon the subject?"[4]

When Lucy broke news of her engagement to the Fluckers, they exploded. Little did it matter that Henry was ambitious or had once attended Boston Latin School. To the Fluckers, he was ordinary. Lucy disagreed. Henry's father, William, a comfortable shipmaster, had died suddenly in 1762, plunging the family into poverty and forcing twelve-year-old Henry to leave school. After his apprenticeship with a printer, Henry supported his widowed mother and younger brother, William. The Fluckers were not impressed. Knox was common, they sniffed, a "man in trade," inappropriate as Lucy's husband.

Her father, Thomas Flucker, was the Crown-appointed secretary of the province of Massachusetts. Her mother, a Waldo, was an heiress to vast tracts of land in the district of Maine. If Lucy insisted upon marrying Knox, they predicted, she would "eat the bread of poverty and dependence," while her married sister, Hannah Flucker Urquart, rode through the streets in a fine carriage.[5]

Added to the Fluckers' objections were Knox's radical politics. Though the British had imposed harsh taxes upon the colonists and sent soldiers to patrol Boston that had been done to restore peace. Could not Lucy understand that everything she enjoyed—the Fluckers' Summer Street townhouse, fine clothes, imported household goods, servants—came from her father's Crown appointments? To Lucy that was not important. "My mother," her eldest daughter explained decades later, "claimed the privilege of thinking for herself on a subject so deeply involving her own happiness."[6]

Interestingly, Lucy's own mother, the beautiful Hannah Waldo, had also defied convention in her youth. In 1751, several days before her long-planned wedding to one Andrew Pepperrell, Hannah spurned him. Six weeks later, she married Lucy's father, Thomas Flucker, a widower whose "natural" or illegitimate daughter, Sallie, later lived with the family. Even so, the Fluckers opposed Lucy's decision. Ultimately they "gave a half-reluctant consent" but "refused to sanction [the marriage] by their presence."[7] On June 16, 1774, six weeks before her eighteenth birthday, Lucy defiantly married Henry Knox at Boston's King's Chapel.

"Be pleased to accept my sincere compliments of felicitation on your late auspicious nuptials with a lady famed for every female excellence," Knox's friend John Murray later wrote. "May that event be productive to you both of all the happiness your hearts can wish."[8]

No such congratulations arrived from Thomas and Hannah Flucker, who left town on Lucy's wedding day. Only two members of the Flucker family attended the ceremony: Lucy's sister Hannah and half-sister Sallie. Nearly a year later, Lucy's brother, Thomas, a British soldier, sent his wishes from Antigua. Radiant with happiness, the bride paid no attention to snubs or the wagging tongues of Boston's wealthy Loyalists. What mattered most—and would throughout Lucy's life—was her marriage to the "best and tenderest of friends," whom she called "her Harry."[9]

Relations between the newlyweds and the Fluckers remained tense and after the April 19, 1775, violence at Lexington and Concord, quickly deteriorated. By then, the Fluckers' friend, General Thomas Gage, commander of the British forces in America, pressed Knox to support the Crown. When the young man refused, Gage threatened arrest if he bolted from the city.

The Knoxes refused to be bullied. Wielding her needle, Lucy stitched Henry's militia sword into her cape. One moonless night, they slipped out of Boston and galloped to the headquarters of the Continental army in Cambridge.

Once Henry enlisted, Lucy moved into a crowded house in Watertown, a few miles from the army camp at Cambridge. From there the teenager wrote to her family, especially to her mother and sister. But no letters arrived in return. The blood spilled at Lexington and Concord had ruptured her ties to the

Fluckers. Years later, Lucy rebuked her sister Hannah for "the great neglect with which I have been treated both by you and my dear mamma."[10]

Henry wrestled with different frustrations. With little time to pack his bookstore manuals on artillery and fortifications he had to rely upon his memory to erect fortifications at Roxbury. Fortunately, Knox was a brilliant man. His intelligence, as Continental army surgeon Dr. James Thacher observed with wry understatement, was "not of the ordinary class."[11]

By early June, Knox insisted that Lucy leave Watertown for the safer western Massachusetts town of Worcester, thirty-five miles from Cambridge. Reluctantly, she complied. Whenever separated from Knox, Lucy slumped, feeling alone and invisible. She wrote Knox that he was "always in my thoughts, whose image is deeply imprinted on my heart." In a rare moment of self-awareness, the young woman even understood that her dependence was probably unhealthy. Henry, she declared, was a man "whom I love too much for my peace."[12] Nevertheless, Lucy continued to cling desperately to Knox, her one anchor in the churning tides of the Revolution.

Knox was equally attached to Lucy. Having served as caretaker for his widowed mother and younger brother, he continued that role after marriage even in the face of war. "I wish to render my devoted country every service in my power," Henry later explained to his wife. His only objection was that it "separates me from thee, the dear object of all my earthly happiness."[13]

The first sign of Knox's prospects as a warrior began on July 6, 1775, when the newly appointed general George Washington toured Knox's fortifications at Roxbury with General Charles Lee. Knox proudly wrote Lucy of the "pleasure and surprise" the two generals expressed over the fortifications he had built from memory.[14] That same letter expressed his excitement—his "pleasure," as he put it—to see Lucy the following week in Worcester.[15] There, Lucy had her own "pleasure" to share with Henry— news that she was pregnant.

Though impressed with Knox's engineering talent, Washington thought the twenty-four year old too young to assume responsibility for creation of the Continental army's artillery corps. To that, Knox retorted in his deep voice, "I am growing older every day."[16] John Adams also urged Knox's commission. The former bookseller, Adams wrote James Warren, speaker of the Provincial Congress and paymaster general of the Continental army, should not be overlooked for he was one of those "young gentlemen of education and accomplishment . . . [who] might become in time and with experience able officers."[17]

In an effort to understand more about Knox's potential, Washington invited him to dine with him and his generals. By September 22, the commander in chief also asked Knox and Lucy to a private meal at his Cambridge home and headquarters, the John Vassal House. Little is known about that dinner, but from the fond friendship that developed between Washington and the Knoxes, it seems Lucy's wit and spirit charmed the reticent Virginian as much as Henry's skills had impressed him. In October, Washington appointed Knox a colonel of the Continental army.

Coincidentally, Congress had just authorized Washington to seize the cannons the British had abandoned at Fort Ticonderoga, New York, the previous spring. Looming over the narrow straits of Lake Champlain at its juncture with Lake George, the stone garrison protected the waterways of America's northern borders.

Ticonderoga was "the key of this extensive country," as Benedict Arnold had warned Congress the previous May after his victory there over the British. To abandon that fort would be foolhardy, leaving "a very extensive frontier open to the ravages of the enemy."[18] For months Congress had ignored Arnold's advice, but finally, after they allowed Washington to seize its guns, the commander in chief assigned that task to Knox.

In Worcester, ignorant of that assignment, Lucy waited vainly for Henry's arrival on a blustery November 15. The next day his letter arrived, blaming his delay on bad weather. Within it was startling news: "Keep up your spirits, my dear girl. I shall be with you tomorrow night." Knox added, "Don't be alarmed when I tell you the general [Washington] has ordered me to go to the westward as far as Ticonderoga, about a three week's journey. Don't be afraid. There is no fighting. . . . I am going upon business only."[19]

The news terrified Lucy. Alone and pregnant, Lucy feared Knox might perish in the northern wilderness. Would she and their unborn child ever see him again? If not, what would become of her? Their reunion could only have been stormy, with Lucy sobbing and Henry defending his promise to fulfill Washington's orders. Later that month, writing from New York City before sailing north on the Hudson, Henry attempted to appease his distraught wife. "Her Harry was and is all anxious for her safety," he wrote. "Keep up your spirits, my Lucy. Preserve your health by every means in your power for the sake of the youth who values you above all earthly blessings."[20]

A day later, that "youth" arrived at the southern tip of Lake George and lodged in a tiny cabin. His roommate was a congenial British prisoner, Captain John André. Neither man could have suspected that their paths would cross again.

The paths to and from Ticonderoga were equally unpredictable. The "three weeks journey" Knox had originally announced to Lucy became fifty-eight days that were plagued with bad weather. Anguished by their separation, he wrote on January 5, "Those people who love as you and I do never ought to part. It is with the greatest anxiety that I am forced to date my letter at this distance from my love. . . . My Lucy is perpetually in my mind, constantly in my heart."[21]

Two hundred miles north thirty-five-year-old Benedict Arnold lay in a military hospital, his leg shattered at the disastrous Battle of Quebec. Among his sorrows was the recent death of his heroic fellow commander, General Richard Montgomery, and that of his thirty-year-old wife, Margaret Mansfield, the previous June.

On a chilly, snow-packed January 24, 1776, Knox cheerfully arrived at Washington's headquarters in Cambridge with the first of Ticonderoga's forty-three cannons and sixteen heavy guns. The rest of the artillery, he explained to the beaming commander in chief, was on its way from Framingham, being pulled on sleds by 1,600 oxen. As Knox reached western Massachusetts, messengers rode ahead with the news and attracted crowds along the Boston Post Road. Among the onlookers were John Adams and Elbridge Gerry, who were then returning from Congress to Boston. Awed, the two delegates stared at the large guns—some eleven feet long. Adams later listed them in his diary as "9 eighteen pounders, 10 twelves, 6 four to nine pounders, 3 thirteen-inch mortars."[22]

In celebration, Washington and his kindly wife, Martha, invited the Knoxes to their Cambridge home. "The General and Mrs. Washington, present their compliments to Col. Knox & Lady, begs the favor of their company at dinner, on Friday half after 2 o'clock," read their invitation.[23] If Lucy's pregnant belly and Knox's 250-pound girth surprised Martha, so did the couple's wit, brains, and charm. By the end of that meal, Lucy had endeared herself to the future First Lady, forging a friendship that would last throughout their lives.

Three weeks later, on an icy February 25, Knox asked an unusual favor from his fellow militia friend Henry Burbeck. Could he position several cannons at Lechmere Point? "These things I should have done myself," Knox explained, "but Mrs. Knox, being exceedingly ill, prevents my leaving of her."[24] In eighteenth-century parlance, the words "exceedingly ill" often referred to childbirth. The next day Lucy delivered a daughter she and Knox named Lucy.

After returning to military duty, Knox ordered twenty cannons placed at Dorchester Heights in southern Boston and concealed under a series of hay-covered fortifications. At dawn on March 4, when General Howe peered through his spyglass at Dorchester Heights, he paled at the sight of Ticonderoga's guns. Behind them filed three thousand Continental soldiers. "My God, these follows have done more work in one night than I could make my army do in three months!" the British general gasped.[25] As he summoned the British for an attack, a thick fog rolled into Boston Harbor followed by howling winds and pounding rain, destroying all hopes for a counterattack. At dawn two days later, on March 6, the discouraged Howe decided to evacuate Boston.

Lucy was ecstatic. Not only had she borne a healthy infant—no easy endeavor in eighteenth-century America—but "her Harry" had become a hero. For a brief few days, life seemed "the very pink of perfection,"[26] as contemporary British writer Oliver Goldsmith had put it. Then, just as suddenly, on March 17, Lucy's life darkened after she learned that the

Fluckers had sailed with the British without a letter of farewell. Soon afterwards, Washington ordered the army to leave Boston. Inevitably that included "her Harry." By April 3, Knox and his artillery corps dutifully marched south towards New York City, the anticipated site of the next British attack. By then, nearly all of Lucy's frightened Tory friends had either scattered or sailed with the British. Lucy's one dependable relative was her brother-in-law, William, who was overwhelmed by the British plunder of Knox's New London Bookstore.

Boston lay in shambles. During the winter months, shivering redcoats had chopped down trees in the Common and ripped apart old buildings for firewood. The Flucker mansion had been looted. Other homes and shops were abandoned, crumbling, ruinous reminders of Boston's pre-Revolutionary splendor. Many of the remaining residents, once trapped in the city under Howe's martial grip, were sickly, malnourished, or dying from epidemics sweeping through Boston.

"Is my Harry well?" Lucy solicitously wrote her husband from Boston. Self-pityingly she then scrawled, "No, that cannot be when he reflects how wretched he has left me. . . . The remembrance of his tender infant must also affect him when he considers it at so great a distance from its father . . . in a place exposed to an enraged enemy."[27]

Contrary to Washington's expectations, that "enraged enemy" had yet to appear in New York. After weeks of waiting, Lucy grew impatient. She saw no reason to avoid joining Henry, especially since wives of other officers had planned trips to New York. "Mrs. Greene and Mrs. Morgan set out on Sunday next," Lucy wrote. "They fully expected me to have gone with them. What is the reason I am not as happy as they . . . loved as well."[28]

Her letter hit the mark, piercing Knox as keenly as a British bayonet. "Although father, mother, sister, and brother have forsaken you, yet my love, your Harry will ever esteem you the best boon of heaven," he replied.[29]

Still, his words were merely paper and ink—not the flesh-and-blood man who would hold her in his arms, dispel her fears, whisper reassurances in the dark of the night. By early June, Lucy had packed the family trunks, bundled up her infant, braved a bumpy carriage ride, and arrived in New York. Reunited with Knox in his Broadway home near Bowling

Green, Lucy happily hosted dinners for his colleagues. Intrigued with the port city of twenty thousand, she and Caty Greene toured its streets, shops, and piers. Often, too, they gaped at the sight of the city's drunks and prostitutes, as well as the "Tory rides" in which tarred-and-feathered Loyalists were paraded through the streets on rails.

One day the Knoxes visited their friends, the Greenes in Brooklyn; on another they dined with the Washingtons in Richmond Hill. But her visit, Knox continually reminded Lucy, was not safe. A British attack was imminent. It was prudent for her and the baby to leave. To that Lucy paid no mind—until the memorable morning of June 29. As she and Henry ate breakfast at their home overlooking New York harbor, an ominous fleet of white sails appeared over the horizon. The British had arrived.

"You can scarcely conceive the distress and anxiety that she [Lucy] then had," Knox wrote his brother William. The city was in an uproar. "Guns firing, the troops to their posts and every thing . . . bustle." Worst of all, Knox had no time to calm Lucy, for "my country calls loudest." Anguished, he added, "My God, may I never experience the like feelings again. They were too much." In the press of his duties, Knox admitted that he "scolded like a fury at her [Lucy] for not having gone before."[30]

Stung by "her Harry's" outburst, Lucy left for Fairfield, Connecticut. Accompanying her were Caty Greene and Mary Johnson Pollard, whose husband was Knox's quartermaster. Both women, Knox confided to William, were ill-suited companions for the vulnerable Lucy. Nathanael Greene's wife, Caty, was moody, a vain, flighty woman who flirted with the army's handsome young officers. Mary had a "melancholy dumpish disposition ... a very unfit companion."[31] Worried that the British would seize the coastal towns near New York, Knox begged Lucy to travel further east, to New Haven. And, he added, she should ignore any other army wives whose husbands, like one named Palfrey, encouraged them to return to New York, who selfishly wanted "to see her because she is a woman."[32]

Lucy moved further east. "I will go to New Haven, indeed I will," she penned from Stamford, Connecticut, in early July, "but first must beg your patience to read this, which I think will show that I am not deserving of the severe censure that I have received. You may remember I left my Harry in a state of mind, that prevented . . . a word to him of the tender kind. . . . This induced me to stay a little time as near as possible, in hopes by some smile of Providence I might be favored with a more affectionate parting."[33]

Especially irksome was Henry's habit "to remind me of my incapacity of judging for myself. I now assure you that I have [a] sense of my own weakness and ignorance and a very high opinion of the abilities of him in whose eyes mine are so contemptible. I am afraid you do not bestow the time to read my scrawls with any attention."[34]

On July 18, after a week of silence, she received Knox's reply. "I am grieved and distraught by receipt of your letter," he began, insisting that he had asked her to leave New York City out of "the most disinterested friendship cemented by the tenderest love."[35]

Relieved by his reassurances of affection, Lucy replied, "I have just received my dear Harry's letter. . . . It gives me great pleasure, that admidst the hurry of pubic business he steals so much time for me. If I wanted proof of his affection this would be sufficient, but thank heaven, that is not the case." Apologetically, Lucy added, "It grieves me that I have ever professed what has given you pain but I [am] sure you will forget, and forgive when you reflect, that my affection for my dear Harry led me into the error."[36]

Paradoxically, the Revolution also created marital tensions for Lucy's parents. Through Tories who had remained in Boston, William Knox heard about the Fluckers' flight from their home and relayed the news to Lucy and Henry. Lucy's father had sailed on the first ship to England. Her mother and sister landed instead in Halifax, Nova Scotia, where they shared a small room in a rented house. From London, Thomas Flucker had invited his wife to join him "if she pleases," suggesting a previous disagreement. Hannah had refused. An argument had apparently ensued. "Thomas won't say whether he wishes her to come or not." William wrote Lucy. Her mother, Hannah, "intends tarrying at Halifax till he comes to her."[37]

The news distressed Lucy. "My heart aches for her [Hannah], as I fear she is in great want of ready money" she wrote her husband.[38] From a Waldo relative she also learned that the British government still paid her father a handsome salary. "Pappa enjoys his 300 pounds a year as Secretary of the Province. Droll, is it not?" she wrote Henry.[39]

More immediately disquieting were reports from Knox about the influx of redcoats and Hessians in New York. From Wallingford, Connecticut, where she and Mary Pollard lived in a borrowed house, Lucy sent Knox fresh clothes. Then, to sate his enormous appetite, she dispatched supplies of cheese and poultry. Knowing the army needed more gunpowder, Lucy dutifully visited the saltpeter mills of nearby New Haven and dispatched samples to Henry.

By then, outbreaks of smallpox in the army prevented thoughts of Lucy's return to New York. Immunity developed one of two ways: from contraction of the disease or inoculation with the live virus. The latter, known as a "variolation," was nearly as dangerous as the illness itself, producing high fevers, pustules, and, occasionally, death. "I wish my dear girl and her babe to be eased of that dread," Knox wrote. It would be best if she returned to Boston where her brother-in-law, William, would arrange the variolation. After that Lucy could visit him in the army camp "at any time you see proper and it shall be thought prudent so to do."[40]

Fate decreed otherwise. By autumn 1776 Washington's army had suffered a string of defeats in New York City, Harlem Heights, and White Plains. Added to Knox's dismay was Lucy's sudden silence. His next letter of November 1 explained he was "exceedingly afflicted" by the absence of her letters.[41]

On November 6, an infuriated Lucy retorted, "You accuse me of neglecting to write by three posts—and impute it to pleasure or negligence . . . [but] neglecting you is a thing I never shall be guilty of."[42] Knox, on the other hand, now seemed completely engrossed in the war. "I imagine by this time that you have almost forgot my very looks and if perchance my name is mentioned you cry what have we to do with women. Out of the last sixteen months we have not been six weeks together. Alas, what a change from the happy days I have seen."[43]

Perhaps her parents' predictions had been correct.

← →

By early December, Washington's ragged men had retreated across the Hudson and through New Jersey to the Pennsylvania side of the Delaware. The ranks of the Continental army, diminished by casualties, deserters, and those taken prisoners, had reached its lowest ebb. "Unless some great and capital change suddenly takes place . . . this Army must inevitably be reduced to one or other of three things. Starve, dissolve, or disperse," Washington grimly warned Henry Laurens, the new president of the Second Continental Congress.[44]

Lacking Congressional support, the commander in chief resorted to a desperate plan. On Christmas Day 1776, Washington ordered 2,400 men to McKonkey's Ferry for a nocturnal crossing of the Delaware. Although the weather remained clear all day, by 11 p.m. Christmas night, high winds and blinding snows slowed the soldiers' crossing. Through it all, Knox's booming voice directed pilots of the flat-bottom boats carrying cannons and horses across the swift-running Delaware. "The floating ice in the river made the labour almost incredible," he later acknowledged.[45] At dawn, after an eight-mile march to Trenton, Washington's forces routed the Hessians in a stunning victory that signaled the turning tide of the Revolution.

The next day, Washington told Knox of his appointment as a brigadier-general. "It was unsolicited on my part though it was not wholly unexpected," he joyfully wrote Lucy on January 2, 1777. "Will it give you satisfaction or pleasure in being informed that the Congress have created me a general officer, a brigadier with the entire command of the artillery. If so, I shall be happy."[46]

Although proud, Lucy sensed that her husband's new rank would require further sacrifices on her part. Henceforth, she must play mistress to Henry's marriage to the Revolution. Soon afterwards, and probably not coincidentally, she decided to leave Wallingford, Connecticut, whose residents she found ill-mannered and crude. "Take care, my love, of permitting your disgust for the Connecticut people to escape your lips," the ever- diplomatic Henry warned her. "Indiscreet expressions are handed from town to town and a long while remembered."[47]

His warning probably came too late. Soon afterwards, Knox received an angry letter from the landlord who had rented the Wallingford house to Lucy and her friend Mary Pollard. His complaint? The crockery in the house had been broken and twenty-five gallons of West Indian rum were missing from the cellar. Possibly the two women had drowned their sorrows in alcohol. More likely, though, a group of locals had entered the house and avenged themselves on Lucy after her departure for Boston.

In late February 1777, the military hero Benedict Arnold also arrived in Boston. A former New Haven apothecary and West Indies trader, the newly widowed officer was an attractive, well-built man, about five feet nine inches tall with a dark complexion and strikingly pale blue eyes. The preceding November he had famously staged a strategic coup at Lake Champlain's Valcour Island that had prevented General Guy Carlton from retaking Ticonderoga. Those who met Arnold rarely forgot his charm and charisma—nor his formidable vitriol, when crossed.

Through Lucy, Arnold met a fifteen-year-old beauty, Elizabeth "Betsy" DeBlois. Enchanted, the warrior showered the brunette with gifts, among them a golden-diamond ring. To advance the romance Arnold begged Lucy to speak in his favor to "the heavenly Miss DeBlois." Delighted, Lucy presented Betsy with the colonel's love letter and arranged for delivery of his trunk of fashionable gowns. Meanwhile, Arnold reminded Lucy that he waited "under the most anxious suspense until I have the favor of a line from you."[48]

Despite Lucy's best efforts, Arnold's suit fell flat. "Miss DeBlois has positively refused to listen to the general, which, with other mortifications will come very hard upon him," Lucy wrote Henry four days later.[49] Among those disappointments was Congress's reluctance to promote Arnold a major general.

Infuriated, the warrior wrote Washington demanding a trial, which the commander in chief discouraged. "Public bodies" he reminded Arnold, "are not amendable for the actions." Arnold's failure to obtain a major generalship, Washington assured him, was "not overlooked for want of merit in you" but rather from an agreement among Congressional delegates that they must award generalships evenly throughout the states.[50]

Still that seemed unfair, especially when, as Knox later wrote Lucy, five younger men were finally promoted over Arnold. That, he anxiously added, probably "pushes [Arnold] out of the service. I hope the affair will be remedied."[51]

Ironically, Arnold's patriotism probably contributed to Betsy's refusal of him. According to one account, her meddlesome Tory mother had objected to Arnold's political views. Soon afterwards, Betsy attempted to elope with a Boston corset maker, but Mrs. DeBlois allegedly stopped them at the altar.

By then, Betsy had returned Arnold's trunk to Lucy. Lacking European imports because of the war, Lucy and her friend Caty Greene rifled through its contents. Nathanael's trim wife found a gown but plump Lucy only a scarf. At the time, Arnold would not let the items go, but the following December Lucy asked for the scarf again. Major David Salisbury Franks, the warrior's aide de camp and a relative of Becky Franks, explained that Arnold "cannot part with any part of the contents of the trunk you mention until he comes to Boston." At that point, he would "give you the preference he desires."[52]

Another distraction that spring was Lucy's sale of her father's looted townhouse. Since women not could hold property in their own name, Lucy arranged with an attorney to place the £5,500 of proceeds in Henry's name. "This affair gives me pain (not that Papa will disapprove of it for he must certainly think it a wise step when he knows the circumstances) but for fear that it should be misconstrued," she wrote Henry on April 3.[53] Implied was Lucy's fear that her father might interpret that as Henry taking permanent possession of those monies rather than sending them to Flucker in London after the war.

Subsequent to the property transfer, Lucy submitted to the variolation against smallpox. "My heart palpitates at the thought of my dearest Lucy being in the least danger," Knox wrote from the army camp on the Raritan near Middlebrook.[54] On April 30, Lucy cheerfully reported that, after three days' illness, she was on the mend. Although she had no mirror, she could feel twenty pockmarks on her face. "I am almost glad you do not see it," she wrote. "I don't believe I should get one kiss, and yet the doctor tells me it is very becoming."[55]

Still Henry refused to let her visit. "You ask me why I give you no encouragement. Your safety and happiness is the sole object of my heart," he again explained. "I however anxious to have you with me cannot consent to a step which will most inevitably . . . reiterate . . . the disagreeable situation" of Lucy's earlier visit to New York.[56]

That note infuriated her. Living perilously with Henry was preferable to being lonely with difficult strangers. The latest example, Lucy wrote from Sewall's Point (contemporary Brookline, Massachusetts), was General William Heath's twenty-six-year-old wife, Mary Heath, who was "so stiff it is impossible to be sociable with her."[57]

For all his insistence that Lucy remain in Boston, Knox expected her to write more often. "I was . . . mortified [disappointed] beyond description in not having a line from you," he lectured her. "What in the name of love is the reason? I write you by every opportunity and expect the same from her who is far dearer to me than life, especially at a time when my anxiety is so great upon the account of your recovery."[58]

The only remedy for those anxieties was a visit. No longer did she care about "the luxuries of life," Lucy insisted. She was "willing to taste nothing but bread and water" if only she could join Henry. Other wives had joined their husbands at Middlebrook. "Happy Mrs. Washington, happy Mrs. Gates. In short, I do not recollect an instance like my own."[59]

By July, Lucy was seething. "I am resolved nothing shall prevent my coming to you in early September, but your positive refusal," she finally announced in a letter dated July 17. "In which case, I will try to be as indifferent as I shall then think you are." Later in that letter, Lucy confessed the reason behind her rage—fears that "her Harry" would "fall into the usual error of absent lovers—that indifference will take place of that refined affection, which you have entertained for me."[60]

Implied was the threat of the women of the Continental army's baggage train, who served as the army's cooks, seamstresses, nurses, and laundresses and trailed a mile or two behind the regiments in carts and crude wagons. Some were married and others single and still others were willing to provide sexual favors in exchange for cash. In his war diary, private Joseph Plumb Martin penned a common slur about the baggage train: "'Tag, Rag and bobtail . . . some in rags and some in jags,' but none in velvet gowns.'"[61]

Fears about his fidelity were ridiculous, according to Henry. "There never was a purer ... affection than what I profess for you," he wrote. He was "indifferent indeed to all the rest of your sex."[62] War councils, drills with his artillery corps, and letters to Congress filled his waking hours, especially during the last discouraging months of 1777. On September 11, General Howe had defeated the Continentals at Brandywine, staged a standoff at Germantown, and, on the twenty-sixth, occupied Philadelphia.

Two weeks later news arrived from upstate New York that marked a change in the course of the Revolution—the patriots' triumph over General Burgoyne at Saratoga. Euphoric, Henry wrote Lucy about his consequently celebratory cannonade. "They [Howe's men] have been very angry for our *feux de joie* . . . and say that by and by [we] shall bring ourselves into contempt for propagating such known falsehood. Poor fellows! Nothing but Britain must triumph."[63]

Nevertheless, in early December, after Howe's skirmish at White Marsh, New Jersey, Washington ordered his eleven thousand men to retreat into the countryside northwest of Philadelphia. "The situation of our army on account of clothing is such as to render a winter's campaign impossible," Henry morosely wrote Lucy. "We have a mind to put an end to the war by starving all the soldiers."[64]

During his trip to New England to recruit soldiers and order munitions that winter, Knox visited Lucy, but their reunion was interrupted by a February 26 note from Nathanael Greene. "The army has been in great distress since you left," Knox's friend wrote to him from Valley Forge. Many of the soldiers had worn out their clothes and were nearly naked. And they were starving. The soldiers were "seven days without meat and several days without bread."[65] In his haste to return to that camp, Knox conceded that Lucy could join him at Valley Forge the following spring.

←→

On May 1, Arnold returned to New Haven and a hero's welcome. The previous September 7, while leading a bold offensive at Freeman's Farm, Saratoga, the Hessians shot Arnold's horse and pierced the warrior's left leg with a musket ball. As the horse fell, it landed on Arnold's wounded limb and splintered his thigh bone. Even before that his leg was in bad shape, having been badly injured a year earlier at Quebec. Now it was so badly shattered that doctors urged an amputation. Though writhing in pain, the warrior refused. For the next five months, Arnold lay in Albany's General Hospital with his leg encased in a wooden contraption.

By December Washington, who considered Arnold his favorite fighting general, conveyed wishes for his speedy recovery and promised that, once recovered, he would be awarded with a new field command. A week after Arnold's return to New Haven, Washington sent him a set of French epaulettes and a sword knot in "testimony of my sincere regard and approbation of your conduct."[66] Arnold consequently decided to visit Washington in Valley Forge, even though his crippled leg meant he had to travel by carriage. Somehow—and here the details become hazy—the war hero agreed to transport Lucy and her toddler with him.

Privately, Arnold still seethed with resentments. After Saratoga, his blustery rival, General Horatio Gates, had claimed sole responsibility for the triumph. Arnold's men knew the truth, that their leader had pounded the enemy at Freeman's Farm without Gates's permission while that general tarried behind. Yet neither the nicknames the soldiers conferred upon Arnold—the "Hero of Freeman's Farm" and the "Eagle of Saratoga"—deflated Gates's boasts or convinced Congress to recognize Arnold's critical contribution. The final insult arrived at Arnold's hospital bedside in December: a notice from Washington that he had been appointed a major general. Congress had not announced it publicly. Instead, the commander in chief was to inform Arnold privately about his change in rank.

Personally, Arnold was also in a funk. That spring he learned that his former Boston sweetheart, Betsy DeBlois was still unwed. With soaring hopes he wrote to her again:

Twenty times have I taken my pen to write to you, and so often has my trembling hand refused to obey the dictates of my heart. . . . Long have I struggled to efface your heavenly image from it. . . . Dear Betsy, suffer that heavenly bosom . . . to expand with friendship at last and let me know my fate.[67]

In response, the Boston belle asked him to stop writing to her.

By mid-May 1777, Arnold, Lucy Knox, and her toddler set off from New Haven. Each snap of the coachman's reins upon the horses brought Lucy closer to Knox. Arnold, meanwhile, brooded over his forthcoming visit to Washington.

On May 20, two days after John André's Mischianza in Philadelphia, the unlikely threesome arrived at Valley Forge.

3

"The Delight, and Comfort of Her Adoring General"

"BOTH LUCYS ARRIVED IN perfect health and are situated in my hut in the center of the park, perhaps better situated than any other ladies in Camp," Henry Knox boasted in a letter to his brother William May 27, 1778. The "park" was Valley Forge, at whose center stood Knox's log hut, adjacent to his artillery center in which stood cannons, howitzers, and field pieces.[1]

While Knox spent his days training his men, Lucy visited with wives of other officers, watched her daughter play with their youngsters, and helped Martha Washington sew shirts and knit stockings for soldiers. She also admired the portrait of "her Harry," painted by the artist Captain Charles Willson Peale, along with those he had done of Washington, Nathanael Greene, and Clement Biddle, commissary general at Valley Forge. Evenings were spent with officers and their wives in communal song fests. Yet, as Knox predicted to William, neither Lucy nor their toddler could enjoy camp life for long, "because the army was preparing for action."[2]

By then the soldiers of Valley Forge were no longer starving, ill-trained men but had been transformed into sturdy warriors. Several factors had contributed to that. In March, a Philadelphia gingerbread baker and seventy helpers had arrived to prepare daily batches of bread. Nathanael Greene, the army's new quartermaster, had also ordered roads cleared and bridges built to speed deliveries of food and supplies. By April, farmers began appearing with wagonloads of crops. Drovers arrived with herds of livestock stalled earlier by winter storms and bureaucratic delays. The result, as Lieutenant-Colonel Samuel Ward Jr. cheerfully wrote his wife on May 5, was that "we

ARNOLD AS A COLONEL

Colonel Arnold

get a piece of good beef or pork, though generally of both—and have as good bread as I ever eat."[3]

Contrary to Lucy's expectations about existing upon "bread and water," the Continental officers and their wives dined on generous portions of meat, salt pork, fish, and vegetables. Had those servings been more scanty, neither she nor Knox would have starved. "Mrs. Knox is fatter than ever, which is a great mortification to her," Nathanael Greene gleefully wrote his wife, Caty. "The General [Knox] is equally fat, and therefore one cannot laugh at the other."[4]

By early spring too, visiting French engineers had encircled Valley Forge with redoubts and other fortifications to protect the camp's twelve thousand soldiers and two thousand log huts. Some men were veterans, others new recruits, but all had trained vigorously under the beloved Prussian drillmaster, Baron Friedrich Wilhelm Augustus Von Steuben, and the Marquis de Lafayette. No longer a "receptacle for ragamuffins," as Knox had bitterly dubbed the army the previous December, Washington's army now consisted of tightly disciplined regiments of warriors.[5]

Soon after Lucy's arrival, rumors swept through the camp about an imminent British evacuation of Philadelphia. Spies reported that the city's "sick, women, children, and prisoners ... [were] already on board ship, and the whole army ready to move at a moment's warning."[6] General Clinton, it was suspected, would march his men through New Jersey towards New York City—a destination Washington planned to block with his troops. During those last days of the army at Valley Forge, Lucy and her daughter consequently left camp to live with their New Jersey friends, the Lots. After the June 28 Battle at Monmouth, though, Knox wrote to his wife that he hoped "in a few days to have the superlative happiness of being with you."[7]

Simultaneously, Washington pondered how to bring order to Philadelphia after the evacuation. After being ruled by two governments in nine months, the city's residents remained politically divided. Some, like Quaker Sarah Logan, feared the patriots' return. "Having so long enjoyed the greatest tranquility & peace under the British government, the apprehensions of again coming under the arbitrary power of the Congress are very dreadful," she noted in her journal.[8]

Other neutralists, like Judge Edward Shippen, doubtless recalling the harsh treatment they had received under the earlier patriot regime, worried about their return. More frivolous were Shippen's teenage daughters' complaints about the prospect of finding suitable "beaux" among the returning Americans. The Continental officers they had met two years earlier had seemed crude, provincial, and indifferently dressed—like others, as Peggy observed later in life, "wholly unaccustomed to [the] genteel life" that she expected as her due.[9]

Twenty-five miles from the Shippens' silken drawing room in Valley Forge, Washington understood that he needed a charismatic leader, a man to inspire a renewal of patriotic sentiment. Newly arrived Benedict Arnold was a likely candidate. Admired as one of America's most courageous warriors, the crippled general seemed well-suited to serve as the military commandant, or governor, of Philadelphia.

Arnold accepted Washington's offer only coolly. A command, even a dull one to restore civilian peace in America's largest city, was better than no command at all. The task Washington had outlined for Arnold seemed mundane: "to preserve tranquility and order in the city and give security to individuals of every class and description."[10] As military commandant, Arnold would remain a commissioned officer while regaining his health and full vitality. In addition, Philadelphia might provide opportunities for new, lucrative enterprises on the side. Such a thing was permissible legally as long as those enterprises supported the patriotic cause. Other officers had done so to support their meager salaries, among them Henry Knox and his friends Henry Jackson and Nathanael Greene.

Privately, Arnold still resented Washington on two counts. First, he believed the Virginian should have insisted upon his Congressional appointment as a major general over younger officers. Second, Arnold blamed the commander in chief for failing to obtain reimbursements for funds Arnold had spent supporting his soldiers in battle. Had he considered Washington's then-tenuous position with Congress, Arnold might have understood why the Virginian could not fulfill his wishes. Instead, ignoring talk about the schemes then threatening Washington in Congress, the narcissistic Arnold remained as tragically nearsighted as the horses he once rode into battle.

Ultimately, though, necessity compelled Arnold to put his ill-founded resentments aside. On Saturday, May 30, he consequently raised his right hand before his friend Henry Knox and vowed:

I, Benedict Arnold, Major General, do acknowledge the United States of America to be Free, Independent and Sovereign States, and declare that the people thereof owe no allegiance or obedience to George the Third, King of Great-Britain; and I renounce, refute and abjure any allegiance or obedience to him; and I do swear that I will, to the utmost of my power, support, maintain and defend the said United States against the said King George the Third, his heirs and successors . . . and will serve the said United States in the office of Major General which I now hold, with fidelity, according to the best of my skill and understanding.[11]

By dawn, June 18, 1778, an eerie silence surrounded the docks of Philadelphia, which were strewn with tables, chests, and other household gear. Tossed overboard by the departing British to make room for military gear, those possessions were the remaining personal effects of the three thousand Tories who had streamed onto British ships and sailed for New York City the preceding day. "This morning, when we arose, there was not one redcoat to be seen in Town," an astonished Elizabeth Drinker noted in her diary "Col. Gordon and some others, had not been gone a quarter of an hour before the American light horse entered the city . . . the few that came in today had drawn swords in their hands, galloped about the streets in a great hurry. Many were much frightened at their appearance."[12]

Among them was David Salisbury Franks, Arnold's aide de camp. In addition to finding a stately residence for the new commandant, Franks was ordered to purchase "European and East India goods" and keep them secret from even "his most intimate acquaintances."[13] Prices for those goods had soared during the Revolution and now, temporarily retired from combat, Arnold planned to profit from their sale. Already he had experimented with that idea when, while still at Valley Forge, he issued a pass, or permission, to suspected Tory Robert Shewell to purchase imports from *The Charming Nancy*, a privateer docked in Philadelphia. Arnold later issued passes for two other vessels for Shewell's shady partners.

Subsequent to the British evacuation, Philadelphia's shops were filled with British goods. Fearful of looting, Washington consequently ordered a curfew for the night after the evacuation. "A bellman went about this evening . . . to desire the inhabitants to stay within doors after night," Elizabeth Drinker jotted in her diary. "If any were found in the street by the patrol, they should be punished."[14]

The next morning, throngs of enthusiastic residents gathered on Philadelphia's streets to welcome Arnold as he rode through in a military carriage. Crowds cheered and church bells clanged for the "Eagle of Saratoga," who would restore order to the torn City of Brotherly Love. "I understand Gen'l Arnold, who bears a good character, has the command of the city, and the soldiers conducted with great decorum," wrote Sally Wister from nearby Germantown. "I now think of nothing but retuning to Philadelphia."[15]

Initially Arnold lived up to his promise. Soon after his arrival, he ordered Colonel Henry Jackson, head of the Massachusetts militia, to "follow the route of the enemy . . . harass them by all means in your power."[16] He also insisted that workers clean Philadelphia's debris-cluttered streets, especially behind the State House, where the British, in a snide farewell, had dumped human and horse carcasses and garbage. As late as June 25, when Knox toured the city with Lucy, the stench was still overwhelming. Philadelphia, he wrote his brother, "stunk so abominably that it was impossible to stay."[17]

During that same period Arnold also signed a Congressional resolve to close the city's shops. That was the brainchild of Congressional delegate and attorney Joseph Reed, vice president of the patriotic Supreme Executive Council, which, as its name implied, governed Pennsylvania. As wiry and tough as his name, Reed formerly served as Washington's aide but later sided with the Virginian's rival, Horatio Gates. Consequently Reed distrusted Arnold even before they met. Others who knew Reed, including Nathanael Greene, regarded him warily, perceiving him as an overly ambitious, avaricious politician who believed "to have power, you must have riches."[18]

To acquire them, the Pennsylvania power broker shrewdly adopted the mantle of militant patriotism. Officially he had convinced Congress to shut the shops so that "quartermaster, clothier, and commissary generals may contract for such goods . . . wanted for the use of the army." Secretly though, Reed wanted first choice of those goods for his own resale and profit.[19]

Arnold had similar ambitions. His new residence, the stately three-floor brick and marble Masters-Penn House on High Street, was filled with costly furnishings, staffed by ten servants, and was home to a luxurious coach and four. Before long, Arnold's flashy lifestyle raised eyebrows among Philadelphia's lean-living patriots. Especially those of Joseph Reed.

Soon after the shop-closure resolve became official, James Mease, the Continental army's clothier general, purchased stacks of clothes at cost and sold them at top dollar on the open market. Fuming, Reed traced those sales back to Arnold, whom he believed was receiving kickbacks. Later, upon learning about the sale of Philadelphia flour in Havana at five times the domestic price and originally stockpiled for the army, Reed's suspicions deepened.

The covert sale of government property was reprehensible, he asserted, for it prevented Americans from purchasing household goods at fair prices on the open market. After all, even affluent Philadelphians like Edward Shippen struggled to obtain certain food and drink. "It will be very difficult to procure Madeira wine at any price," the judge complained to his elderly father in early July. "There is no such thing as syrup, the sugar bakers having all dropped the business a long while."[20]

Believing the United States owed him a debt, Arnold vowed to collect it by cultivating friendships among Philadelphia's most wealthy and influential citizens. Among them was Robert Morris, Philadelphia's richest merchant, as well as New Yorkers Robert R. Livingston, Gouverneur Morris, and John Jay. Inevitably Arnold's friendships attracted still more public notice, further eroding his image as Philadelphia's neutral peacekeeper.

Simultaneously, the city's new patriotic leaders scorned those once friendly with the British, dubbing them the "disaffected." So vitriolic was public sentiment against them that one Congressional delegate insisted they pay a collective fine of £100,000—in today's terms, millions of dollars. One of their well-publicized targets was the women of the Mischianza. Those participants, thundered General "Mad Anthony" Wayne, leader of the Pennsylvania militia, should lay their costumes "at the feet of those virtuous daughters of America who cheerfully gave up ease and affluence in a city, for liberty and peace of mind."[21] Reed went even further, proposing that five hundred known British sympathizers be tried for treason and hanged. Ultimately, reason and appeals for leniency prevailed. Nevertheless, the "disaffected" continued to be treated like second-class citizens, excluded from public galas like the July Fourth celebration at the Masonic temple.

Still, Peggy Shippen and her friends gadded about town in their imported finery and attended concerts and plays, impervious to the snubs and cold stares of Philadelphia's patriots. Peggy's best friend, Becky Franks, privately snickered about the patriots' drab homespun dresses, crudely nailed leather shoes, and dull entertainments. "Oh! The ball," Becky gossiped to the Shippen sisters after one gala. "Not a lady there. The committee of real Whigs met in the afternoon and frightened the beaux [men] so much that they went to all the [fashionable] ladies . . . to desire they'd stay home. . . . I'm delighted that it came to nothing, as they had the impudence to laugh as us."[22]

To soften relations between the two groups and meet Philadelphia's fashionable young beauties, Arnold hosted a ball at the fashionable City Tavern with a guest list that included Tories and neutralists, as well as patriots. Inevitably the "disaffected" emerged triumphant, their beaded gowns gleaming in the candlelight, their two-feet-high hairdos towering over the caps of patriot women in their crude clothes. Horrified, Reed complained to Nathanael Greene that Arnold's guest list included "not only common Tory ladies but wives and daughters of persons proscribed [listed] by the state."[23]

By late August 1778, the Shippen sisters and their friends had fully redeemed their status as Philadelphia's most admired belles. The precipitant was again political, this time driven by demands for a municipal ball in honor of the August 7 arrival of French minister plenipotentiary Count Conrad Alexandre Gerard. Aghast to discover that Philadelphia could not supply enough stylish patriotic women to fill the ballroom and impress Gerard, city leaders consequently added Peggy Shippen and other ladies of the Mischianza to the guest list.

"We have a great many balls and entertainments, and soon the Assemblies will begin," Mary White Morris, the tall young wife of Robert Morris, wrote her mother that summer." Even our military gentlemen are too liberal to make any distinction between Whig and Tory ladies. If they make any, it is in favor of the latter. . . . [It] originates at [Arnold's] headquarters.[24]

Through the Robert Morrises, Arnold met their relative Judge Edward Shippen and, inevitably, Shippen's daughter Peggy. Theories vary about where that introduction took place, among them the Shippen drawing room, the City Tavern, the ball for Count Gerard, or one Arnold's galas held at his home. By late summer the crippled general was escorting Peggy to dinners, receptions and the theater, smitten with her beauty, wit, and spirit. When criticized for courting the neutralist (or possibly Tory) daughter of Judge Shippen, Arnold merely shrugged. After all, as military governor of Philadelphia he was obliged to restore peace. What better way to smooth political differences and unite opposing factions than through such a romance?

For all her superficial sophistication, Peggy was overwhelmed. To her, as to other Philadelphia beauties who clustered around the handsome general at galas, Arnold, his game leg propped upon a stool, seemed a warrior of mythic proportions. That his heroic military record was complemented by his gallant manners, and that he was cultured and appreciated high living only added to his appeal. Hobbling about on a white, jewel-encrusted cane and a built-up shoe to compensate for the two inches lost in height to his crippled leg, Arnold's disability reminded others of his heroism at Montreal and Quebec City; at Valcour Island and Saratoga, New York; and at Ridgefield, Connecticut.

His courtship with Peggy Shippen immediately titillated Philadelphia society. "I must tell you that Cupid has given our little general a more mortal wound than all the hosts of Brittons could," Mary White Morris reported to her mother. "Miss Shippen is the fair one."[25]

By September, Arnold's ardor had spilled over in two letters—one to Edward Shippen and the other to Peggy. The first assured the judge that he had no interest in the Shippen money. "My fortune is not large, though sufficient . . . to make us both happy. I neither expect nor wish one [a dowry] with Miss Shippen. My public character is well known; my private one is, I hope, irreproachable." Nor did Arnold consider the Revolution an obstacle. "Our difference in political sentiments will, I hope, be no bar to my happiness," he smoothly observed. "I flatter myself the time is at hand when our unhappy contest will be at an end, and peace and domestic happiness be restored to everyone."[26]

On the twenty-fifth. Arnold wrote to Peggy, repeating almost verbatim his love letter sent two years earlier to Betsy DeBlois: "Twenty times have I taken up my pen to write to you, and as often has my trembling hand refused to obey the dictates of my heart," he began. His passion was "not founded on personal charms only; that sweetness of disposition and goodness of heart, that sentiment and sensibility which so strongly mark the character of the lovely Miss P. Shippen, renders her amiable beyond expression and will ever retain the heart she has once captivated." Only the last line of his letter was new: "Whatever my fate may be, my most ardent wish is for your happiness; and my last breath will be to implore the blessings of heaven on the idol and only wish of my soul."[27]

Neither Peggy nor her father responded initially. One objection they may have had was Arnold's social status. Though now a major general, he was formerly a middle-class Connecticut apothecary. Another was the nineteen-year gap in age between Arnold, then thirty-six, and Peggy. A third was his crippled leg, and a fourth, that the widowed general was the father of three sons, then cared for by his sister in Connecticut, who would likely join his Philadelphia household.

During that autumn of 1778, the Shippens were also preoccupied with the forthcoming marriage of daughter Betsy, who, on December 17, would marry her cousin, the judge's protégé, Neddy Burd. Just before that wedding, with its twenty-five bridesmaids, Betsy had panicked. "How is it with your highness now have you got over all your little palpitations," her cousin

Elizabeth Tilghman later teased, "shameless girl, how could you have been so naughty as to have so many witnesses to your actions?"[28]

Sitting by her jittery sister Betsy's side the night before the ceremony, Peggy began worrying about the prospect of her own wedding night. Legend has it that the eighteen-year-old virgin took a "solemn oath never to change her state." Soon afterwards, though, she retracted that vow. Instead she giddily bet an older family friend a pair of gloves there would be "twelve marriages among her acquaintances" before the next Christmas.[29]

Four days after Betsy's wedding, Judge Shippen wrote his father, "I gave my daughter Betsy to Neddy Burd last Thursday evening and all is jollity and mirth." Peggy, he added, "is much solicited by a certain general on the same subject. Whether this will take place or not depends on circumstances. If it should, it will not be until spring."[30]

The judge remained uneasy. Conceivably, Peggy's marriage to the commandant could advance his own ambitions for a new court appointment, but counterbalancing that were rumors about Arnold's unsavory business deals in New Haven. Moreover, by late 1778, the commandant's reputation within Philadelphia's political hothouse had begun to wither.

The trouble began when Arnold's aide, David Salisbury Franks, ordered nineteen-year-old sergeant William Matlack to fetch Arnold a barber. When the man failed to appear, Franks cursed the sergeant, who, in turn, complained to his father, the secretary of the Supreme Executive Council. Before long Arnold received an irate letter from the elder Matlack: "At a time when you were one of the militia, what would have been *your* feelings had an aide of your commanding officer ordered *you* to call his barber? Free men will be hardly brought to submit to such indignities."[31]

To that Arnold coldly replied, "The respect due to the citizen is by no means to be paid to the soldier any further than his rank entitles him to it. . . . [As] an orderly sergeant, it is his duty to obey every offer of my aides."[32] Exchanges between the two grew increasingly acrimonious before Matlack related them to Reed, who added Arnold's responses to his list of grievances against the commandant.

Soon, the list had grown even longer. In October *The Charming Nancy*, then partly owned by Arnold, arrived at Egg Harbor, New Jersey, loaded with West Indian goods and promptly looted by the British. Most of the cargo, however, was still intact, leading Arnold to have it stored in a warehouse. Then he asked the army's quartermaster, John Mitchell, to round up sixteen wagons and have it hauled to the city. The use of government equipment for private purposes was illegal but done so frequently that Arnold never mentioned to Mitchell that the cargo was private property.

Another of Arnold's missteps was a pass he illegally issued to one Hannah Levy so she could enter British-occupied New York City. Denied permission at the border, she again appealed to Arnold. This time he applied to the Supreme Executive Council for a "legal" pass. Mrs. Levy, the council informed Arnold, was a Loyalist whose male friend had attempted to smuggle a letter "inimical to the safety and liberties of the United States" across enemy lines.[33] "Pennsylvania officials had long been frustrated over the exercise of Continental authority within their borders," Joseph Reed complained to Congress months later, "and especially with the imperious conduct of the military commander of Philadelphia."[34]

In November, Reed and Matlack began to excoriate Arnold to the newspapers. "I cannot think that the commanding officer views himself exposed to any real danger in this city," sneered their letter in the influential *Pennsylvania Packet* under the byline of "Militia Man." "From a public enemy there can be none, from Tories, if any such there be amongst us, he had nothing to fear, they are all remarkable fond of him."[35]

To Reed, who had ascended to the presidency of the Supreme Executive Council in December 1777, that was only prelude. Soon afterwards he filed a complaint about Arnold's military misconduct with the Supreme Executive Council. Among his accusations were the commandant's hostility to Matlack, illegal use of army wagons to haul *The Charming Nancy*'s cargo, and his issue of an illegal pass for a suspected spy. Infuriated, Arnold replied, that he was "at all times ready to answer my public conduct to Congress or General Washington, to whom alone I am accountable."[36]

A bitter argument followed, sending tremors of anxiety through Congress. With Washington's army in New Jersey, the delegates' sole protection from British attacks was the Pennsylvania militia, whose salaries the Supreme Executive Council paid. If Arnold remained governor of the city, Reed threatened blackmail: he would withdraw the militia "until the charges against [Arnold] are examined."[37]

For many months, Congress had looked askance at Arnold. As delegate, General John Cadwalader explained, "Every man who has a liberal way of thinking highly approve[s] his conduct," but he had become "very unpopular [among] men of power in Congress."[38] Arnold returned that negative assessment. Congress, he complained to Nathanael Greene, was "distracted and torn with party and faction . . . debt accumulated to an . . . incredible sum, the currency daily depreciating, and Congress, if possible, depreciating still faster."[39]

Little did Arnold seem to care that his own reputation had lost its currency. By mid-winter 1779, his one desire was to return to civilian life, with Peggy at his side.

Fueling that desire was a letter from General Philip Schuyler, Arnold's friend and military colleague, which explained that the authorities of New York State planned to award Arnold land for his heroism at Saratoga. If he could "obtain a tract of any consequence," Arnold responded, he was willing to become a citizen of New York. In return, he would establish "a settlement of officers and soldiers" to protect the state's borders.[40] Intrigued with the prospect of living like a landed European aristocrat, Arnold then reported to Judge Shippen that he anticipated "something handsome" with which to bestow a generous prenuptial settlement upon Peggy.[41]

For months, the romance had simmered along uncertainly as Peggy remained noncommittal even to her favorite sister, Betsy Shippen Burd. When a friend asked in a December 30 letter if Peggy would soon wed, Betsy replied, "Everyone tells me so with such confidence that I am laughed at for my unbelief. Does she know her own mind yet?"[42]

Betsy's new husband, Edmund Burd, claimed Peggy did: "My expectations have been answered. From what I gather a lame leg is at present the only obstacle." Arnold, he added, "from the slight knowledge I have of him to be a well-dispositioned man . . . one who will use his best endeavors to make P. happy and I doubt not, will succeed."[43] From Lancaster, Pennsylvania, Peggy's grandfather, the patriarch Edward Shippen, also heartily approved "another match in the family, this one to the 'fine gentleman.'"[44]

Gossips continued their chatter through January, prompting Elizabeth's Tilghman's declaration on the twenty-ninth: "I had like to have forgot the gentle Arnold . . . when is he like to convert our little Peggy? They say she intends to surrender soon. I thought the fort could not hold out long. Well, after all, there is nothing like perseverance and a regular attack."[45]

By then, the teenager had conditionally accepted the "gentle" Arnold's proposal—pending her father's approval. One hundred and twenty years after this period, a Shippen descendent claimed in the *Pennsylvania Magazine of History and Biography* that Judge Shippen had had no choice but to consent to the marriage. Whenever he expressed doubts about Peggy's proposed marriage, she reverted to her childhood pattern of weeping, taking to her bed, refusing to eat or drink, and, ultimately, becoming ill.

Ultimately, Judge Shippen consented. Possibly he did so because his own marriage twenty-eight years earlier to Peggy's mother, Margaret Francis, had been a love match. "If I had obtained a girl with a considerable fortune no doubt the world would have pronounced me happier," the future judge once wrote his father. "Happiness does not consist in being thought happy by the world, but in the internal satisfaction and contentment of the mind."[46]

By late winter 1779, news of Peggy's engagement became public knowledge. During Henry Knox's visit to Congress in early winter, Arnold proudly introduced him to Peggy. Knox was immediately impressed that "our friend Arnold is going to be married to a beautiful and accomplished young lady, a Miss Shippen—of the best families in this place," he gushed to his brother William.[47]

Only one event tainted their joy: the Supreme Executive Council's smear campaign. Disgusted with Reed's attacks, Arnold left Philadelphia on February 6 or 7, 1779, and headed to the Continental army camp at Middlebrook to ask Washington for advice. From there he planned to travel to upstate New York to meet with General Schuyler. No sooner had his coach reached the Delaware River at Bristol Ferry when a messenger handed Arnold a proclamation from the Supreme Executive Council that accused him of military misconduct. The proclamation had been shrewdly timed to coincide with Arnold's departure from Philadelphia to spark rumors of his supposed defection to the British.

By Tuesday, February 9, the council's accusations had appeared in the *Pennsylvania Packet* newspaper and sent to the governors of other states. Arnold's behavior, the *Packet* declared, was "oppressive to the faithful subjects of this state, unworthy of his rank and station, highly discouraging to those who have manifested their attachment to the liberties and interests of America, and disrespectful to the supreme executive authority."[48]

The eight charges included Arnold's friendship with persons of "disaffected character"; sailing a vessel (*The Charming Nancy*) from British-held Philadelphia to an American port; the closure of city shops for his own private profits from sale of those goods; the imposition of menial services on militia men and Arnold's defense of that behavior; the awarding of a prize (a ship) for his own profit; the use of public wagons to transport private cargo; an illegal attempt to permit a British sympathizer to enter occupied New York; an "indecent and disrespectful refusal" to explain the use of those wagons to the council; and, finally, "discouragement and neglect "of patriotic individuals while friendly to "those of another character."[49]

At the Shippen townhouse on South Fourth Street, Peggy and her family were as stunned by those notices as they were suspicious of Reed's accusations. Remembering the patriots' harsh treatment of the judge in 1776–1777 and the family's frightened retreats to the countryside, the Shippens considered the Supreme Executive Council's accusations one more example of power run amok.

From Middlebrook on February 8, Arnold confirmed that assessment to Peggy. Washington and his officers had "treated [me] with the greatest politeness," he wrote his fiancée, and "bitterly excoriate Mr. Reed and the council for their villainous attempt to injure me."[50] To clear his name, Washington suggested Arnold ask for a Congressional hearing. But Peggy's fiancé would not hear of it: a court-martial, he believed, was preferable, for then he would be judged by his peers. The Supreme Executive Council, Arnold bitterly responded in the *Pennsylvania Packet*, exemplified "as gross a prostitution of power as ever disgraced a weak and wicked administration."[51]

Adrift in a sea of uncertainty and public censure, Arnold lingered in Middlebrook for several days before canceling plans to visit Schuyler. Longing for reassurance, he wrote Peggy:

My Dearest Wife
Never did I so ardently long to see or hear from you as at this instant. I am all impatience and anxiety to know how you do. Six days' absence without hearing from my dear Peggy is intolerable. Heavens! What must I have suffered had I continued my journey; the loss of happiness for a few dirty acres [in New York State].[52]

Disheartened by the storm of accusations around him, he added:

I can almost bless the villainous roads and the more villainous men who oblige me to return. I am heartily tired with my journey and almost so with human nature. I daily discover so much baseness and ingratitude among mankind that I almost blush at being of the same species and could quit the stage without regret were it not for some few gentle, generous souls like my dear Peggy.[53]

Among those few "generous souls" was Henry Knox, whose letter to his brother William complained that the newspapers carried "highly [unfair] charges against General Arnold by the State of Pennsylvania." To Knox, as to his wife, Lucy, Reed's accusations seemed absurd. "I shall be exceedingly mistaken if one of them can be proven," Knox confided to his brother. Arnold was then returning to Philadelphia, he added, "and will, I hope, be able to vindicate himself from the aspersion of his enemies."[54]

Ultimately Arnold rejected the concept of a court-martial. Instead he appealed to Congress, which, in turn, handed over the accusations to a special committee. After an anguished debate, all but two of the charges were dropped. Reed was outraged, protesting so forcefully that on April 3

Congress agreed that Arnold must be judged on four accusations of the Supreme Executive Council.

Peggy, meanwhile, continued to believe in Arnold's innocence. She was eighteen, in love, implicitly trusted her fiancé, and had the support of her relatives. "I think all the world are running mad. What demon has possessed the people with respect to General Arnold? He is certainly much abused; ungrateful monsters, to attack a character that has been looked up to," wrote her cousin, Elizabeth Tilghman, to Betsy Shippen. "Poor Peggy how I pity her; at any rate her situation must be extremely disagreeable. She has great sensibility, and I think it must often be put to trial."[55]

Discretion was bred into the Shippens' bones. Whatever arguments, embarrassments, or regrets the family expressed were hidden behind their handsomely polished front doors. The accusations against Arnold were unjust, the Shippens publicly maintained, yet another instance of political chicanery from the fanatically patriotic Reed and his intimidated Congressional cronies.

By March 19, Arnold had resolved to change his plans, resigning that day as commandant of Philadelphia. He also released General Schuyler from his offer for an upstate New York residence. Instead, either by scraping together or borrowing assets, he purchased Mount Pleasant, an elegant property just outside Philadelphia for £16,240. Built of white stone, the Georgian mansion on the banks of the Schuylkill included ninety-six acres of lawn, a formal garden orchards, and outbuildings. According to John Adams, it was "the most elegant seat in Pennsylvania."[56] Now part of Philadelphia's Fairmount Park, Mount Pleasant was never meant to be Arnold's residence. Instead it was to serve as an income-producing rental, placed in trust for Peggy and her future children as financial protection in the event of his death.

On Thursday, April 8, a white-gowned Peggy and Arnold, leaning on the arm of an aide, were married in the Shippen drawing room. Among the witnesses were Peggy's relatives, bridal attendants, Arnold's sister Hannah, and his three sons, newly arrived from Connecticut. Of the subsequent celebration, Judge Shippen wrote, "We saw company for three days. This, with punch drinking, etc. is all the entertainment that was given."[57]

Six days later an enchanted Elizabeth Tilghman gushed to Betsy, "Will you my dear give my best love to Mrs. Arnold, tell her that I wish her every happiness that this world is capable of affording, and that she may long live the delight and comfort of her adoring General."[58]

4

"Our Sweetest Hopes Embittered by Disappointment"

BY THE WINTER OF 1779 Lucy Knox was happily ensconced in a fieldstone farmhouse in the hills of Somerset County, New Jersey. After the June 28 Battle of Monmouth, Henry had urged Lucy to join him in the army camp at White Plains where she and her daughter stayed until mid-autumn. So pleasant was that reunion that when Washington ordered the Continentals to a winter encampment in New Jersey, the Knoxes saw no need to separate again. Lucy, consequently, had traveled with her daughter to a hamlet near Middlebrook, New Jersey, near the contemporary town of Bound Brook.

To Washington, the encampment was an ideal site from which to protect the Hudson Highlands, spy upon the British movements in New York City, and protect patriotic New Jersey from an enemy attack. Located at the crossroads of the state, Middlebrook was also "as near our supplies as possible," a place where "our cattle can be driven to us," with easy access to Pennsylvania and supplies of flour.[1]

Instead of a log hut, Henry, Lucy and their little daughter lived in a Dutch farmhouse owned by the elderly Jacobus Vandeveer, whose house stood two and a half miles west of the army camp. There at the foot of the Watchung Mountains, Knox fulfilled his dream of establishing a military school, or "college." Called the Pluckemin Artillery Cantonment, heavy field pieces and cannons guarded the entrance to the square-shaped campus at whose borders stood barracks, an armorer's shop, a military forge, and a munitions laboratory. The centerpiece of Knox's first war college was a cupola-topped hall where soldiers studied tactics, military engineering, and gunnery. A foreign visitor, amazed that its construction was only "the work of a few weeks," praised the results for their "look of enchantment."[2] Needing funds to train more men, Knox traveled to Philadelphia in January to meet with Congress.

Lucy, heavy with a second pregnancy, had remained in Pluckemin, waiting anxiously for the arrival of two relatives, Elizabeth and Sarah Winslow. The two women had left Boston in 1775 and settled in New York City, but by 1779 longed to return to their home town. Nearly penniless but knowing that the Knoxes lived nearby, Elizabeth and her niece, Sarah, had appealed for help. Lucy and Henry had complied, assuring them they would "afford them every assistance necessary," in spite of their political differences. It was "absolutely necessary" for them to leave New York, Knox wrote his brother, since one of their relatives was sailing for England, which would have left the two Winslows "friendless and without protection."[3]

Just before Knox left for Philadelphia, the two women arrived. Little is known about that visit, although Sarah seems to have been the more spirited of the two, so street smart that the Knoxes' somber Rhode Island friend Nathanael Greene labeled her a "hussy." Lucy, nevertheless, warmly welcomed them. Undoubtedly they chatted about life in New York City under the British and gossiped about its Loyalist Bostonian residents. More important for Lucy's purposes, though, was that their visit served as a family reunion, evoking memories of the high-toned life they had shared in Boston before the Revolution—the splendid dinners, drawing-room receptions, and formal teas Lucy enjoyed as a girl.

If the Winslows provided a window to Lucy's past, the forthcoming gala at Pluckemin previewed her future. By mid-February, workers swarmed over the Pluckemin campus to prepare the first-anniversary celebration of the Franco-American alliance. Tables, chairs, blue-plate dishes, and utensils soon appeared in the academy building and transformed it into a banquet hall for four hundred guests. Outside, carpenters hammered boards into a towering colonnade one hundred feet long, "a temple , or frame, of 13 Corinthian arches . . . each . . . containing an illuminated painting emblematic of the Revolution."[4] Each mural contained an inspiring picture of the Revolution, among them the battle at Lexington, the founders of Congress, the triumph at Saratoga, a portrait of Louis XVI, and the anticipated fall of England. On the appointed day, a sunny Thursday, February 18, Washington and his wife, Martha, arrived in mid-afternoon. So too did dignitaries like Benjamin Franklin, Henry Laurens, Alexander Hamilton, and General "Mad Anthony" Wayne, followed by throngs of the most "respectable ladies and gentleman of the state of New Jersey," Dr. James Thacher noted in his journal.[5]

At 4 p.m., thirteen cannons sounded, signaling the start of the festivities. After toasts and a dinner, fireworks lit up the clear winter sky. Then, as music wafted from the banquet room, "the ball was opened by Mrs. Knox and General Washington in the Academy building," reported the *Pennsylvania Packet*.[6] Though in her ninth month of pregnancy, the be-gowned Lucy danced a minuet with Washington, glorying in her role as the event's presiding hostess. Afterwards, musicians struck up a lively tune as thirty couples appeared on the dance floor, ready "to foot it to no indifferent measure."[7]

To the astonishment of the guests, Washington and Caty Greene joined hands and danced tirelessly to song after song, each seemingly daring the other to quit. "We had a little dance at my quarters a few evenings past," Nathanael Greene proudly recalled. "His Excellency and Mrs. Greene danced upwards of three hours without once sitting down. Upon the whole we had a pretty little frisk."[8]

In contrast to Caty's "frisk," Lucy spent most of that night conversing with Martha Washington, dignitaries, officers, and their wives, forming what the *Packet* described as a "circle of brilliants."[9] Conversations in other parts of the room dwelled upon the course of the Revolution. When the flirtatious *Packet* reporter asked a young woman "if the roaring of the British lion in his late speech did not interrupt the spirit of the dance," she saucily retorted, "Not at all. It rather enlivens, for I have heard that such animals always increase their howlings when most frightened."[10] The celebration was so dazzling, gushed the *New Jersey Journal*, that "the power of description is too languid to do justice to the whole of this grand entertainment."[11]

Afterwards, Knox boasted to his brother: "We had above seventy ladies, all of the first *ton* [class] in the State. We danced all night; between three-hundred and four-hundred gentlemen: an elegant room. The illuminating fireworks, etc. were more than pretty."[12]

Ten days after the Pluckemin Grand Alliance Ball, Lucy "was brought to bed of a beautiful daughter," Knox announced to William. "Though we wished her a son. . . . It is a divine child—we shall call it Julia."[13] Soon afterwards he reported, "Mamma has been so well as to ride out every day for the . . . post."[14] By May 2, Lucy even traveled to Middlebrook to watch the Continental army parade before French minister Gerard.

Quite unexpectedly, a week later Lucy became "most alarmingly ill," so feverish and weak that she could no longer nurse Julia.[15] Then her skin turned yellow, leading the doctors to conclude that she suffered from "jaundice occupied by bilious obstructions."[16] Lucy had contracted infectious hepatitis, a disease associated with poor sewage and contaminated water often found in overcrowded sites like army camps. Soon afterwards, little Julia and her four-year-old sister, Lucy, also fell ill.

At the same time, at British headquarters at 1 Broadway in New York City, General William Clinton, commander of the North American forces, schemed to weaken Washington's supply lines along the Hudson. By June 1, he led eight thousand men along the Hudson's rocky, western shores above the Palisades and seized a key garrison at Stony Point. The next day Howe's men took Verplanck's Point on the opposite shore, effectively blocking a key crossing of the Hudson at King's Ferry. The loss of that station, Clinton gleefully noted in his narrative on the Revolution, "obliged the enemy to pass and repass the Highlands twice" through a mountain road, extending their journey by more than sixty miles.[17] Alarmed, Washington ordered the army to the Hudson on June 4 and posted them at various strategic positions along the Hudson Highlands as he contemplated a counterattack.

Worried about his ailing wife and children, Knox had marched reluctantly to the Hudson. By June 14 he learned that Lucy was well enough to enjoy an outing. "I long to hear how my dear Julia is," he wrote that day from headquarters at New Windsor near Newburgh, New York. "Heaven preserve her—kiss her and my angelic Lucy [their daughter] for me."[18] But ten days later came alarming news: baby Julia was gravely ill. "Good Heavens, my Lucy, what affliction did your letter . . . inflict upon me," Knox hastily replied on June 29. "Julia, poor innocent, is not in half so much pain as is its unhappy mother. To add to her and my distress, I am absent, unable to assist. . . . I long to see you, to be assured from your own lips that you are getting better daily. I long to hear the little prattle of my lovely Lucy and to see the expressive countenance of Julia."[19]

That was not to be. On July 2, the Knoxes' infant daughter died. Though obliged to remain on the Hudson with the army, a local legend insisted that he returned to Pluckemin. According to that story, Knox arrived just as members of the local Dutch Reformed Church refused to bury Julia in the churchyard. The reason? Because he and Lucy were Congregationalists. Coincidentally, the Knoxes' elderly landlord, Jacobus Vandeveer, had been denied that right because his daughter had died insane. The old man, it was said, led Knox to a grave beyond the churchyard fence. "General, this is my ground," he explained. "Bury your child here." Years later a more enlightened generation of churchgoers moved the cemetery fence to encompass the graves of Julia Knox and Vandeveer's daughter.[20]

Naturally news of the baby's death stunned Knox's colleagues and their wives, many of who were either pregnant or had recently given birth. "How our brightest prospects are blasted, and our sweetest hopes embittered by disappointment. May guardian angels protect you against such evils," Nathanael Greene wrote his pregnant wife, Caty, who had returned to Rhode Island. Lucy, he added, seemed to accept the baby's death "with a degree of fortitude that marks a philosophic temper."[21] But that was far from the truth: Lucy was so devastated that, after the baby's death, she rarely wrote Knox.

"I have not had the happiness to hear from you since your Letter of the 28th. . . . I entreat if you have opportunities that you would . . . embrace them and confer that pleasure on your Harry," Knox begged her from his post at West Point on August 18. To cheer her, he promised she could soon join him. He too ardently wished for "that period when my Lucy and I shall be no more separated, when we shall set down free from the hurry, bustle and impertinence, of the world, in some sequestered vale where the education of our children and the preparation on our own parts for a pure and more happy region shall employ the principal part of our time in acts of love to men and worship to our maker."[22]

True to his promise, Lucy and their daughter, little Lucy, joined him on the Hudson in late August. Other than Major Henry Lee's August 19 triumph against the British at Paulus Hook (today's Jersey City) on the Hudson's western shore, the summer passed quietly, leading Washington to deem West Point a "happy spot."[23] Had they been polled, the Knoxes would probably have agreed. Within a few weeks of their reunion, they were expecting another child.

If, as British lexicographer Samuel Johnson observed, "the applause of a single human being is of great consequence," Arnold's marriage to Peggy Shippen was a monumental life shift. [24] Not only was the bride beautiful, but, as the general later confided to a General Robert Howe, she was also remarkably sexy." I myself had enjoyed a tolerable share of the dissipated joys of life, as well as the scenes of sensual gratification," Arnold admitted, "but when set in competition with those I have since felt and still enjoy," there was no comparison.[25]

Peggy was equally enchanted with the older, more sexually experienced Arnold. Long after their honeymoon and first years of marriage she continued to praise Arnold as "the best of husbands."[26]

The one cloud hovering over the newlyweds were the accusations of the Supreme Executive Council. Five days before the Arnolds' wedding, Washington announced a court-martial to examine the council's four original charges. So heavily did that weigh upon Arnold that, half through his honeymoon, he grumbled to his friend John Jay, then president of the Second Continental Congress, "I cannot resist my surprise, that a court-martial should be ordered to try me for offences, some of which the committee of Congress in their report say, 'there appears no evidence.'"[27] Even Jay's considerable powers of persuasion, nevertheless, would not change the Supreme Executive Council's decision.

Nor did Peggy's tender reassurances soothe Arnold, who became obsessed with the damage done to his public reputation. The perception of a man's honor, as the popular British decorum book *Letters, Sentences and Maxims* had advised readers, was key to worldly success: "Your moral character must be not only pure, but like Caesar's wife, unsuspected. The least speck or blemish upon it is fatal."[28]

To blemish his character was precisely Reed's intent, Arnold groused to Washington. The man had deliberately "kept the affair in suspense for near two months . . . and will use every artifice to delay the proceeding of a court-martial." The only remedy was "an early day . . . fixed for it as [soon as] possible." He thus hoped Washington would notify the Supreme Executive Council of that date as soon as possible "so that the court may not be delayed for want of their evidence." Explaining that he preferred a trial in Philadelphia, where records were more accessible, than one in Middlebrook, Arnold conceded that wherever it was scheduled he "will be ready at the shortest notice."[29]

In confidence Washington explained why the court-martial had to be held at Middlebrook: "It would have given me great pleasure to have indulged you with a court at Philadelphia," he wrote to Arnold, "but such is the weak state of the line in respect to general and field officers that it would have been impossible without entirely divesting the army of officers of that rank."[30]

Reed, meanwhile, fumed over Washington's agreement to an early trial date. In a thinly veiled threat, he warned the commander in chief, "Such is the dependence of the army upon the transportation of this state, that should the court martial treat it as a light and trivial matter, we fear it will not be practicable to draw forth wagons for the [army] in the future, be the emergency what it may."[31] More time, Reed insisted, was needed to collect evidence and call witnesses. The trial must be rescheduled for a later date.

To protect the already disquieted Arnold from Reed's monumental hostility, Washington simply informed the general that the trial date had been postponed. "As Congress have stamped ingratitude as a current coin, I must take it. I have nothing left but the little reputation I have gained in the army," Arnold bitterly retorted on May 5 in a letter to Washington. "Delay in the present case is worse than death. I want no favor, I only ask for justice. . . . If your Excellency thinks me a criminal, for heaven's sake, let me be immediately tried and if found guilty, executed."[32]

One can only imagine how Arnold's turmoil affected Peggy. Such matters were beyond her experience, indeed beyond that of nearly all Revolutionary-era women, whose sphere was the home and hearth. Knowing little about the nuances of military law or the righteousness of the accusations against her husband, her only recourse was to calm Arnold with kisses and caresses. If she sensed that those accusations against him boded ill for their future, Peggy kept them to herself. Raised in an era when women were valued for their sexuality, solicitude, and silence, the eighteen year old stood loyally by Arnold's side. Only decades later did Peggy finally comprehend the sacrifices she had made as Arnold's wife. "My life," she admitted in 1801 to her father, Judge Shippen, "has been a most trying and eventful one."[33]

Even before his vitriolic letter to Washington of May 5, Arnold weighed his options. What more could he lose by defection? "A patriot is a fool in ev'ry age," English satirist Alexander had written in 1738. [34] Arnold now shared that view: The Revolution was ill-conceived from the start. The idea that a British colony could survive on its own had been naïve. Undermining it was a politically divisive Congress that had failed to support the army and confounded the ideals originally inspiring the Revolution. Since Arnold was already suspected of being a traitor, why not profit by becoming one— and stop the unnecessary bloodshed along the way? So, presumably, the tortured general raved through the first weeks of his marriage as his bride sympathetically listened.

On Saturday, May 1, Arnold summoned Joseph Stansbury to his home. The man, a 1767 émigré from London, was not only Philadelphia's most fashionable china merchant but also a writer of anti-Revolutionary poems. During the British occupation of 1777–1778, Stansbury had been rewarded with the post of commissioner of the city watch. After the patriots reclaimed Philadelphia, Stansbury switched sides again by swearing loyalty to the Revolution. Covertly, though, he remained a Tory.

Years later, Stansbury claimed he initially thought Arnold summoned him to the Masters-Penn House to order more china. Instead, the crippled general had stunned him by explaining "his intention of offering his services to the commander in chief of the British forces . . . that would most effectually restore the former government and destroy the then-usurped authority of Congress, either by immediately joining the British army or cooperating on some concerted plan with Sir Henry Clinton."[35]

To accomplish that, Arnold proposed disguising his identity through the alias of Gustavus Monk—Monk for short. Flushed with promises of a handsome reward, Stansbury thus agreed to become Arnold's secret agent. A week later the china merchant rode through patriot-held New Jersey, sailed across New York harbor, and entered the city. There he connected with a Loyalist poet, the Reverend Jonathan Odell, who was acquainted with another amateur poet, the British officer John André. By 1779, André had ingratiated himself with General Henry Clinton and served as one of his most trusted aides. As Howe had before him, Clinton admired André's intelligence, finesse, and talents. So fond was the widowed commander in chief of the younger officer that he often hosted André at his country house in The Fields, today the corner of First Avenue and Fifty-second Street.

By Monday morning, May 10, Odell had arranged for Stansbury to meet with André at British headquarters (and Clinton's home) at No. 1 Broadway. Patiently the British officer listened to the Philadelphian's message that a certain American named Monk offered to reveal key information about the Continental army. Added to his astonishment was Stansbury's message from his old friend Peggy Shippen—now Peggy Shippen Arnold—conveying her regards.

"Such sudden proposals," a flustered André wrote Clinton, created "confusions . . . when one must deliberate and determine at once" a decision. By afternoon the British commander in chief agreed that he was willing to consider the American's offer. "We meet Monk's overtures with full reliance on his honorable intentions and disclose . . . the strongest assurances of our sincerity," André explained. Nevertheless, that information must produce a significant triumph for the British, either by "seizing an obnoxious band of men . . . or enabling us to attack [and] defeat a numerous body."[36]

To seal the deal, André handed Stansbury a letter of instructions that explained the three ways that Monk could transmit information. The first was through the use of ciphers, or numbers coded to the letters of a certain "long book," like *Blackstone's Commentaries on the Laws of England.*

Another was by using invisible ink to write a message that would be inserted between the lines of a conventional letter. That was known as "interlining"—a technique André hoped to persuade Peggy to use in letters from her friend Peggy Chew. "The lady might write to me at the same time with one of her intimates," André explained to Stansbury. "She will guess whom I mean, the latter remaining ignorant of interlining. . . . I will write myself to the friend to give occasion for a reply. This will come by a flag of truce . . . every messenger remaining ignorant of what they are charged with. The letters may talk of mischianza [entertainment] & other nonsense."[37]

A third and final technique involved the writing of a seemingly conventional letter on a matter like "an old woman's health" that secretly alluded to a timely military situation.

André's next paragraph has intrigued historians for decades. While copying his report about the meeting for Clinton, André intuitively identified Monk as "Arnold." Then, realizing his slip, André crossed out the name and substituted "Monk." Worried that border guards might seize his instructions, André insisted that Stansbury take "mysterious notes" from it, "burn it, or rather leave it sealed with me." Ultimately, the china merchant copied "mysterious notes," which he later conveyed to Arnold.[38]

During Stansbury's visit to New York, Arnold received two letters from Washington. The first announced June 1 as the new date for the court-martial; the second, defended the Virginian's diplomatic relations with the

Supreme Executive Council. "I feel my situation truly delicate and embarrassing. On one side, your anxiety, very natural in such circumstances," Washington agreed. "On the other . . . the impropriety of precipitating a trial so important in itself left me no choice [but to agree.]"[39]

Arnold had no choice but to accept the new trial date. Nothing, he replied to Washington, "can be more disagreeable than the cruel situation I am in at present, not only as my character will continue to suffer until I am acquitted by a court-martial, but as it effectually prevents my joining the army . . . as soon as my wounds will permit." He intended to do so, Arnold falsely promised, "to render my country every service in my power at this critical time; for, though I have been ungratefully treated, I do not consider it as from my countrymen in general, but from a set of men, who void of principle, are governed by private interest."[40]

Even as Arnold wrote those slippery words, he suffered an attack of gout in his right leg, which left him even more disabled than usual. Stress, as is well known today, can often exacerbate a latent constitutional illness.

Although nearly a year had passed since the British evacuation of Philadelphia, the city's leading belles remembered their British beaux fondly—so passionately, in fact, that they annoyed Grace Galloway, the disgruntled wife of a fled Tory. After having tea with Nancy and Peggy Chew on May 5, Grace complained in her diary that "all their discourse was of the [British] officers [who] sent cards and messages." In return, the girls celebrated the birthdays of six officers that year "by meeting together, drinking their health in a glass of wine." In fact, "the girls "brag[ged] so much of their intimacy that I was quite sick of it."[41]

Those flirtatious correspondences, in turn, led André to write his former sweetheart, Peggy Chew, in the hope that Peggy Shippen Arnold would secretly interline her reply. "I hardly dare write to you after having neglected your commissions and not apologized for my transgressions," André ingenuously penned. "I would with pleasure have sent you drawings of head-dresses had I been as much a milliner here as I was at Philadelphia in the Mischianza times, but from occupation as well as ill health, I have been obliged to abandon . . . what relates to the ladies.

"[I] should, however, be happy to resume it had I the same inducements as when I had the pleasure of frequenting yours and the Shippen family. I trust I am yet in the memory of the little society of Third and Fourth Street, and even of the *other Peggy*, now Mrs. Arnold, who will, I am sure, accept of my best respects."[42]

In all likelihood, Peggy Chew was thrilled. She may have shared the letter with her friend, Peggy Shippen Arnold, but if so, the latter did nothing about it. In the aftermath of her wedding, things had not gone as Peggy planned. Her husband ranted continually about the injustices of his countrymen, then gloomily retreated into his library. Nor had Peggy become the sole mistress of the Masters-Penn mansion. Instead she was obliged to share that role with her sister-in-law. Just before the wedding, the tall, plainly dressed Hannah Arnold arrived from New Haven with Arnold's three sons. Years earlier, she served as her brother's house-keeper in that city and ran his apothecary business while he traded in the Caribbean. After the 1775 death of Arnold's first wife, Margaret Mansfield, Hannah had stepped in again to raise his children. Legend has it that when a Frenchman courted Hannah, Arnold threw him out of his house because he was a Catholic.

Whether that story is apocryphal or not, the thirty-six-year-old, unmarried Hannah not only knew Arnold's tastes but was a far more experienced home manager than young Peggy. A subsequent letter reveals that she superficially accepted Peggy but harbored secret resentments toward the stylish, luxury-loving, teenage Philadelphia belle.

Arnold's dark moods persisted through May, fueled by tensions over the court-martial and wary responses from the British over his treasonous offer. In a ciphered message to André on May 23, the crippled general insisted, "It will be impossible to cooperate unless there is mutual confidence."[43] To stimulate that confidence, Arnold offered key information: "General Washington and the army move to the North [Hudson] River as soon as forage can be obtained. Congress ha[s] given up Charles Town, South Carolina. . . . They are in want of arms, ammunition and men to defend it. Three or four thousand militia is the most that can be mustered to fight on any emergency." That riveted Clinton's attention. Within a year, the British had seized Charleston.

Arnold's letter also demanded certain financial rewards: "I will expect some certainty, my property here secure and a revenue equivalent to the risk and service done. I cannot promise success: I will deserve it." In closing he revealed Peggy's acceptance, if not direct complicity, in his deal to serve as a spy: "Madame Ar[nold] presents you her particular compliments."

By Tuesday, June 1, Arnold had appeared at Middlebrook for the court-martial. By late afternoon or early evening that day, messengers had arrived reporting Clinton's attack on Stony Point. Promptly, Washington dashed off a note to Arnold. "I am sorry to inform you that the situation of affairs will not permit a court martial to proceed on your trial at this time," he wrote. "The Army should at least advance towards the North [Hudson] River with all practical expedition."[44] As described above, among those preparing to leave New Jersey was Arnold's friend Henry Knox, then fretting over the ailing Lucy, their newborn Julia, and his older daughter.

After his return to Philadelphia, Arnold resumed correspondence with André. By then, he and British General Henry Clinton had asked for the names and identities of members of Congress, presumably for nefarious purposes. Once they were received, "generous terms would follow our success and ample reward and honors."[45] In a subsequent letter, Clinton also demanded that Monk obtain an active post in the army. As commander of a battle, the spy could easily pretend surprise with a British triumph and still escape blame. That battle, he again stressed, must be a major one—"a complete service . . . involving a corps of five or six thousand men [for which Arnold/Monk] would be rewarded with twice as many thousand guineas."[46]

Arnold was not impressed: ten or twelve thousand guineas was hardly fair compensation. As wary of being ambushed as a spy as when on the battlefield, Arnold consequently insisted upon additional protections. Essentially, Clinton had placed him in an impossible position: he could not obtain a high military post until the court-martial had cleared his name. To speed the trial, Arnold begged Washington to set a new date. "As a part of the British army are gone down the North River, I hope the time is now arrived to appoint as early a day as possible," he wrote on July 16. Moreover, he added, he was finally well enough to accept a field command: "My wounds are so far recovered, that I can walk with ease and I will soon be able to ride on horseback."[47]

Coincidentally General "Mad Anthony" Wayne had recaptured Stony Point that same day, enhancing Arnold's expectations for a new trial date. Still Washington balked. "You may be assured it is not my wish to delay your trial a single moment," he explained. "At the same time you must be sensible, that I cannot fix with precision on any day, during the more active part of the campaign."[48]

In New York, an equally frustrated André finally decided upon a new tack. On August 16 he wrote Peggy Shippen Arnold to renew their friendship. His letter, the British officer genially explained, "meant to solicit your remembrance, and to assure you that my respect for you and the fair circle in which I had the honor of becoming acquainted . . . remains unimpaired by distance or political broils. It would make me very happy to become useful to you here." Graciously, André added, "You know the Mischianza made me a complete milliner. Should you not have received supplies for your fullest equipment from that department, I shall be glad to enter into a whole detail of capwire, needles, gauze, &c., and, to the best of my abilities, render you in those trifle services from which I hope you would infer a zeal to be further employed."[49]

Sixteen months earlier, during the spring of 1778, André's design of gauzy turbans and other finery had thrilled Peggy. Now, though, his offer of similar favors was laced with peril. As the steamy days of that Philadelphia summer cooled into early autumn, the usually polite, and now pregnant, Peggy did not reply.

5

"Fortitude under Stress"

CITIZEN DISCONTENT ROCKED PHILADELPHIA during the summer of 1779 when food supplies dwindled and prices for basic commodities soared. "There is hardly any flour, salt or coffee, tea or sugar, spirits or wine to be got in the town owing to the regulation of the mobbing committee," complained Grace Galloway in her diary. "The country people will not bring butter and they [the patriots] stop them on the road and take their marketing from them."[1] In reality, wealthy patriots like Robert Morris, chief financial agent of Congress, had paid the farmers in gold for their crops that were stored to feed French reinforcements expected to arrive from Rhode Island.

That left workers "desperate from the high price of the necessaries of life," as Benedict Arnold recalled.[2] On October 4, a group of armed protestors who had opened the gates to the jail learned that Morris was visiting the unpopular lawyer James Wilson. As the group advanced towards Wilson's house, an officer alerted Arnold of the trouble. Gamely he rushed before the men to calm them, but was swept into the crowd. "The press of the mob was so great that it was difficult to keep our feet," Arnold recalled. Soon he found himself "crowded among the . . . prisoners, which they had taken into custody in their march through the city."[3]

As the vigilantes swept him past the Masters-Penn House, Arnold caught a glimpse of Peggy and another woman peering from a second-story window. "The moment she saw me in the crowd, she screamed out and fainted," he recounted.[4] Within moments, the mob carried Arnold to Wilson's house. There, as an army colonel tried to dispel their rage, shots rang out, scattering the crowd and prompting Arnold to dash into Wilson's house. A second time the mob advanced wielding hammers and iron bars, broke into the house, killed one man, and wounded others. Only with the thunder of hoofbeats announcing the arrival of Joseph Reed and the Pennsylvania militia did the vigilantes disappear.

"They rescued the prisoners, but thought proper to send them to prison where they are this night," Elizabeth Drinker scrawled in her diary.[5] Among those apprehended were Arnold, Morris, and Wilson. The next morning, the bruised general returned to his distraught wife, Peggy, who pleaded with him to remain indoors. But Arnold, as his bride was already unhappily learning, rarely listened to others. The next day he went out and was again menaced by more angry men.

"A mob of lawless ruffians have attacked me in the street and threaten my life," Arnold immediately complained to Samuel Huntington, the new president of Congress. "There is no protection to be expected from the authority of the state [Joseph Reed] for an honest man. I am . . . requesting Congress to order me a guard of Continental troops."[6]

Like everything political Arnold touched in 1779, his request backfired. "The President informed General Arnold that his application ought to be made to the Executive Authority of the state of Pennsylvania," Huntington archly replied.[7] Arnold would have to apply to Reed personally for an order of protection. Clearly that was impossible.

Terrified for her husband and their unborn baby, Peggy surrendered whatever allegiance she had—if she ever had any—for the patriotic cause. It could not have been coincidental that on October 13, she finally answered André's letter of August and agreed to resume their correspondence. "Mrs. Arnold presents her best respects to Capt. André, is much obliged to him for his very polite and friendly offer of being serviceable to her. . . . Mrs. Arnold begs leave to assure Captain André that her friendship and esteem for him is not impaired by time or accident. The ladies to whom Capt. A. wished to be remembered are well and present their compliments to him."[8]

Peggy's "millinery" letter, as historians later called it, arrived at British headquarters at an auspicious moment. On October 23, André was promoted as a major and appointed as Clinton's Deputy Adjutant General.

"Good fortune still follows me," the twenty-nine year old euphorically wrote his mother and sister in England. "The Commander-in-chief has raised me to the first office in the army . . . I am Adjutant General. . . . I . . . can hardly look back at the steep progress I have made without being giddy!"[9]

In contrast to André's relationship with Clinton was Arnold's tense relationship with his patriotic commander in chief. Most of the Continental army had remained in the Hudson Highlands through November, leading Washington to delay a date for the court-martial. By early December, ten thousand Continental solders were ordered to the hills of Jockey Hollow at Morristown, New Jersey. During that trek, blinding snows hobbled their progress in the first of several blizzards of the "hard winter" of 1779–1780, the coldest of the century. In his journal, Joseph Plumb Martin wrote that he and his fellow soldiers were "naked, fatigued and starved, forced to march many a weary mile in winter, through cold and snow, to seek a situation in some (to us, unknown) wood to build us habitations to starve and suffer in."[10]

Onc the soldiers were camped at Jockey Hollow, Washington set Thursday, December 20 (or, by some records, the twenty-third), for the court-martial at nearby Norris Tavern. Earlier that week, Peggy, her belly swollen with pregnancy, had embraced her husband, wished him good luck, and watched his carriage lumber down icy Market Street in the direction of Morristown.

At 10 a.m. on December 23, Arnold appeared before a twelve-man jury that sat at long wooden tables near a roaring fire in the barroom, the tavern's largest space. As Arnold predicted, he was to be tried by his fellow soldiers. Among them were General Robert Howe, who served as the presiding judge, and Arnold's friend Henry Knox as vice chairman. Four of the witnesses sat nearby: Timothy and William Matlack, David Franks, and Alexander Hamilton. The fifth, John Mitchell, quartermaster of the Philadelphia militia, was not yet present.

Serving as his own counsel, Arnold pleaded not guilty. As he leaned on his cane, the famous warrior deftly foiled one accusation after another. As one officer confided to a friend, "It is expected he will be acquitted with honors."[11] On December 30, the court temporarily adjourned just before a double blizzard blanketed Morristown. "On the 3rd . . . we experienced one of the most tremendous snowstorms ever remembered; no man could endure its violence many minutes without danger to his life," Dr. James Thacher recalled. "The snow is from four to six feet deep, obscuring the very traces of the roads."[12]

That month, as two other blizzards swept over the region, burying Philadelphia and New York in five feet of snow, both Peggy and Lucy remained in suspense: Peggy, in luxurious surroundings at the Masters-Penn mansion, and Lucy, at Knox's simpler quarters in Morristown. Had the two women met, they would have discovered much in common that chilly January. Born to privilege and linked to the Revolution through their husbands, both women were pregnant and both hoped for Arnold's acquittal.

From Morristown, Arnold wrote to Peggy, complaining the trial was stalled because quartermaster Mitchell had failed to appear. Infuriated, the former belle sent a servant to Mitchell's office, begging him to travel to Norris's Tavern. "I never wanted to see you half so much," she also wrote to Arnold on a blustery January 4. "You mentioned Sunday for your return [but] I will not flatter myself I shall see you even then, if you wait for Colonel Mitchell."[13] Finally, on January 19, Mitchell arrived at Norris's Tavern. However, his testimony was so evasive that the jury discounted it.

Two days later, Arnold presented his closing statement. "My time, my fortune, and my person have been devoted to my country in this war. And if the sentiments of those who are supreme in the United States in civil and military matters are allowed to have weight, then my time, my fortune, and my person have not been devoted in vain." In a plea for sympathy, he explained his resentment of the "uncommon attention . . . employed in propagating suspicions, invectives, and slanders to the prejudice of my character. The presses of Philadelphia have groaned under the libels against me; charges have been published, and officially transmitted to the different states, and to many parts of Europe."[14]

Those accusations, Arnold insisted, were "calculated to raise a prejudice against me, not only among the people at large, but in the minds of those who were to be my judges." After a heart-rendering account of his courageous deeds on the battlefields, the crippled general concluded, "I have looked forward with pleasing anxiety to the present day when, by the judgment of my fellow soldiers, I shall . . . stand honorably acquitted of all the charges brought against me and again share with them the glories and dangers of this just war."[15]

His presentation had its intended effect. On Wednesday, January 26, the jury acquitted Arnold of all charges but his grant of an illegal pass to *The Charming Nancy*. Described as "imprudent and improper . . . the court in consequence of their determinations respecting the first and last charges exhibited against Major General Arnold, do sentence him to receive a reprimand from his Excellency, the Commander-in-Chief."[16]

Arnold was stunned. He had anticipated a full acquittal. Washington's reprimand would be humiliating—and unwarranted. "For what? Not for doing wrong but because I might have done wrong; or rather, because evil might follow the good that I did," Arnold complained to the sympathetic Silas Deane."[17] Seething, Arnold stormed out of Morristown, returned to Philadelphia, and to Peggy's waiting arms.

One event raised Arnold's spirits a month later. On March 19, 1780, Peggy delivered a sturdy baby boy named Edward Shippen Arnold.

During the court-martial, conditions at Jockey Hollow grew increasingly grim. "We have had the most terrible winter here that I ever know," Nathanael Greene wrote his kinsman Governor William Greene of Rhode Island. "Almost all the wild beasts of the fields, and the birds of the air, have perished with the cold. All the bays, rivers and creeks are froze up."[18] Each storm was followed by sub-zero temperatures that delayed food deliveries to the army camp. "The troops, both officers and men, have born their distress with a patience scarcely to be conceived." Washington advised Samuel Huntington in Congress. "Many of the latter have been four or five days without meat entirely and short of bread."[19]

The soldiers became desperate. "We were absolutely, literally starved," noted Private Joseph Martin in his diary. After four days without food, he gnawed a piece of black birch bark off a stick. Then, "I saw several of the men roast their old shoes and eat them . . . some of the officers killed and ate a favorite little dog."[20] On January 7, other soldiers slogged through five-foot drifts to nearby private homes and plundered them for food.

Horrified, Washington ordered Nathanael Greene to apologize to county judges for the behavior of his men. "The present situation of the army with respect to provisions is the most distressing of any we have experienced since the beginning of the war. For a fortnight past, the troops, both officers and men, have been almost perishing," Greene's notice warned.[21] Should the residents of New Jersey refuse to donate food, Washington would be forced to resort to martial law. Soon afterwards, donations of grain and herds of cattle arrived at camp. Still the storms continued—twenty-six of them by winter's end.

To dispel the gloom, Washington and his officers pooled funds to hold dances in one of Morristown's empty warehouses. The first of those "dancing assemblies," on February 23, coincided with another storm that prevented most of the female guests from attendance. Although six months pregnant, Lucy managed to appear, however. "Last Wednesday commenced the great Military Assembly at Morristown," an attending officer wrote General William Irvine. "His Excellency opened the ball with Mrs. Knox. As the weather was cool, there were but sixteen ladies and from fifty to sixty gentlemen present."[22]

For Lucy, the effort of plodding through the snow to the ball was worth it. Not only did it provide amusement from that long, dreary winter, but it also reconfirmed her role as the social leader for subsequent military galas.

The following May, Lucy delivered a healthy baby boy, named Henry Jackson after the Knoxes' friend and head of the Massachusetts militia. Unlike the Knoxes' daughter Julia, who died in infancy, the Knoxes' first-born son would survive to adulthood.

The "hard winter" of 1779–1780 turned into a hard spring for Arnold. No longer serving as Philadelphia's commandant, Arnold also faced declining income from other factors—failed trading schemes, sketchy lenders, un-recompensed military expenditures, and an expensive lifestyle. To reduce expenses, Arnold leased out the Masters-Penn mansion and moved his family into one of Judge Shippen's smaller rental properties. Whatever disappointment Peggy may have felt, she, like "the General," as she referred to him, blamed his misfortunes on the misguided American cause.

By April, Arnold even asked for a loan from the new French minister Anne-Cesar, the Chevalier de la Luzerne. "I have shed my blood for my country and she is ungrateful. The disorder which the war has occasioned in my private affairs, may force me into retirement . . . if I cannot borrow a sum equal to the amount of my debts," he explained.[23]

A diplomat, Luzerne agreed to meet Arnold, but afterwards coolly replied in a letter, "You desire a service from me which would be easy to perform, but which would degrade us both. When the minister of a foreign power gives, or if you will, lends money, it is usually for the purpose of corrupting those who receive it." To avoid that, Luzerne proposed a loan under one condition: that Arnold make that loan public knowledge. If not, the Frenchman sneered, "your friends will be eager to secure you as soon as you adopt a system of order and economy."[24]

More public was Washington's April 6, 1780, reprimand of Arnold. Necessarily stern in tone, the sympathetic Virginian attempted to soften the rebuke by initially alluding to Arnold's distinguished military record.

> The Commander-in-Chief would have been much happier on the occasion of bestowing a commendation on an officer who has rendered such distinguished service to his country as Major General Arnold. But in the present case a sense of duty and a regard to candor oblige him to declare that he considers his conduct in the instance of his issuance of the permit, as peculiarly reprehensive, both in a civil and military view, and in the affair of the wagons as imprudent and improper.[25]

Washington penned a second, private letter to the crippled general. "Our profession is the purest of all. Even the shadow of a fault tarnishes the luster of our finest achievements," he reminded Arnold. Given that understanding, he hoped the former military hero would "exhibit anew those noble qualities, which have placed you on the list of our most valued commanders." Once Arnold did so, Washington promised to "furnish you, as far as it may be in my power, with opportunities for regaining the esteem of your country."[26]

But it was too late: Clinton's promise of a lucrative financial award now obsessed Arnold. To achieve it, he had to win a strategic military command, preferably the one at West Point. Situated on a rocky ledge at a sharp turn in the Hudson forty miles north of New York City, the granite fort was dubbed by the British the "Gibraltar of America." To Washington it was the "key to America" because of its commanding position on the Hudson, which linked New England and upstate New York with patriotic territories to the south. The conquest of West Point would mean disaster for the American cause, severing New England from the lands to the south, disrupting communications and supply streams, and, ultimately, disabling the Continental army. In view of this, in 1778, Washington consequently ordered the installation of the "Great Chain," an 1,097-foot-long chain of iron links that ran just below the Hudson's water line, stretching from West Point to Constitution Island on the opposite shore—and blocking all enemy traffic.

One way to win command of West Point, Arnold schemed, was through support from friends like General Philip Schuyler. In April 1780, the unsuspecting New Yorker had consequently proposed the idea of such a promotion to Washington after Schuyler arrived in Philadelphia to attend Congress. No sooner did Schuyler propose Arnold's appointment then Washington discounted the idea. "I am so well persuaded of the safety of West Point," he replied, "that I have dismissed all the militia . . . for the defense of the posts on the North [Hudson] River."[27]

Meanwhile, Arnold continued his relentless negotiating with the British. In mid-May he insisted that his risks as an informant required a guarantee of £10,000, "half in indemnification for the loss of his personal American assets, the other half for the still-unrecompensed military funds" that he once advanced to his soldiers.[28] At that moment, neither André nor

Clinton replied, for both were then sailing north after their May 12 triumph in Charleston.

Arnold left Peggy and their newborn son in Philadelphia that June and rode to Connecticut to sell his New Haven properties. Along the way he stopped at West Point and asked an unwitting General Howe for a tour of the garrison. West Point was poorly defended and even more poorly manned, Arnold subsequently reported to the British, adding that he did not think the chain would be an impediment to their victory. "I am convinced the boom or chain thrown across the river to stop shipping cannot be depended upon," Arnold opined. "A single ship, large and heavy-loaded with a strong wind and tide would break the chain."[29]

In Connecticut, though, Arnold's hopes for achieving a financial windfall faltered. Not only did the state legislature deny him the funds Arnold had claimed in lieu of those Congress had failed to pay, but he was also unable to sell his New Haven home. Disgusted, he lowered the price of the house, handed it over to an agent, rode through Westchester County, and recrossed the Hudson.

Meanwhile, in a glittering Philadelphia drawing room, Peggy flirted in a low-cut gown with Robert R. Livingston, the thirty-four-year-old chancellor of the State of New York, suggesting that he ask Washington to replace the West Point commander, General Howe, with Arnold. Livingston agreed to do so. In fact, as he confided to the lovely former belle, Washington welcomed the idea but thought Arnold would be insulted with such a dull post. Not at all, Peggy fanned and fluttered to the charmed Livingston.

Arnold, meanwhile, continued to press the British for a firm commitment to his request for funding. With bravado based on nothing but hopes, he announced to André on July 12 that he would "take the command of W.P. immediately on the fleet's arrival or at any rate in the course of this month." As an additional lure, Arnold wrote that he possessed "a drawing of the works on both sides of the river done by the French engineer . . . [also] a plan of communication whereby you should be informed of everything projected at headquarters."[30]

Three days later, again Arnold demanded "compensation for services agreed on and a sum advanced for that purpose."[31] When André failed to reply, Arnold grew insistent, demanding £20,000 before he would deliver his information. Finally, reluctantly, on July 24, André conceded that "the sum even of 20,000 pounds should be paid to you. You must not suppose that in case of detection or failure . . . you would be left a victim, but services done are the terms on which we promise rewards; in these you see we are profuse; we conceive them proportioned to your risk."[32]

Before his trip to Connecticut, Arnold understood that his letters were best sent from Philadelphia to avoid interception from spies in the Hudson River Valley. Peggy, or so it was later alleged, consequently, passed them to her husband's agent, who, in turn, dispatched them to New York. One such letter assured the British that Washington's forces were too weak to attack New York City and mentioned the imminent arrival of French reinforcements. To untrained ears, Arnold's letter sounded merely social: "Upon the whole our affairs which do not wear a pleasing aspect at present, [but] may soon be greatly changed."[33]

The words were more prophetic than Arnold anticipated. After General Wayne's July 16 re-conquest of Stony Point, Washington announced that he intended to appoint Arnold to a special command. Arnold thrilled at the words: the special command must have been West Point. Just after crossing King's Ferry on his return from Connecticut, he met Washington on horseback. Unable to retain his curiosity any longer, Arnold asked about the post. The commander in chief replied with enthusiasm: "Yes, you are to command the left wing, the post of honor."[34]

Arnold, who was usually a consummate actor, could not hide his disappointment. "Upon this information his countenance changed, and he appeared to be quite fallen," Washington recalled. "Instead of thank[ing] me or expressing any pleasure at the appointment, [Arnold] never opened his mouth."[35] Others were equally stunned. Washington's aide, Tench Tilghman (a patriotic cousin of the Shippens), recalled that after the announcement, Arnold suddenly limped more than usual and complained that his leg was too weak for horseback duty. Again Washington encouraged the former military hero to reconsider the post offered to him. But, Arnold insisted, his fragile health prevented it. He was, he said, better suited to assume the command at West Point. Baffled, Washington wondered at Arnold's reluctance.

Peggy was as ill-prepared for the announcement as her husband. A day or two later, while attending a gala at the mansion of her relatives Mary and Robert Morris, her conversation was interrupted by another guest, who congratulated her on Arnold's appointment as commander of the army's left flank. "The information affected her so much as to produce hysteric fits," Morris observed. Alarmed, he, Mary, and others tried to calm Peggy, assuming the twenty year old was upset by the dangers of Arnold's new position. "Efforts were made to convince her that the General had been selected for a preferable station," Morris added, but "the explanations . . . to the astonishment of all present produced no effect."[36]

On Tuesday, August 3, Washington learned that the British fleet, which had sailed east to attack the French in Newport, Rhode Island, had reversed course and were returning to New York. Immediately, he contacted Arnold and ordered him "to proceed to West Point and take the command of that post and its dependencies from Fishkill to King's Ferry. . . . You will endeavor to obtain every intelligence of the enemy's motions. . . . You will endeavor to have the works at West Point carried on as expeditiously as possible by the garrison under the direction and superintendence of the engineers."[37]

Arnold was ecstatic. Indeed, he would fulfill Washington's expectations for "intelligence of the enemy's motions" but not as the commander in chief had intended.

With Washington's announcement, relief swept over Peggy. In contrast, his sister Hannah was appalled. Apparently Arnold had written to her in August that, while Peggy and his infant son "Neddy" would join him at West Point, she should remain in Philadelphia with the nearly eight-year-old Henry, the youngest son from Arnold's first marriage. Infuriated that she and the boy were not included (the older ones being in boarding school),

Hannah retorted, "Ill nature I leave it you, as you have discovered yourself to be a perfect master of it. Witness yours of August 18th." Nor did she see any advantage to Arnold's relocation. "As you have neither purling streams nor sighing swains at West Point, 'tis no place for me; nor do I think Mrs. Arnold will be long pleased with it."[38]

Then, in a vicious snipe at Peggy, Hannah added, "Though I expect it may be rendered dear to her for a few hours by the presence of a certain chancellor; who, by the by, is a dangerous companion for a particular lady in the absence of her husband." In fact, Hannah continued, "I could say more than prudence will permit. I could tell you of frequent private assignations and of numberless *billets doux*, if I had an inclination to make mischief. But as I am of a very peaceable temper I'll not mention a syllable of the matter."[39]

The "certain chancellor" Hannah alluded to was Robert R. Livingston, with whom Peggy had flirted to win support for Arnold's command of West Point.

Subsequent to his arrival at West Point on a rainy August 5, Arnold noted the fort's crumbling walls, decayed nearby forts, and lackluster protection from 1,500 men. Guns, magazines, wagons, horses, and stockpiles of food remained in short supply. In an effort to secure supplies for the British Arnold wrote Thomas Pickering, the newly appointed quartermaster general, on August 16, "Everything is wanting. . . . The barracks here will not contain more than eight hundred men or any kind of camp equipment; there is not a tent at West Point, and it is with great difficulty that one can be made to cover the troops . . . without these supplies the garrison will be in a wretched uncomfortable situation next winter."[40] Arnold's subsequent letter to Washington (copied to the British) also explained that West Point's six-foot walls offered little protection. The garrison, he explained, could easily be attacked from the land side by transporting cannons on back-country roads from the south.

Still British general Clinton remained so wary of Arnold's reliability that he had ordered spies to track Arnold's movement through Connecticut and New York that summer. By late August 1780, convinced that the

American turncoat's proposals were sincere, Clinton finally agreed to pay Arnold £20,000—but on one condition: the British must be assured they could capture three thousand soldiers at West Point.

For Arnold, that was nearly a deal-breaker. In an attempt to further weaken the garrison, he had ordered hundreds of soldiers to the surrounding region to perform trivial tasks: chopping wood and making bricks. Ironically, the unsuspecting Washington then played into Clinton's demands by dispatching one of Knox's artillery units to West Point, swelling the troop count to three thousand men.

Still, Arnold remained on edge. A network of spies and double agents roamed the territory between the Hudson Highlands and New York City, and might report his schemes to the patriots. André, too, worried, fearing that at the last minute the traitor might bolt. To quickly conclude the capture of West Point, André urged a secret meeting. It would take place at Dobbs Ferry on the Hudson's eastern shore, well below West Point. To that Arnold had eagerly agreed. On Sunday, September 10, he consequently sailed downriver for an overnight stay at Belmont, the manor house of Hudson River landowner and attorney Joshua Hett Smith.

Simultaneously, André sailed upriver on the *Vulture*, a British sloop of war, accompanied by the graying Colonel Beverly Robinson, one of New York's most wealthy and powerful Loyalists. As commander of West Point, Arnold had deliberately chosen to live at Robinson's abandoned country house. That property, two miles south of West Point on the opposite shore (modern-day Garrison, New York), provided perfect cover for meetings with Robinson, who would allegedly plead to reclaim his property from Arnold.

Ultimately, a series of failed communications prevented the September 11 meeting between André and Arnold. As Arnold's barge appeared on the horizon near Dobbs Ferry that Monday morning, British gunboats stationed upriver of the *Vulture*, knowing nothing about the rendezvous, fired. Frantically Arnold's oarsman headed for shore, after which the general waited for hours for André's all-clear message. On the opposite shore, André waited for a similar message from Arnold. Finally both men gave up.

Three days later, Arnold boarded the barge again and continued down-river to Smith's manor house to await the arrival of Peggy and their infant, Neddy, from Philadelphia. A quarter of a century later, Smith claimed in his memoir that he felt honored to have hosted the famous general and his family overnight. Only later, Smith insisted, had he learned the truth. "Little did I then conceive I was dispensing hospitality to a man whose defection from the cause . . . afterwards astonished the whole world."[41]

Smith's defense has long been questioned. His eldest brother, William, a former royal chief justice of New York, had not only defected to the British but was one of General Clinton's closest advisors. That, in turn, heightened suspicions among the patriots that other members of the Smith family were Tories. Hostilities ran so high against the Smiths, Joshua later claimed, that he and his wife, Elizabeth Gordon, escaped to his Hudson River property. Indeed, one of Smith's motives for ingratiating himself with Arnold involved his hopes for extra protection or "motives of security."[42] Sensing the attorney's vulnerability, the crippled general had accordingly drawn Smith aside.

In a few days, Arnold explained, he intended to meet a certain British gentleman on a business matter. Would Smith be willing to row that man and Robinson from the *Vulture* to his home on Haverstraw Bay? Assured the meeting was legal and conducted under a flag of truce, Smith agreed. To ensure confidentiality, the attorney even promised to clear the manor house by escorting his wife and nephews to relatives in Fishkill.

That Thursday, September 14, Arnold's aide, David Franks, arrived with "the greatest treasure you have"—his wife, Peggy.[43] The young mother had arrived weary from a bumpy, ten-day journey with her servant, a slave who drove the carriage, and a baby nurse for her son, Neddy. Just before the trip, the baby had apparently hurt his head, for Peggy's sister-in-law, Hannah, had referred to Neddy as "the poor little sore-headed boy" in one of her notes.[44]

Arnold's passionate love for Peggy, whose "life and happiness" meant all, as even Hannah admitted, inspired him to plan every detail of her trip along with providing her with a list of travel instructions.[45] Among them, "You must by all means get out of your carriage in crossing all ferries and going over all large bridges to prevent accidents." Peggy must also use her own sheets in lieu of the soiled ones often found at inns. Since it was summer, Arnold also advised his wife to "put a feather bed in the light wagon which will make an easy seat, and you will find it cooler and pleasanter to ride in when the roads are smooth than a closed carriage." She must also avoid long carriage rides, which "might fatigue you or the dear boy."[46]

Franks was also ordered to stay either at certain inns or with any of several of Arnold's acquaintances. By the fifth night of the trip, Peggy and her party were advised to stay at a gentleman's farm near Paramus, the Hermitage. There they would be hosted by Anne Watkins and her daughter, Theodosia Prevost. The latter, the twenty-nine-year-old mother of five, was married to British officer James Marcus Prevost, then stationed in South Carolina. In spite of the usual hostilities towards Loyalists, Theodosia and her mother had shrewdly escaped eviction. Subsequent to the June 28, 1778, Battle of Monmouth, Theodosia had invited General Washington to rest at the Hermitage, where, she promised, the "accommodations will be more commodious than those to be procured in the neighborhood" and assured Washington that she would be "particularly happy to make her house agreeable to His Excellency, and family."[47]

Washington, knowing that the family was politically divided, had accepted that invitation. During his stay at the Hermitage, from July 11 to 14, the commander in chief had supervised care of his wounded men, planned the army's next move, and tended to other military business. Meanwhile, his officers flirted with Theodosia's female relatives and guests. One such officer was twenty-two-year-old James Monroe, who described Theodosia as "a lady full of affection, of tenderness and sensibility, separated from her husband, for a series of time by the cruelty of the war . . . fortitude under distress, cheerfulness, life and gayety, in the midst of affliction."[50]

PART II

Tender Wives

6

"As Good and Innocent as an Angel"

"PLEASE TO PRESENT MY best respects to Mrs. Knox," Arnold wrote Knox on August 8, 1780, four days after assuming command of West Point. "A line from you at any time when you are at leisure will be very acceptable," he added, hoping to wheedle more military information from Knox."[1]

The Continental army was then in crisis, its ranks dwindled to ten thousand men, its supplies nearly exhausted, and morale at its lowest ebb since the start of the Revolution. Not only had the British conquered Charleston in May but only 5,300 French soldiers and 7,000 French sailors had arrived in Newport, Rhode Island, in mid-July—many fewer than anticipated. No sooner were General Rochambeau (Jean-Baptiste Donatien de Vimeur) and Admiral Ternay (Charles-Henri-Louis d'Arsac) settled then they heard about the army's wretched condition. That, combined with reports about America's bankrupt credit, led them to stall in Rhode Island rather than embrace Washington's plan for a joint attack on British New York. "Send us troops, ships and money but do not depend on these people nor upon their means. They have neither money nor credit," General Rochambeau warned France's foreign minister, Vergennes, also known as Charles Gravier.[2]

By Thursday, September 14, after weeks of embarrassment and delay, Washington agreed to meet the French leaders in Connecticut. "I shall be at Peekskill," he informed Arnold. "You will be pleased to send down a guard of a captain and fifty at that time and direct the quarters to have a night's forage for about forty horses. You will keep this to yourself, as I want to make my journey a secret."[3]

Arnold was more than "pleased." Immediately he dispatched Washington's "secret" schedule to André and Clinton as more proof of his value as a spy. By September 15 he also assured Washington he would provide the necessary protections, as well as "deliver in person" other information.[4] To Washington, as to other high-ranking officers, Arnold's former bitterness seemed to have disappeared. The new commander of West Point seemed committed to help the Revolution triumph over the British.

On Friday, September 15, the day after Peggy's arrival at Joshua Hett Smith's manor house, she, Arnold, and their party were rowed upriver to Colonel Beverly Robinson's country house. Set above the Hudson in a high meadow, surrounded by pastures and orchards, the rambling, two-story clapboard house was one of the Loyalist's properties before the patriots seized it. Arnold's decision to live there struck a discordant note with his West Point predecessor, General Robert Howe, who, having lived there himself, pointed out its inconvenience, lying two miles south of the fort on the Hudson's opposite shore. "At present I apprehend no danger in these quarters," Arnold scoffed, insisting the house was "convenient for an invalid."[5] Unmentioned, of course, were Arnold's underlying reason for taking this particular house: woods screened the property from the river.

Shrewdly, too, Arnold had hired the impeccably patriotic Richard Varick, a twenty-seven-year-old veteran of Saratoga and former secretary to General Schuyler. Varick, who was privately studying law, had gratefully accepted Arnold's part-time position and thrilled at the idea of meeting his beautiful wife. "The presence of Mrs. Arnold will certainly make our situation in the barren Highlands vastly more agreeable and will more than compensate for every deficiency of nature."[6]

Those "deficiencies" referred to the isolation of the Hudson Highlands, whose hills and deep valleys were sparsely pocketed with homes and farms. Even to Smith, whose country manor lay twenty miles south, Robinson's property seemed "dreary . . . environed with mountains, and no way calculated for the residence of a lady of Mrs. Arnold's taste, she being . . . [an] example and ornament of the politest circles."[7]

If the Hudson Highlands touched a raw nerve in Peggy from her earlier residences in the country, no one knew it. Primed by Arnold, she understood that Robinson's house was an ideal place for Arnold's treason. Secrecy was of utmost importance, especially in the presence of the observant Franks and Varick. If Arnold's leap to the British was to succeed, Peggy must play the innocent as his cheerful and charming young wife.

Peggy's first test came on Sunday, September 17, while she and Arnold were hosting a dinner with West Point's chief of artillery, the battle-scarred General John Lamb. Among the guests were Joshua Hett Smith and his family, who had stayed overnight on their way to Fishkill. That day tensions as powerful as the currents churning the Hudson one hundred feet below lay beneath the polite banter in Robinson's beamed dining room. Smith, thrilled to be dining with the famous General Arnold, talked long and loud through the meal, as his host feigned interest in his comments. Varick and Franks though, puzzled by Arnold's warmth to a suspected Loyalist, fumed, as the former recalled during a subsequent court inquiry.[8] Money, they feared, lay behind the commander's friendliness. Was it possible that Smith had lured their financially strapped employer into another illegal trading scheme?

Adding to these tensions was the arrival of a messenger who handed Arnold a sealed letter whose seal he broke before his guests, scanned and nervously stuffed into his pocket. When General Lamb inquired about the sender, Arnold explained it was from Robinson, who requested a meeting to recover his confiscated home. The message had indeed arrived from Robinson, but it actually contained a seditious signal. Robinson was aboard the *Vulture*, a British man-o'-war, in Haverstraw Bay awaiting the arrival of Major André. Arnold's meeting with the British major was, consequently, imminent.

After lunch, Arnold, Franks, and Lamb barged south to meet Washington at Smith's house near Haverstraw and accompany him to Peekskill. During their trip across the river, the commander in chief mentioned that he planned to come back up the Hudson on Saturday, September 23, to tour West Point and spend the night at the Robinson's with Arnold and Peggy.

Privately, Arnold welcomed that information, key news to forward to the British to obtain his reward of £20,000.

Possibly Franks sensed something was amiss. Or perhaps the day's tensions had worn on Arnold, who subsequently hurled so many "insults and ill treatment" upon Franks, that the aide decided to find another position.[9]

Back at Robinson's, Varick was equally disgruntled. Subsequent to Arnold's departure, he had remained at the table with Peggy and the Smiths. Inevitably, the conversation turned to the Revolution. "America might have made an honorable peace with Great Britain when the commissioners came out in 1778," Smith opined. To that, Varick had sharply disagreed and soon the two men were quarreling. Peggy, meanwhile, grew jittery, then she began chattering hysterically, as if to block out the dissension. It was not the first time Arnold's wife seemed rattled. "She would give utterance to anything and everything on her mind," Franks recalled. As a result, he and Varick already knew to be "scrupulous of what we told her or said within her hearing."[10]

Accordingly, the next morning, Monday, September 18, when Peggy defended Smith as "a very 'warm and staunch Whig,'" Varick attributed her comment to her high-strung nerves. Subsequent events later proved Peggy's behavior to be a case of the lady doth protest too much, per Shakespeare's Queen Gertrude. That Monday Varick, nevertheless, had no reason to suspect Peggy of deception.

Later that afternoon, while reading Arnold's reply to Robinson's letter, Varick again became suspicious. The tone of the letter was so warm, he complained to Arnold, that it seemed "the complexion of one from a friend, rather than one from an enemy."[11] To disarm Varick, Arnold amended the letter tone and directed Robinson to address his request to the civil authorities. Then, he surreptitiously slipped a second letter into the envelope that read, "I shall send a person to Dobbs Ferry or on board the *Vulture* on Wednesday night the 20th instant, and furnish him with a boat and flag of truce. The ship must remain where she is until the time mentioned . . . [when] the gentleman in New York [André] . . . will be permitted to come."[12]

In the double-speak of a spy, Robinson replied on the nineteenth, "I am sorry . . . that it is not proper to allow me to see you, my business being entirely of a private nature. . . . I was induced to make my application to you in hopes of meeting with a favorable reception from a Gent of your character. . . . I have nothing more favorable to say to you . . . other than to wait for a more favorable opportunity of doing something for my family."[13] Arnold understood: André would soon board the *Vulture* and meet him at a specific time and place on the shore at Haverstraw Bay.

Joshua Hett Smith stopped at Robinson's on his return from Fishkill the following morning to report that a "Mr. John Anderson"—André's alias—would appear at his manor house near Haverstraw Bay late that night, Tuesday, September 19. The following morning, September 20, an apologetic message arrived from Smith. His tenant farmers, the brothers Samuel and Joseph Cahoon, who were supposed to row Anderson from the *Vulture* to Haverstraw the preceding night, had refused to cooperate. Enraged, Arnold stormed out of the house, leaving a bewildered Peggy behind. After bellowing orders, his startled boatman rowed him to Stony Point. There Arnold borrowed a horse, galloped to Haverstraw, burst into Smith's house, and insisted upon seeing the Cahoons.

It was near sundown as he was "going for the cows," Samuel Cahoon recalled, when Smith brought him before the scowling general, who demanded he row a certain British gentleman from the *Vulture* to Haverstraw Bay that very night. "I said I could not go, being up the night before, and told him I was afraid to go," the farmer recalled. "But General Arnold urged me to go, and told me if I was a friend to my country I should do my best."[14]

Intimidated, Samuel convinced his brother, Joseph, to return with him to Arnold. Drams of whisky, bribes of flour, and, finally, threats of imprisonment followed. "If I did not assist . . . for the good of my country and Congress he would put me under guard immediately," Samuel said.[15] At midnight, the Cahoons and Smith rowed with muffled oars six miles downriver to the *Vulture*.

By 1 a.m. the morning of Thursday, September 21, Arnold was waiting at a landing beneath Long Clove Mountain at Haverstraw Bay. Through the inky darkness, he spotted an approaching rowboat with three men and a cloaked figure seated in the stern. Once the vessel landed, the passenger disembarked and walked towards a thicket. There Arnold greeted him. The slender, fine-featured man was Major John André. But he was not wearing a disguise. Instead, beneath his blue cloak was his scarlet uniform. As the men talked, André refused to cross British lines to Smith's manor house on the American side. Clinton had forbidden him to do so, as well as to wear a disguise. Both, the British general had warned André, were the behaviors of a common spy.

Although disgruntled, Arnold provided André with information about West Point, after which the two men argued about the size of his reward. By 4 a.m. Smith interrupted them to warn of the approaching sunrise. Worried about their visibility in the dawning light and the possibility of being shot by the British, the Cahoons balked at rowing André to the *Vulture*. That left the British major trapped. Consequently he had to ride with Arnold through American lines two miles to Smith's country house.

After a hurried breakfast, Arnold and André gazed down upon the river at the *Vulture*, bobbing quietly at anchor. Suddenly cannon fire burst across the Hudson at Teller's Point, today's Croton Point. Arnold was stunned: no cannons had previously been stationed there. A day earlier, though, the doughty commander, Colonel James Livingston, worried about the *Vulture*'s proximity, had ordered heavy guns delivered from Verplanck, which he fired upon the ship at dawn. The "very hot fire . . . continued two hours, and would have been longer but luckily their magazine blew up," Robinson recalled.[16] So badly damaged was the *Vulture*'s hull, rigging, and gangway stanchions that its captain, Andrew Sutherland, launched longboats to tow the battered ship downriver for repairs.

André and Arnold were flabbergasted, for the retreat of the *Vulture* left the British officer stranded in enemy territory. Arnold quickly proposed two possible solutions. Joshua Hett Smith, he assured the edgy André, would see to his safe return to British territory. To ensure that, Arnold coolly issued two passes. The first allowed Smith to travel "with a boat and three hands, and a flag to Dobbs Ferry," from where André could cross the Hudson to British territory. The second allowed Smith and a "Mr. John Anderson" (the alias for a disguised André) to ride through Westchester County to neutral ground and reach the British border.[17]

Intuitively, André distrusted the second option. Westchester County was dangerous, especially in its southern reaches, a no-man's land where skirmishes between patriots, or "cowboys," and ruffians, or "skinners," men with no political allegiances, robbed travelers in exchange for permission to proceed to British lines.

Dismissing André's objections, Arnold foisted maps and papers about West Point upon him, insisting he carry them back to Clinton in his boots. Smith, Arnold reassured the agitated British officer, would ensure his safe return to New York.

By Friday morning, September 22, Arnold had returned to the embrace of a relieved Peggy. During his absence, Varick and Franks had confided in her. The general, they feared, "had some commercial plan" through Smith involving a Mr. John Anderson. If that was true, Varick and Franks said they intended to quit.[18] After hearing Peggy's report, Arnold drew his secretary and aide aside and promised to cut off his relationship with Smith. Privately, he intended to see the country lawyer only once more, in any case, and then only to confirm André's safe return to the British.

The next morning, Saturday, September 23, Smith arrived at Robinson's to report that he had delivered André to safe territory. The night of the crossing, he had disguised André in an old velvet jacket, frayed lace shirt, and beaver-skin cap, and had crossed Kings Ferry, arriving at Verplanck, where they slept in a farmhouse. At dawn on Friday, they paid a woman for a breakfast of cornmeal gruel and rode south through Westchester County. Along the way Smith, complaining of an attack of ague—a malaria-like syndrome of fever and chills to which he was prone—convinced André to complete the last few miles of the journey alone to the British border. To that, the British officer had happily agreed.

After hearing Smith's account, Arnold invited him to stay for the midday meal. During the fish course, the butter ran out. Peggy called for more, but a servant explained that their supply was gone. "Bless me, I had forgot the olive oil I bought in Philadelphia. It will do very well with salt fish," Arnold replied, adding it cost him "eighty dollars" in Continental money. "'Eighty pence,' [meaning] that a dollar was really no more than a penny,'"

Smith countered. Varick, resenting Smith's crack, snapped, 'That is not true, Mr. Smith.'" What followed, according to General Lamb, was "a very high dispute," which grew so acrimonious that Peggy, "observing her husband in a passion, begged us to drop the matter."[19]

After an awkward silence the meal ended and Smith returned to Haverstraw. Arnold then ordered Franks and Varick into his office where the trio argued. Varick declared Smith a "damned rascal, a scoundrel and a spy." Acidly, Arnold bellowed, "If he asked the Devil to dine with him, the gentlemen of the family should be civil to him, I'm always willing to be advised by the gentlemen of [my] family but by God [I will] not be dictated by them."[20] Exasperated, Franks left the house and rode to Newburgh to deliver a military notice.

In the wake of Franks's departure, Varick presented Arnold with a letter from an aide to the governor of New York State warning of Smith's untrustworthy and "loose character." Solemnly, the general listened. Then, to the younger man's surprise, Arnold apologized for "treating [him] with such cavalier language" and promised to refrain from seeing Smith again.[21]

Later that evening, Varick developed flu-like symptoms, ran a high fever, and collapsed in bed. When servants told Peggy about his illness, she dashed to his side. Varick recalled that the "amiable lady had spent an hour while I lay in a high fever, made tea for me, and paid me the utmost attention in my illness."[22] Like other Revolutionary era-women, Arnold's wife was an accomplished nurse. That she did not abandon Varick to her servants convinced everyone in the Robinson's household that Peggy would never deliberately hurt others.

Between Thursday, September 21, and Friday, September 22, as sailors repaired the *Vulture*, neither Captain Sutherland nor Robinson had expected André's return. By Saturday, September 23, though, they grew alarmed. "It is with the greatest concern that I must now acquaint your Excellency that we have not heard the least account of him since he left the ship," Robinson finally informed Clinton on Sunday. "I shall do everything in my power to come at some knowledge of Major André."[23]

That same day, Washington announced a change of plans: he would arrive at the Arnold's residence on Monday morning, September 25. Accompanying him were the Marquis de Lafayette, twenty-three-year-old Alexander Hamilton, Henry Knox, and two French engineers. That morning, at around 9 a.m., as servants completed preparations for breakfast, Hamilton and Lafayette arrived to report that Washington was delayed. On their way to Robinson's, the commander in chief, Knox, Lafayette, and the engineers had turned down a path towards the Hudson. "General, you are going in the wrong direction: you know that Mrs. Arnold is waiting breakfast for us, and that road will take us out of our way," Lafayette reminded Washington.[24]

"Ah, Marquis, I know you young men are all in love with Mrs. Arnold and wish to get where she is as soon as possible," the commander in chief had jovially replied. "You may go and take your breakfast with her, and tell her not to wait for me. I must ride down and examine the redoubts on this side of the river, and will be there in a short time."[25]

Soon after Hamilton and Lafayette appeared for breakfast, Arnold received a letter. A Mr. John Anderson had been captured in Westchester County. Within the man's boots were treasonous papers about West Point. Arnold, Franks recalled, immediately "went upstairs to his lady."[24] Above, in their bedroom, an agitated, whispered conversation took place as Arnold and Peggy realized their own lives were at risk.

"In about two minutes his Excellency General Washington's servant came to the door and informed me that his Excellency was nigh at hand," Franks added. "I went immediately upstairs and informed Arnold of it. He came down in great confusion and ordering a horse to be saddled, mounted him and told me to inform his Excellency that he was gone over to West Point and would return in about an hour."[26]

Waves of fright swept over Peggy, set her trembling, and, perhaps, as historians later suspect, prompted her to burn her husband's incriminating letters in the bedroom's fireplace. As Arnold's wife, Peggy would be subjected to questioning, possible imprisonment, and, if found guilty, hanged for treason. Those thoughts raced through Peggy's head, and then a plan formed: she would become mad, jolted into insanity by the shock of

Arnold's betrayal of America. It would not be difficult; as a child, indeed as a half-grown woman, Peggy had thrown tantrums and feigned fits to get her way. Now her life depended upon her successful display of still another outburst.

As Peggy plotted her course of action, Washington arrived for breakfast. After the meal, he left for West Point where he anticipated meeting Arnold. Peggy, cowering in her bedroom, asked her housekeeper to check on the ailing Varick. Then, willing herself into a frenzy, she tore at her hair and clothes, weeping, her sobs accelerating in volume.

Suddenly an earth-piercing shriek emanated from the Arnolds' bedroom, prompting Varick to throw off his bedclothes and dash upstairs. There stood a nearly unrecognizable Peggy. Instead of being tastefully dressed and coiffed, the young blonde was "mad to see him, with her hair disheveled and flowing about her neck," Varick later wrote his sister. "Her morning-gown with few other clothes remained on her—too few to be seen even by gentlemen of the family, much less by many strangers. Peggy was raving, distracted. She seized me by the hand with this—to me—distressing address and a wild look; 'Colonel Varick, have you ordered my child to be killed?'"[27]

Shocked, the young man wondered at the outburst from "this most amiable and distressed of her sex whom I most valued. Then, she fell on her knees at my feet with prayers and entreaties to spare her innocent babe. A scene too shocking for my feelings, in a state of body and nerves so weakened by indisposition and a burning fever." Varick immediately summoned Dr. William Eustis from West Point. By then Franks, having returned from his errand at Newburgh, Varick, and the physician "carried her to her bed, raving mad."

Repeatedly, Varick attempted to calm her. "When she seemed a little composed, she burst again into pitiable tears and exclaimed to me, alone on her bed with her, that she had not a friend left here," he explained. After all, he reasoned, she had "Franks and me, and General Arnold would soon be home from West Point with General Washington." To that, Peggy wildly retorted, "No, General Arnold will never return; he is gone, he is gone forever; there, there there, the spirits have carried [him] up there, they have put hot irons in his head—pointing that he was gone up to the ceiling." By then, Varick sensed "something more than ordinary having occasioned her hysterics and utter frenzy."

Washington, meanwhile, puzzled by Arnold's absence at West Point, returned to his home in mid-afternoon. Hamilton handed him a packet of dispatches after which he was asked to summon Knox and Lafayette. "Arnold has betrayed us!" Washington exclaimed, holding the letters in his trembling hand. "Whom can we trust now?"[28] That was the only time, said Lafayette, "that Washington ever gave way, even for a moment, under a reversal of fortune. I was the only being who ever witnessed in him, an exhibition of feeling so foreign to his temperament."[29] Hamilton and Lafayette's aide, James McHenry, immediately raced to Verplanck in hopes of arresting the traitor. It was too late. Arnold had already boarded the *Vulture*.

Upstairs at the Robinsons', Peggy continued to rave about "a hot iron on her head and no one but General Washington could take it off, and [she] wanted to see the general."[30] Hearing that, the unsuspecting Dr. Eustis summoned Varick and Franks, roaring, "For God's sake send for Arnold or the woman would die."[31] Judging from Peggy's comments, the two aides suspected that after confessing treason to his wife, Arnold had defected. Fearful of overstepping their authority, Franks and Varick brought Washington to Peggy's bedside, hoping the general could confirm their suspicions.

Peggy stared vacantly at Washington. "She said, no, it was not [him]. The general assured her he was, but she exclaimed, 'No! that is not General Washington! That is the man who is going to assist Colonel Varick in killing my child.' She repeated the same sad story about General Arnold; poor, distressed, unhappy, frantic and miserable lady," Varick recalled.[32]

Washington then left the bedroom. "Come gentlemen; since Mrs. Arnold is unwell and the General is absent, let us sit down without ceremony."[34] Washington calmly told Lafayette, Knox, and Hamilton. "Never was there a more melancholy dinner," Lafayette recalled. "The general was silent and reserved and none of us spoke of what we were thinking about. . . . Gloom and distrust seemed to pervade every mind."[33]

← →

At Verplanck, where Hamilton discovered Arnold had escaped to the *Vulture*, a messenger handed him a letter. Addressed to Washington, the traitor had written:

> The heart which is conscious of its own rectitude cannot attempt to palliate a step which the world may censure as wrong. I have ever acted from a principle of love to my country, since the commencement of the present unhappy contest between Great Britain and the colonies. The same principle of love to my country actuates my present conduct, however it may appear inconsistent to the world, who very seldom judge right of any man's actions.[34]

"Too often," Arnold claimed, he had "experienced the ingratitude of my country" and now expected nothing else. He had only one request: "From the known humanity of your Excellency, I am induced to ask your protection for Mrs. Arnold from every insult and injury that a mistaken vengeance of my country may expose her to. It ought to fall only on me: she is as good and innocent as an angel, and is incapable of doing wrong. I beg she may be permitted to return to her friends in Philadelphia, or come to me, as she may choose."[35]

Within that envelope Arnold also enclosed a letter for Peggy, which read:

> Words are wanting to express my feelings and distress on your account, who are incapable of doing wrong, yet are exposed to suffer wrong, I have requested his Excellency General Washington to take you under his protection and permit you to go to your friends in Philadelphia—or to come to me. I am at present incapable of giving advice. Follow your own intentions. But do not forget that I shall be miserable until we meet. Adieu—kiss my dear boy for me. God almighty bless and protect you, sincerely prays
>
> Thy affectionate and devoted
> B. Arnold
>
> P. S. Write me one line if possible to ease my anxious heart.[36]

Even Arnold's note did not calm Peggy, who remained "frantic with distress." Her reaction, an overwhelmed Hamilton wrote his fiancée, Elizabeth Schuyler, was "the most affecting scene I was ever witness to. At one moment, she raved, another she melted into tears, sometimes pressing her baby to her breast and lamenting its fate by the imprudence of his father. All the sweetness of beauty, all the loveliness of innocence, all the tenderness of a wife, and all the fondness of a mother showed themselves in her appearance and conduct." Consequently, he added, "We have every reason to believe that she was entirely unacquainted with the plan, and that the first knowledge of it was when Arnold went to tell her that he must banish himself from his country and from her forever."[37]

Lafayette, too, was hoodwinked. "The unhappy Mrs. Arnold did not know a word of this conspiracy," he insisted to Chevalier Luzerne. "Her husband told her before going away that he was flying never to come back, and he left her unconscious . . . we did everything we could to quiet her; but she looked upon us as the murderers of her husband, and it was impossible to restore her to her senses. The horror with which her husband's conduct has inspired her, and a thousand other feelings, make her the most unhappy of women."[38]

The next morning, Tuesday, September 26, Hamilton returned to Peggy's bedside. Though more composed, "she is not easily to be consoled . . . very apprehensive of her country will fall upon her (who is unfortunate) for the guilt of her husband. I have tried to persuade her that her fears are ill-founded, but she will not be convinced." The young woman's suffering, Hamilton added, was "so eloquent that I wished myself her brother, to have a right to become her defender. As it is, I have entreated her to enable me to give her proofs of my friendship."[39]

As outraged by Arnold's betrayal of Peggy as of America, he wrote, "Could I forgive Arnold for sacrificing his honor, reputation, and duty, I could not forgive him for acting a part that must have forfeited the esteem of so fine a woman." Yet to his astonishment, Peggy continued to worry about Arnold and replied to his letter. Her message has not been preserved, but judging from Hamilton's comment, it was loving. "At present," wrote the perplexed Hamilton, "she almost forgets his crime in his misfortunes and her horror at the guilt of the traitor is lost in her love of the man."[40]

Exhausted by hours of crying and hysterics, Peggy fell into a restless sleep. Her marathon display of insanity, the grandest theatrical performance of her life, had successfully deceived Washington and Hamilton.

7

"A Momentary Pang"

"THE RAIN FELL IN torrents, and it was the darkest and most dismal night I have ever known," recalled army surgeon mate Dr. Isaac Bronson of the first hours of Tuesday, September 26.[1] By 8 a.m. a soggy group of soldiers had arrived at the Arnold residence with an agitated Joshua Hett Smith in tow. Hearing the commotion, Washington appeared on the porch, eyed the prisoner coolly, then withdrew into the house.

Soldiers had awakened Smith at midnight as he slept in a relative's house in Fishkill and forced him at bayonet point to march the eighteen miles to Arnold's house. After confinement in a back room, the irate attorney was brought before Washington from whom he demanded an explanation. "Sir," Washington icily replied, "do you know that Arnold has fled and that Mr. Anderson, whom you piloted through our lines, proves to be Major John André, the Adjutant General of the British Army, who is now our prisoner? I expect him here under guard of one-hundred horses to meet his fate as a spy." Pointing to a tree outside the window, the commander in chief added, "Unless you confess who were your accomplices I shall suspend you both on that tree."[2]

As Washington predicted, one hundred Continental dragoons on horses soon pounded into the yard with Major John André in their possession. The prisoner sat upon a horse, Dr. Bronson recalled, with an expression that was "impossible to describe."[3]

MAJOR JOHN ANDRÉ,

Adjutant General to his Majesty's Forces in North America
under the Command of Sir Henry Clinton.

Publish'd Sept.r 20, 1784, by I.K. Sherwin, Engraver to his Majesty, and his Royal Highness the Prince of Wales,
N.o 66. St James's Street, and Sold by Robert Wilkinson, N.o 125 Fenchurch Street.

Major John André

Washington's attitude towards the British spy was measured. "I would not wish André to be treated with insult," he observed. But since André was not a "common prisoner of war," the officer "could not be entitled to the usual indulgence they receive and so is to be most closely and narrowly watched."[4] Notably, André and his old friend Peggy Arnold spent that night in the same house but did not communicate. They may not have even known of each other's presence.

Fearing that Arnold's betrayal would provoke a British attack, Washington immediately tightened security for West Point. "Put the division on the left [flank] in motion as soon as possible with orders to proceed to King's Ferry," he wrote Nathanael Greene at headquarters in Tappan, New York.[5] With equal urgency, Knox ordered the region's heavy guns repositioned to repulse an enemy attack along the Hudson. "The strangest thing in the world has happened. Arnold has gone to the enemy," Knox warned Major Sebastian Bauman, head of artillery at West Point. "It is incumbent on us to be on our guard."[6]

Before long, messengers were galloping across the region, conveying the news to each army post. At Preakness, New Jersey, one officer recalled that "dark moment . . . in which the defection of Arnold was announced in whispers. It was midnight, horses were saddling, officers going from tent to tent ordering their men, in suppressed voices, to turn out and parade. No drum beat; the troops formed in silence and darkness . . . in consternation, for who in such an hour, and called together in such a manner, and in total ignorance of the cause, but must have felt and feared the near approach of some tremendous shock."[7]

According to Dr. James Thacher, "At three o'clock this morning an alarm was spread throughout our camp. Two regiments from the Pennsylvania line, were ordered to march immediately to West Point, and the whole army to be held in readiness to march at a moment's warning . . . in consequence of the discovery of one of the most extraordinary events in modern history . . . the treacherous conspiracy of Major General Arnold, and the capture of Major John André, adjutant general."[8]

At daybreak on Tuesday, September 26, General Greene ordered all soldiers to hear an announcement:

> Treason, of the blackest dye, was yesterday discovered. General Arnold, who commanded at West Point, lost to every sentiment of honor, of private and public obligation, was about to deliver up that important post into the hands of the enemy. Such an event must have given the American cause a dangerous, if not a fatal wound; happily, the treason has been timely discovered, to prevent the fatal misfortune. The providential train of circumstances which led to it, affords the most convincing proofs that the liberties of America, are the object of Divine protection.[9]

Had André initially been more cautious in his plans or less trusting of Arnold, he might have avoided capture. Once trapped in Haverstraw, though, the British officer had no choice but to disguise himself in Smith's old clothes before they crossed the Hudson that Friday evening, September 22. At dawn the next day, after spending the night in a Verplanck farmhouse, André and Smith ate a hurried breakfast and mounted their horses.

The closer they rode towards neutral territory, Smith recalled, "the more his [André's] countenance brightened into a cheerful serenity, and he became very affable. In short, I now found him highly entertaining," As they approached Pine's Bridge in Tarrytown, the country lawyer gave André half his cash, presented him with a map, and directed him towards British lines. André seemed so "affected at parting," Smith claimed, that he had even offered "a valuable gold watch in remembrance of him, as a keepsake, which I refused."[10]

For several miles André traveled alone before stopping at a bridge to consult his map. Three scruffy young men suddenly emerged from the woods and blocked his way. The tallest, wearing a German sharpshooter's coat, pointed a musket at André, who muttered, "I hope you belong to our party." The second man asked André, "Which party?" Assuming that the coat belonged to a Hessian, André replied, "The lower," meaning the British. Then, to confirm his status, André displayed his gold watch. "I am an officer in the British service and have now been on particular business in the country," he explained. "I hope you will not detain me."[11] Suspicion hardened the faces of the trio. "My God, I must do anything to get along!" André exclaimed. "My lads, you had best let me go or you will bring yourselves into trouble, for, by stopping me, you will detain the General's business. I am going to Dobbs Ferry to meet a person there and get information for him."[12]

Paulding, the wearer of the German jacket, explained that he and his companions "did not mean to take anything from him," but one of his companions, Isaac Van Wart, demanded André's money. After realizing that the traveler had only a few coins, the trio stripped him. In André's socks they found Arnold's papers on West Point. Paulding, the only one of the trio who could read, studied them for a moment. "This," he exclaimed, "is a spy!"[13]

Accounts differ as to what happened next. André's captors claimed that he attempted to bribe his way to freedom with his watch, horse, 100 guineas, and the promise of household goods. André insisted that he was even more generous and had offered the trio a sizeable sum to be paid at the British border. After a whispered argument, the trio decided to turn André over to soldiers at the nearest military post.

Before leaving, Paulding fired his musket, notifying other "irregulars" that something important had happened. It was then, Van Wart recalled, that "big drops of sweat" poured off André's face. "You never saw such an alteration in any man's face . . . only a few moments before, he was uncommonly gay in his looks, but after we had made him prisoner, you could read in his face that he thought it was all over with him. After traveling one or two miles, he said, 'I would to God you had blown my brains out when you stopped me!'"[14]

At the North Castle post, Lieutenant Colonel John Jameson ordered the prisoner and his papers sent on to Arnold. André was relieved, convinced the American general would free him and have him returned to the British. But as he and his guards rode towards the Hudson, a messenger intervened and ordered their return to North Castle. Military protocol demanded that, insisted secret service officer Major Benjamin Tallmadge: the prisoner must appear at the Arnold residence only after Washington arrived there on

Monday. Never dreaming that West Point's commander had instigated the treachery, Tallmadge consequently reported the capture of a John Anderson—and unwittingly provoked Arnold's flight.

The next day André's guard at a second post in South Salem observed that the British captive "looked like a reduced [impoverished] gentleman. His small clothes (beneath his jacket) were nankeen [a yellow cloth]. . . . His coat, purple, with gold lace, worn, somewhat threadbare, with a small-brimmed hat tarnished on his head." One hint of the prisoner's true identity were his whitetop boots, which British officers wore on informal occasions. Another was André's hair. When a barber combed it, white power fell onto the prisoner's clothes, suggesting the recent wearing of a wig and convincing his guard he had "no ordinary person in charge."[15]

After learning that Washington, rather than Arnold, would supervise his capture, André decided to confess the truth. His real name, he wrote the commander in chief, was John André, not Anderson. He had entered neutral territory to "meet a person who was to give me intelligence," only to be "betrayed . . . into the vile condition of an enemy in disguise within your posts." Consequently André said that he hoped he would be "branded with nothing dishonorable, as no motive could be mine, but the service of my king, and I was involuntarily an imposter."[16]

The letter did not soften Washington. Nor, when the dragoons delivered André to the Arnold residence that rainy Tuesday morning, September 26, had the Virginian chosen to meet him. To do so, reasoned Washington, might weaken his judgment. André had violated the international laws of war. He had behaved as a common spy. Death by hanging was the usual punishment.

On Tuesday, September 26, Peggy seemed calmer but spent the day in bed weighing where to go: to Arnold in British New York or to her parents' home in Philadelphia. By the following morning, a rainy Wednesday, she had decided upon the latter. After accepting sympathetic farewells from Washington and Hamilton, Peggy was escorted into Arnold's light carriage with her baby and, at a signal from her escort and Arnold's aide, David Franks, wheeled away.

The roads north and south of West Point buzzed with activity. Hundreds of Continental soldiers filed along them. Some stood guard; still others served as lookouts along the Hudson. Heavy guns and cannons had been repositioned for attack. Continental regiments from New Jersey marched towards West Point, as locals, spooked by rumors of other nearby traitors, retreated into their homes and farms. "Heavens on earth! We are all astonishment, each peeping at his next neighbor to see if any treason was hanging about him; nay, we even descended to a critical examination of ourselves," Colonel Alexander Scammel observed. "The surprise soon settled down to a fixed detestation and abhorrence of Arnold."[17]

As Mrs. Arnold's carriage creaked along the muddy roads towards New Jersey, Peggy stared into the driving rain, shrinking from the taunts and jeers of residents who recognized the vehicle. Occasionally Franks stopped at inns and farmhouses to purchase food and drink but often had the door slammed into his face. Finally, on September 28, Arnold's carriage rolled into the town of Kakait. There, Franks met a Mr. Reed, "the only man who would take us in at the place or give our horses anything to eat," he wrote Varick. "We got here, I very wet, Mrs. Arnold, thank God in tolerable spirits. . . . I have hopes to get them home without any return of her distress in so violent a degree."[18]

A few miles away, in a farmhouse near army headquarters in Preakness, New Jersey, Lucy Knox must have been jolted by news of Arnold's treason. Once that military hero had been her friend, the warrior whose affection she attempted to win for Betsy DeBlois, the same man who had gallantly escorted her and her baby to Valley Forge. How was that possible? Arnold was the renowned hero of Valcour Island, the courageous Eagle of Saratoga, the Hero of Freeman's Farm, the man who had sacrificed his fortune and his leg for the American cause—the general whom "her Harry" continued to admire even after the court-martial. It was true that the Supreme Executive Council had persecuted him and Congress had not appropriately honored his courageous performance on the battlefield.

Still, Arnold's betrayal of the patriotic cause was reprehensible, a desecration of the thousands of lives lost in battle and a mockery of the lofty ideals that inspired the Revolution. To signify her own faith in the war, Lucy had styled her long dark hair in the shape of a tricornered Continental military hat, forming a "a pyramid which rose a foot above her head," as the French general Chastellux noted soon afterwards.[19] Moved by Knox's description of Peggy's anguish resulting from Arnold's treason, Lucy, too, probably sympathized with her counterpart, the defiant bride of Philadelphia.

By September 29 Peggy's carriage approached Paramus for a second overnight stay with Theodosia Prevost. The house was filled with guests, but after they left, Peggy allegedly made a startling confession. "She was heartily tired of the theatricals she was exhibiting," she told Theodosia. Moreover, she confessed that she had "corresponded with the British commander . . . was disgusted with the American cause; and those who had the management of public affairs—and that through great persuasion and unceasing perseverance, she had ultimately brought the general into an arrangement to surrender West Point to the British."[20]

The story not only implicated Peggy as a fellow traitor but as instigator of Arnold's treason. Aaron Burr, who would marry the newly widowed Theodosia in 1782 and later became America's third vice president, often repeated that story to others after the Arnolds' deaths, and an account of it appeared in Matthew Davis's 1836 *Memoirs of Aaron Burr*.

In the late nineteenth century, Lewis Burd Walker, a Shippen descendant, attempted to refute the accusation by publishing a rationale for Burr's comments in the influential *Pennsylvania Magazine of History and Biography*. According to Walker, Burr was visiting at the Hermitage when Peggy arrived. He offered to escort her to Philadelphia. Supposedly she accepted, but as they rode together in a carriage, Burr, a notorious womanizer, tried to seduce Peggy, who rejected him. "Indignantly repelled," Walker wrote, Burr later "treasured up his revenge and left a story behind him worthy of his false and malignant heart."[21]

But Walker's story was specious. Not only had the ever-loyal David Franks escorted Peggy and her child to the Hermitage, but he also delivered her in early October to the Shippens' home in Philadelphia.

← →

By the time Peggy's carriage left the Hermitage, on Wednesday, September 27, Arnold's betrayal had been announced in Philadelphia. Immediately, Joseph Reed and the Pennsylvania Supreme Executive Council ordered the city sheriff to "make a diligent search for General Arnold's papers."[22] No sooner were the files located than authorities discovered André's August 16, 1779, "millinery" letter to Peggy.

On Saturday, September 30, a notice, probably written by Reed, appeared in the *Pennsylvania Packet* asserting that the letter proved Peggy's role in Arnold's treason. "Our correspondent concludes . . . on the fallacious and dangerous sentiments so frequently avowed in this city that female opinions are of no consequence in public matters," the *Packet* shrilly announced. "Behold the consequences. Col. Andrie [*sic*], under the mask of friendship and former acquaintance at Meshianzas [*sic*] and balls, opens a correspondence in August 1779 with Mrs. Arnold, which has doubtless been improved on his part to the dreadful and horrid issue . . . and which but for the overruling care of a kind Providence, must have involved this country and our allies in great distress, and perhaps utter ruin."[23]

Aghast at the public accusations, the Shippens protested that André's letter was nothing more than a gracious offer to supply Peggy with materials for stylish new bonnets. As her brother-in-law, Burd (who served as the family's spokesman), asserted, those accusations were ludicrous: "The impossibility of so delicate and timorous a girl as poor Peggy being in the least privy or concerned in so bold and adventurous a plan is great. . . . It is not possible she should have engaged in such a wicked one." Even General Washington, Burd added, "certifies 'that he has every reason to believe she is innocent & requests all persons to treat her with that humanity & tenderness due to her sex & virtues.'"[24]

The same Saturday of the *Packet* notice, the beat of a solitary drum summoned Philadelphians to the streets. Behind the drummer marched six soldiers, a commander, and a wagon displaying an effigy of Arnold. The dummy had two faces and held a mask in his right hand. In his left, the figure clutched a message from Satan, announcing his completion of mischief.

Behind the dummy stood the devil, "shaking a bag of money at the general's left ear" and grasping a pitchfork poised to drive the traitor into hell "as the reward due for the many crimes which the thief of gold had made him commit."[25] As the wagon paraded by the Shippens' home and passed through other city streets, spectators shouted, whistled, and hooted. Later they set Arnold's effigy on fire. "The public clamor," Burd grimly noted, "is high."[26]

Adding to the animosity were the *Packet*'s exposes of Arnold's illegal business schemes. Among his correspondence Arnold had preserved one of Peggy's letters that further ruined her reputation as a sweet-tempered young woman. Written after a concert at the French minister's house, Peggy's note jeered at several other women also in attendance. Philadelphia society was consequently outraged, producing "much offense." Even so, Burd criticized the *Packet* for printing it. To him, it seemed "rather hard that those observations which are intended merely for the eye of a husband should be made public and criticized."[27]

In the midst of that uproar, on October 2 or 3, Peggy arrived at the Shippen house, where her sympathetic parents fussed over her. Almost immediately "she fell into a kind of stupor," which Burd attributed to her "violent transitions from one kind of grief to another." For days, the young woman remained ill, so emotionally distraught that she could not be comforted. Her outbursts were understandable, Burd opined, reflecting the family's view: "A girl of the most refined feelings, of the most affectionate disposition and dotingly fond of her husband, must be affected in a very extraordinary manner upon such an unhappy event. She keeps to her room and is almost continually on the bed. Her peace of mind seems to me entirely destroyed."[28]

Indeed, there was more to Peggy's despair than the Shippens knew. Contradictory emotions roiled over her: grief over Arnold's thwarted plans and their mutual hopes for a large reward; relief that her husband was safe, coupled with doubts about their marriage. Would she ever see Arnold again? Since he was safely ensconced among the British, would she, could she, join him in a new life in England? Or would she remain in Philadelphia, neither married nor single, residing in her parents' home to raise her son alone?

Peggy's supportive but unsuspecting relatives expressed disgust with Arnold, declaring that her marriage to him seventeen months earlier had been a mistake. "The sacrifice was an immense one at her being married to him at all," Burd fumed. His father-in-law, Judge Shippen, worried that his beloved daughter would never recover her stability. Should Peggy be put "into the hands of so bad a man, her mind might, in time, be debased, and her welfare . . . endangered."[29]

For all her angst, Peggy remained curiously loyal to Arnold. To the Shippens' consternation, she seemed to want "to be persuaded there was some palliation of his guilt . . . and that his conduct had not been so thoroughly base and treacherous as it was generally thought."[30] Peggy's tenderness, the Shippens concluded, was typical of her affectionate nature, not to the character of the infamous man she had wed.

Then came rumors that the Supreme Executive Council planned to exile Peggy. "We tried every means to prevail on the Council to permit her to stay among us, and not to compel her to go to that infernal villain her husband in New York," Burd wrote to his father. In an effort to placate the council, Judge Shippen had Peggy sign a paper promising "not to write General Arnold any letters whatever, and to receive no letters without showing them to the Council if she was permitted to stay." For several days, Peggy's future looked brighter, according to Burd, with signs that council members seemed "to favour our request."[31]

Finally, on October 27, the council reached a decision.

The Council, taking into consideration the case of Mrs. Margaret Arnold (the wife of Benedict Arnold, an attainted traitor with the enemy at New York), whose residence in this city has become dangerous to the public safety; and this board, being desirous, as much as possible, to prevent any correspondence and intercourse being carried on with persons of disaffected character in this state, and the enemy at New York, and especially with the said Benedict Arnold, therefore, resolved, that the said Margaret Arnold depart this state within fourteen days from the date hereof, and she do not return again during the continuance of the present war.[32]

Once again, Judge Shippen tried to reason with the council. "She is very young and possessed of qualities which entitle her to a better fate," than being forced to return to her villainous husband.[33] Other family friends, like John Jay, sympathized. "Poor Mrs. Arnold; was there ever such a villain? His wife is much to be pitied. It is painful to see so charming a woman so sacrificed," he wrote to Robert Morris.[34]

No amount of pleading would change the Supreme Executive Council's decision.[35] On November 9, the Shippens' carriage rolled across New Jersey, reaching British lines at Paulus Hook (today's Jersey City) on November 13. There, Judge Shippen bid a tearful good-bye to Peggy and his infant grandson, Neddy, as they boarded a boat for New York City. "My poor daughter Peggy's unfortunate connection has given us great grief," Judge Shippen later wrote his father.[35]

A day later, Burd wrote his own father, "If she could have stayed, Mr. Shippen would not have wished her ever to be united to him [Arnold] again. It makes me melancholy every time I think of the matter. It is much more so to be obliged, against her will, to go to the arms of a man who appears to be so very black."[36]

Peggy's reaction to her exile has not been recorded. Family letters suggest that she still loved Arnold and believed his attempted delivery of West Point to the British had been a courageous and even a noble deed.

On Tuesday, September 26, Knox's horror over Arnold's betrayal was matched by his recognition that the British prisoner was the same man he had shared a cabin with four years earlier at Lake George. Later that Tuesday, Continental dragoons escorted André and Smith to West Point, and, by Thursday, André was transported downriver and lodged at Casparus Mabie's Tavern in Tappan, New York, near Washington's headquarters.

Letters from the British demanding André's release had already reached the commander in chief. From the *Vulture*, Colonel Beverly Robinson arrogantly defended the prisoner's behavior. His letter claimed that the British officer "went up with a flag at the request of General Arnold, on public business with him, and had his permit to return by land to New York." Ignoring the fact that the "public business" happened to be treason, the

Loyalist contended that André's imprisonment was a "violation of flags, and contrary to the custom and usage of all nations." Moreover, "every step Major André took was by the . . . direction of General Arnold, even that of taking a feigned name."[37]

General Clinton also wrote Washington, insisting that he had permitted André to meet Arnold "at the particular request of that general officer"[38] Within Clinton's packet was a letter from Arnold, written at the British general's insistence. "I have the honor to inform you, sir, that . . . a few hours must return Major André to our Excellency's order, as that officer is assuredly under the protection of a flag of truce . . . for the purpose, of a conversation which I requested to hold with him," Arnold wrote. "Thinking it proper he should return by land, I directed him to make use of the feigned name of John Anderson, under which he had, by my directions come on shore, and gave him passports to pass my lines to the White Plains on his way to New York."[39]

Washington, who doubted the existence of a flag, since André had not mentioned one in his confession, appointed a fourteen-man board of general officers to weigh the matter in a court-martial. André's trial began on Friday, September 29, at Tappan's Dutch Church, with Nathanael Greene as president and Henry Knox as one of the judges. Today, an abstract of those proceedings from John Laurence, the board's general advocate, is the sole remaining record of what transpired.

According to that document, André appeared that morning before his judges, still dressed in Smith's old clothes, and described the events leading to his capture. The rowboat that had brought him from the *Vulture* to the shore near Haverstraw had carried no flag, André explained, for he expected to return to the British sloop that same night. Only later, when forced to ride with Arnold to Smith's manor house, did André realize he had been tricked into crossing into American lines. After the *Vulture* was attacked and towed downstream, André realized he was trapped. The only way he could escape was to don Smith's old clothes as a disguise.

Ultimately, wrote Laurence, the jury concluded that André had violated several international laws of war. The officer "came on shore from the Vulture sloop of war in the night of the 21st Sept last on an interview with Genl

[A]rnold in a private and secret manner; that he changed his dress within our lines and under a feigned name, and in a disguised habit being then on his way to New York, and when taken he had in his possession several papers which contained intelligence for the enemy." In conclusion, "Major André, adjutant general to the British army, ought to be considered a spy from the enemy and, that agreeable to the laws and usage of nations, it is their opinion he ought to suffer death."[40] The next day, Saturday, September 30, Washington approved orders for André's execution to occur on Sunday, October 1, at 5 p.m.

Washington's subsequent letter to Clinton explained that André had "confessed with the greatest candor, 'that it was impossible for him to suppose he came on shore under the sanction of a flag.'"[41] Even with a flag, the officer's intent and behavior would still have violated the international laws of war. A similar notice was dispatched to Clinton. Within that packet were two other letters, one from Peggy to Arnold (now lost) and another, an anonymous letter written in a style suspiciously similar to that of Alexander Hamilton.

"Though an enemy, his [Andre's] virtues and his accomplishments are admired. Perhaps he might be released for General Arnold, delivered up without restriction or condition. Major Andre's character and situation seem to demand this of your justice and friendship. Arnold appears to have been the guilty author of the mischief and ought more properly to be the victim, as there is great reason to believe he mediated a double treachery and had arranged the interview in such a manner that if discovered in the first instance, he might have it in his power to sacrifice Major Andre to his own safety."[42]

An anguished Clinton pondered the concept of an exchange but ultimately rejected it, reasoning that it would discourage future informers from cooperating with the British. In a feverish attempt to save André, Clinton asked for a meeting with the Americans. Surely there had been some mistake. The Board of General Officers must not have been "rightly informed" before reaching their decision. Clinton's deputies would consequently arrive aboard the schooner *Greyhound* the next day, Sunday,

October 1, on the shores of the Hudson at Sneeden's Landing "as early as wind and tides will permit."[43]

Reluctantly, Washington agreed to the meeting, appointed Nathanael Greene to arrange the parley, and postponed André's execution until noon, Monday, October 2. To André, Clinton piteously wrote, "God knows how much I feel for you in your present situation, but I dare hope you will soon be returned from it—believe me, dear Andre."[44]

The meeting accomplished nothing. In it, Greene reiterated the Board of General Officers' decision that neither the existence nor absence of a flag had relevance to the case against André. He had violated the international laws of war. If the British agreed to return Arnold, the Americans would release André. If not, the British officer must be executed.

In a back room at the stone-walled Mabie's Tavern, André came to terms with his imminent death. Humbled, generous-spirited, and impeccably polite, he had not reported Arnold's insistence that he carry incriminating papers across enemy territory. Nor had he implicated Smith for abandoning him during the last few miles of neutral territory. Instead, André blamed his capture upon himself. "Had he been tried by a court of ladies, he is so genteel, handsome and polite a young gentleman that I am confident they would have acquitted him," his moved guard Tallmadge opined.[45]

Hamilton was also touched by André's genteel humility. He wished, as he wrote his fiancé, that he was "possessed of André's accomplishments for your sake, for I would wish to charm you in every sense."[46]

Foremost among André's concerns was the effect of his death upon Clinton. "I am bound to him by too many obligations and love him too well to bear the thought, that he should reproach himself, or that others should reproach him," he tearfully confided to Hamilton.[47] Through the future statesman's efforts, André was finally allowed to write to Clinton. His letter expressed his desire to remove "any suspicion . . . that I was bound by your Excellency's orders to expose myself to what has happened. . . . I am perfectly tranquil in mind and prepared for any fate to which an honest zeal for my king's service may have devoted me. . . . With all the warmth of my heart, I give you thanks for your Excellency's profuse kindness to me."[48]

André had one other wish: to be shot as a soldier, rather than hanged as a common spy. "Sympathy towards a soldier will surely induce your Excellency and a military tribunal to adopt the mode of my death to the feelings of a man of honor," he wrote Washington. "Let me hope, sir . . . that I am not to die on a gibbet."[49] To avoid causing the prisoner more anguish, the Virginian did not reply.

On the sunny morning of October 2, five hundred people waited outside Mabie's Tavern as others streamed into the area. An observer reported that suddenly an unnaturally pale André appeared on the porch, flanked by soldiers on one side and a fife and drum corps on the other, and "had run down the steps [of the tavern] as quickly and lively as though no execution were taking place."[50] As musicians played the "Dead March," soldiers escorted him past Tappan's Dutch church and up a long hill. Upon the summit stood a gallows and beneath it a two-horse baggage cart upon which rested a black coffin. Nearby was a freshly dug grave. "Gentleman, I am disappointed. I expected my request would have been granted," André said with a frown as he saw the gallows, then added, "I am reconciled to my death, but not the mode."[51]

Having scanned the faces of the spectators, André mounted the wagon, stood on the coffin, removed his hat, and lowered his shirt collar. "It will be but a momentary pang," Dr. James Thacher heard him say.[52] Seizing the noose, André brought it over his head, tied a knot under his left ear, and placed a handkerchief over his eyes. When asked for his last words, the British officer raised his handkerchief. "I pray you to bear me witness that I meet my fate like a brave man."

After tying André's arms, a second kerchief was knotted above his elbows. At the hangman's signal, a whip cracked, driving the horses forward, leaving Major John André hanging from the gallows. Messengers immediately carried reports of André's execution south to Philadelphia.

Within a day of that news, Peggy arrived at her parents' home at South Fourth Street in a state of nervous collapse. After her own death, in 1804, Peggy's heirs found among her possessions the gold locket André had once given her containing a lock of his hair.

8

"Haste Happy Time When We Shall Be No More Separate"

"SHALL MEN ALWAYS BE the enemies of men. . . . Is society, at least, susceptible of amendment, if not perfection?" asked the Marquis of Chastellux in his 1772 book *An Essay on Public Happiness*.[1] With that question in mind, the forty-six-year-old author sailed from France to Rhode Island in July 1780 as a major general with General Rochambeau. Two months later, on a rainy Friday, November 24, Chastellux met Henry Knox, whom he instantly liked. As the Frenchman noted in his travel journal, later published as *Travels in North-America*, Washington's chief of artillery was "very fat but very active and of a gay and amiable character." That same Friday, Knox led Chastellux down a thickly wooded path to meet his wife, Lucy, who was happily "settled in a little farm" with her children.[2]

Lucy's clothes, Chastellux observed, were "ridiculous without being neglected"—tidy and clean but apparently an odd imitation of current fashion. Equally striking to him was her hairdo, arranged like a three-cornered military hat and "all decked out with scarves and gauzes in a way that I am unable to describe." Regardless of Lucy's appearance, he admired her warmth, devotion to Knox, and the domesticity of a "real family" she provided for him near the army camp.[3]

During that visit, Chastellux observed Knox's pride in his family. Weeks earlier, in a letter to his brother, William, Henry had written of his new son, "We think our gosling quite a cygnet." Moreover, Lucy, his "dearest partner, enjoyed [a] fine state of health since last August." Best of all, she had "for the greater part of the time been with me" during the past months of the war.[4]

Overshadowing Knox's domestic harmony were the army's depleted resources. With few funds available from a financially pinched Congress, Knox, Greene, and other generals sent a circular on October 7 to the patriotic states of New England. "Our present condition promises them [the enemy] the speedy accomplishment of their wishes," the notice warned, our "army consisting of an inadequate thousands, almost destitute of every public supply . . . subsisting month after month on one bare ration of bread and meat."[5] With the return of cold weather in December, conditions grew even worse.

From headquarters, Knox complained to his brother, "The soldier, ragged almost to nakedness, has to sit down . . . and with an axe . . . to make his habitation for winter . . . punished with hunger into the bargain." [6] Privately, Knox was also financially strapped. Like other officers he suffered a "total stoppage of pay [which] has put me to many difficulties."

Enlisted men in the Continental army suffered from similar "stoppages." On January 1, 1781, eleven regiments from Pennsylvania under General Wayne mutinied and killed three officers, then marched from the Morristown encampment and seized Princeton, New Jersey. From there the mutineers planned to confront Congress and demand back pay. Despite the horror of the officers' deaths, the mutineers' complaints were real, observed Dr. James Thacher, because the men had received only "a mere shadow of compensation . . . a total want of pay for twelve months and a state of nakedness and famine to excite . . . the spirit of insurrection."[7]

By January 5, Washington desperately issued another circular to New England legislators. "It is vain to think an army can be kept together much longer under such a variety of sufferings unless some immediate and spirited measures are adapted to fund at least three-months pay for the troops," he warned the states.[8] To speed that message he had "prevailed upon Brigadier General Knox to be the bearer of this Letter."

Knox consequently rode to New England to meet with members of various state legislatures. So persuasively did he portray the "aggravated calamities and distresses" resulting from the soldiers' lack of pay that several states sent small amounts of aid. [9] The most generous were Massachusetts and New Hampshire, which provided their soldiers and noncommissioned officers with twenty-four dollars in specie.

By January 10, General Wayne and Joseph Reed had reached a compromise with the mutineers. Half of the men took furloughs until March, with a bonus for reenlistment, and the other half were discharged.

From Arnold's perspective, Congressional reluctance to provide financial support for the Continental army was only one of several mistakes made by leaders of the Revolution. Five days after André's execution, Arnold addressed a letter "To the Inhabitants of America." Published in the October 11 issue of New York's *Royal Gazette* and as a broadside, the letter declared that the American alliance with France was misguided.

The Americans, according to Arnold,

> have been duped by a virtuous gullibility . . . to give up their fidelity to serve a nation . . . aiming at the destruction both of the mother country and the provinces. Before the insidious offers of France, I preferred those from Great Britain, thinking it infinitely wiser and safer to cast my confidence upon her justice and generosity, than to trust a monarchy too feeble to establish your independence.
>
> I bear testimony to my old fellow soldiers and citizens, that I find solid ground to rely upon the clemency of our sovereign . . . that it is the generous intention of Great Britain, not only to have the rights and privileges of the colonies unimpaired together with their perpetual exemption from taxation, but to add such further benefits as may consist with the common prosperity of the empire.[10]

Arnold's letter fell flat, failing to persuade the patriots of his motives. Nor did it convince his new commander in chief, Sir Henry Clinton, who believed the traitor was more motivated by pounds than by politics. Convinced that Arnold had sacrificed André's neck to save his own, Clinton, nevertheless, plied the turncoat with questions about American defenses, armaments, and supplies. Arnold's defection was "likely to produce great and good consequences," Clinton optimistically wrote Lord George Germain, Britain's secretary of state for America.[11] Consequently, Clinton had appointed the American the "colonel of a regiment, with the rank of brigadier general of provincial forces."

Though he now occupied a rank lower than his former position in the Continental army, Arnold's compensation was £450 a year, a sum that enabled him to live in a spacious townhouse at 3 Broadway, one door down from Clinton. Aspiring to still larger rewards, the American indelicately reviewed his meeting with André in an October 18 letter to the still-grieving Clinton. Admitting that André had promised him only £6,000, Arnold insisted the young officer "was so fully convinced of my proposal of being allowed ten thousand pounds sterling for my services, risk and the loss" that he expected "to use his influence and recommend it to Your Excellency." No sum of money, Arnold self-righteously added, "would have been an inducement to have gone through the danger and anxiety I have experienced, nothing but my zeal to serve his Majesty and the common cause."[12]

Coolly, Clinton issued a draft for £6,000. Determined to prove his worth, Arnold published another provocative notice in the *Royal Gazette* urging his former military peers to desert the Revolution. "To the Officers and Soldiers of the Continental army who have the real Interest of their Country at Heart, and who are determined to be no longer the Tools and Dupes of Congress, or of France," his message began. Anyone who joined his so-called American Legion would receive guaranteed wages, a good rank, and "lead a chosen band of Americans to the attainment of peace, liberty, and safety . . . rescuing our native country from the grasping hand of France."[13]

After reading it, Washington wryly wrote Congress he was "at a loss which to admire most, the confidence of Arnold in publishing, or the folly of the enemy in supposing that a production signed by so infamous a character will have any weight with the people of these states."[14] Indeed, by December only three sergeants, twenty-eight soldiers, and a drummer had signed with the American Legion.

To Americans, the name Benedict Arnold had become anathema, a synonym for *traitor*. Several efforts were made to kidnap him in New York.

On October 4, Congress ordered the Board of War to strip Arnold's name from the records. Fort Arnold at West Point was renamed Fort Clinton for the American general, George Clinton. In Connecticut, the Masons blotted Arnold's name from their rolls; residents of Norwich shattered the grave markers of his father and infant brother in the cemetery; and in New Milford, citizens marched effigies of Arnold and Satan through town, accompanied by exploding firecrackers. A popular ditty reflected America's public opinion:

> Base Arnold's head, by luck, was saved, poor André' was gibbeted /
> Arnold's to blame for André's fame, and André's to be pitied.[15]

Simultaneous with Arnold's efforts to acquire more funds, Peggy had arrived in New York from Philadelphia to share a spacious townhouse and garden on the Battery at the southern end of the island with her husband. In public the twenty-year old seemed glum, even depressed as she mingled in ornate English gowns with high-ranking British and American Loyalists at balls, concerts, and plays.

"Peggy Arnold is not so much admired here for her beauty as one might have expected," Loyalist refugee Rebecca Warner Rawle Shoemaker confided to her daughter in Philadelphia in November. "All allow she has great sweetness in her countenance, but wants animation, sprightliness and that fire in her eyes." Nevertheless, the Arnolds "have met with every attention indeed." In addition, the former American general now held a "very genteel appointment . . . in the service, joined to a very large present . . . fully sufficient for every demand in genteel life."[16]

Beneath the Arnolds' luxurious lifestyle lay sorrows that Mrs. Shoemaker astutely surmised. "The former American general's 'particular situation,'" she opined, "is such as must give her [Peggy] great pain & anxiety."[17] Nevertheless, within two weeks of her arrival in New York, Peggy had become pregnant. Like her political opposite, Lucy Knox, Peggy must have wondered if she would ever see the Shippens again.

No less disturbing was the way the British regarded her compared to her husband. Invariably, they warmed to Peggy's pretty face and quick wit, but they treated Arnold politely and with little warmth. Typical of their attitude was a comment by an officer that "General Arnold is a very unpopular character in the British Army, nor can all the patronage he meets with from the commander-in-chief procure his respectability."[18] To win that respectability Peggy refined the role she once played as a belle in British-occupied Philadelphia, appearing as a stunning, good-will ambassador to smooth Arnold's reception in New York's military society.

If Lucy's transformation as a partner to the patriotic Knox began at Pluckemin, Peggy's evolution as the disarming wife of a traitor commenced in New York. Youthful passion and defiance, the twin forces that led both women to marry men beneath their social station, had already extracted an enormous price. Love and devotion would be their repayment, transforming those headstrong brides into resilient, forgiving wives.

Reports of growing agitation in the Carolinas, stirred by the swelling numbers of patriots from Georgia and Virginia commanded by General Nathanael Greene, had disquieted British general Henry Clinton. "Unless he [Cornwallis] immediately attacked North Carolina, we must give up both South Carolina and Georgia and retire within the walls of Charleston," wrote Clinton in his narrative on the American war.[19] To strengthen British presence in the south, the commander ordered Arnold, who was growing restless in New York, to seize the strategic town of Portsmouth, Virginia. Arnold prepared to wage war against his former countrymen and, on December 20, set sail with three regiments totaling 1,600 men.

Along the coast stormy weather intervened, scattering the transports that carried most of Arnold's men. By the thirtieth, nearly all the vessels had reconvened and entered Hampton Road, the waterway joining Chesapeake Bay with the James River. Still, one ship and three transports carrying four hundred men were missing, but Arnold pushed ahead. After landing in Virginia, marching to Richmond, and arguing with Governor Thomas Jefferson over the tobacco crop, Arnold vengefully burned the city.

By early January 1781, convinced that the British would win the war, Arnold's confidence soared. Any setback or defeat against the Continental army became his personal triumph. News about the mutiny among the

Continentals in New Jersey consequently thrilled him. "This event will be attended with happy consequences," he gleefully wrote Clinton, indicating his hope that more mutinies would follow. "We anxiously wait in expectation of hearing that the malcontents have joined His Majesty's army in New York."[20]

Once again, Arnold underestimated the depth of contempt he elicited. When Clinton sent men to win over those mutineers, the Pennsylvanians recoiled. Recalling the "treachery and meanness like that of Benedict Arnold," they notified the authorities who, in turn, had the British spies tried and executed.[21] With few battles to wage in Virginia that winter, Arnold grew bored. "A life of inaction will be very prejudicial to my health," he complained to Clinton and requested a return to New York.[22]

But greed soon proved more "prejudicial" to Arnold than inaction. As often was the case in his earlier life, Arnold quarreled with his peers, this time with Commodore Thomas Symonds over "prizes," or the ships (and cargos) that officers often retained as rewards for those victories. So bitterly did they argue that Symonds finally refused to patrol the Chesapeake, which enabled the patriotic Lafayette to cross the bay with his soldiers. Disgusted and also riddled with gout, Arnold sullenly returned to New York.

During Arnold's six-month absence, Peggy had thrived. Even with her advancing pregnancy, she had dazzled New York with her beauty, vivacity, and chatter. Among her friends were those not seen in nearly two years—Loyalists and former Philadelphia belles who had fled that city with the British in June 1778. Her favorite was the witty, dark-eyed Becky Franks, who continued to flirt with British officers much as she had in Philadelphia. As usual Becky caustically opined about those around her. "Few New York ladies know how to entertain company in their own houses unless they introduce the card table," she scoffed. "I will do our ladies, that is in Philadelphia, the justice to say they have more cleverness in the turn of an eye than the New York girls."[23]

Among the most clever of these exiles was Peggy, who had seemingly forgotten her tumultuous days on the Hudson and in Philadelphia, and had recovered her old spirit and style. Arnold's wife was "amazingly improved in beauty and dress, having really recovered a great deal of the bloom she *formerly* possessed, but did not bring in with her," Rebecca Shoemaker wrote her daughter. During a ball at Clinton's headquarters on Broadway, Peggy was widely acknowledged, praised as the "star of the first magnitude, and had every attention paid her as if she had been Lady Clinton."[24]

By June 20, 1781, General George Washington had ordered the Continental army to Peekskill, from where he hoped to launch his stalled plan to attack New York with French reinforcements. Nestled upon hills near the Hudson, the Continental camp's "pleasing variety of vegetables and flowers perfume the air, and the charming music of a feathered tribe delights our ears," observed army surgeon Dr. James Thacher. Soon afterwards that natural tranquility was shattered by "that martial band, the drum and fife, bugle and horn and shrill trumpet, which set the war-horse in motion."[25]

Lucy Knox, who was again pregnant, consequently left Peekskill with her children and traveled north with Gertrude Schuyler Cochran, the wife of Dr. John Cochran, chief physician and surgeon of the Army. After two years of living together, the Knoxes' separation deeply distressed them. "Although we are not bad in accommodating ourselves to our circumstances, yet I . . . feel the inconveniences we labor under . . . in proportion to the increase of our family," Henry complained to his brother, William. "I sincerely pray God that the war may be ended this campaign, that public and private society may be restored."[26]

Heightening the Knoxes' frustrations was the unpredictability of the mail, leaving each uncertain about the other's location. At Livingston Manor, inland on the opposite Hudson shore from Peekskill, Lucy waited vainly for Henry's letter. Finally, on July 26, she wrote to him that she planned to "set off tomorrow for Albany," since there was "no chance of hearing from you."[27]

In Philipsburg (today's Sleepy Hollow section of Tarrytown), Henry also resented his distance from Lucy: "I have never found my absence from her so truly insupportable as the present. I am alone amidst a crowd and unhappy without my companion. Haste happy time when we shall be no more separate." The war, he complained, "has deprived us of the right enjoyment of six years, long years of our life—a period infinitely too long to be enjoyed by other objects than the business of love."[28]

A few brief exchanges followed, but after August 3, Henry's correspondence stopped, plunging Lucy into her old fears of abandonment. "I am at a loss whether to write you or not, four posts have passed without a line from you," she scrawled on August 12. Even their friend, General Benjamin Lincoln, who had seen Knox at Peekskill, "brought no token of remembrance." Lucy's letter then dissolved into a screed. Rather than supporting the Revolution as in the past, she now cursed it. "We hear nothing of the movements of the army, and poor I am constantly sick with anxiety. Oh, horrid war! How has thou blasted the fairest prospect of happiness, robbed of parents, of sisters and brother, thou art depriving me, of the society of my husband: who alone could repair the loss."[29]

Ironically, new military developments would unite the Knoxes once more. That same week, Washington learned that Admiral Francois Joseph Paul de Grasse had sailed from St. Domingue with 29 ships and 3,200 men bound for Chesapeake Bay. With Cornwallis at Yorktown, there was no time to waste. In a rushed consultation, Washington and Rochambeau agreed to dispatch their armies to Virginia and reconnoiter with Lafayette's forces at the Chesapeake. Should Cornwallis attempt to escape to the sea, de Grasse's fleet would block him and force a confrontation with the combined Franco-American forces at Yorktown.

From North Carolina, General Greene, knowing nothing of those plans and believing Washington was attacking New York, wrote Knox, "Methinks I hear the cannon roar while I am writing. . . . The splendor of such a siege, will sink our puny operation [in North Carolina] into nothing." Where, Greene asked, "has Mrs. Knox taken post during your operations? I beg you will present her my most affectionate regards; and I hope you will not get in the way of a four and twenty pounder, but will return to her with whole bones."[30]

On Tuesday, August 28, Peggy delivered a second sturdy son whom she and Arnold named James Robertson, after New York's Loyalist governor. That same hot summer's day, Clinton ordered Arnold to prepare for battle in Connecticut, where he was to destroy the Americans' privateer base. A week later, Arnold left Peggy and his newborn son and sailed with two regiments to New London, twelve miles from his native town, Norwich.

By noon, September 6, Arnold had subdued New London, reducing its key military targets—arsenals, warehouses, and privateers—to flames. On the opposite side of New London Bay, an exhausted regiment of Americans in the high-walled Fort Griswold, having twice repulsed the British, finally raised a white flag of surrender. As custom dictated, its commanding officer, Colonel William Ledyard, surrendered his sword to one of Arnold's officers, who, against military tradition, slaughtered him with it. A riot followed, leading to the death of eighty of the surrendered patriots. By then, Arnold, who had previously ordered Lieutenant Colonel Edmund Eyre to countermand the attack at Fort Griswold, had not waited for the outcome. Apparently oblivious to the massacre, Arnold led a column into New London to destroy its military targets, including the home of its militia captain, the revolutionary general Gurdon Saltonstall; the mill; the printing office; and a dozen ships at mooring.

Suddenly, at the moment of the massacre, the ground shook, as one of those ships, a warehouse, filled with gunpowder, exploded. Flames, fanned by winds, spread to New London's residential sections, burning homes and shops, panicking its citizens, and leaving ninety-seven families homeless and the town in ashes.

Accusations of negligence were hurled at Arnold from every direction—from his men, the patriots of New London, and the British of New York—etching his name even deeper into history as one of its darkest villains. General Clinton, nevertheless, commended Arnold for "his very spirited conduct in New London" and assured him that he believed the brigadier-general had taken "every precaution in his power to prevent the destruction of the town."[31]

The Continental army and its patriots, nonetheless, perceived the destruction of New London as one more example of Arnold's heartlessness. Jared Sparks's 1835 biography of Arnold compared him to Nero. The former American general was "delighted with the ruin he had caused, the distresses he had inflicted, the blood of his slaughtered countrymen, the anguish of the expiring patriot, the widow's tears and the orphan's cries. And what adds to the enormity is, that he stood almost in sight of the spot where he drew his first breath."[32]

When Washington, Knox, and Rochambeau arrived in Philadelphia on Friday, August 31, they found burnt, crumbling homes left over from the earlier British occupation ringing the city. The streets, Dr. James Thacher observed, were "extremely dirty and the weather warm and dry . . . dust like smothering snow storm, blinding our eyes and covering our bodies." To boost morale for the forthcoming battle in Virginia, Washington paraded his officers and their aides in "rich military uniform, mounted on noble steed."[33] Behind them sounded the fife and drum, followed by marching regiments of the common soldiers.

That night, cannons boomed as Philadelphians illuminated their streets, shops, and homes in honor of Washington's arrival. The following morning, French soldiers marched through the streets, nattily dressed in white uniforms trimmed with green. With the exception of Lucy Knox's initial stench-filled visit to Philadelphia after the British evacuation, this was her first in-depth look at the City of Brotherly Love. Impressed with its stately Georgian homes on Society Hill and its splendid ballrooms and theaters, Lucy decided to wait out her pregnancy there.

Her friends, the avuncular Washington and Martha, convinced her otherwise. "The General and Mrs. Washington, prefers Mrs. Knox to take a trip to Virginia and she seems inclined to accept the offer," Knox wrote to his brother, William. If so, Lucy planned to take their son, nicknamed Hal, to Mount Vernon with her and would leave her daughter in a boarding school watched over by her friends Rebekkah and Colonel General Clement Biddle.[34]

To prepare for Yorktown, Knox asked Congress to order an enormous collection of arms from the states, among them three-, six-, and twelve-pound guns; three hundred musket cartridges; countless rounds of ammunition; and twenty thousand flint and one thousand powder horns. By September 8, the Continental army was thus readied for battle. "Our prospects are good and I shall hope to inform you in fifteen days that we have Lord Cornwallis completed invested," Knox predicted to William. His wife, Lucy, he wrote, "in the next five or six days will set out for Virginia to reside with Mrs. Washington."[35]

Washington arrived at Mount Vernon the next day—his first visit in six years—followed a day later by Rochambeau and his aides. By September 12, the two generals and their aides rode down the tree-lined path from the gracious plantation house bound for Williamsburg and Yorktown. Riding up that same path a day or two later to Mount Vernon came Lucy and infant son Hal. Few details remain about that visit, save for Lucy's reminiscences. "Often have I heard her describe the agitated life they then led—the alternations of hope & fear, the trembling that seized them on the arrival of the daily express," recalled her eldest daughter, Lucy Thatcher Knox.[36]

Walking the lush grounds overlooking the Potomac, sipping tea, or engaged in needle work in one of Mount Vernon's wainscoted parlors, the two matrons must have made a remarkable contrast; Martha, its soft-spoken mistress, and Lucy, her warm but high-strung "northern" guest.

"I met a very kind reception from the good lady of this place," Lucy reported to Knox on September 29. Appreciative as she was of Martha's hospitality, Mount Vernon made her "ardently to wish for a home." With remarkable insensitivity, Lucy wrote her husband on the eve of the Battle of Yorktown, "I see but one possible way to obtain one. You know my meaning [leaving the army]. I wish for nothing inconsistent with your happiness and future peace, but could you reconcile it to your feelings, I think it would make me happy."[37]

Long accustomed to Lucy's childish outbursts, Knox simply replied, "I was made happy my dearest and only love by your letter . . . . Yesterday the enemy evacuated their outposts which gives us a considerable advantage in point of time. Our prospects are good & we shall soon hope to impress our haughty foe with a respect for the combined arms."[38]

Knox's massive collection of arms impressed even seasoned soldiers like Joseph Plumb Martin. "Our commanding battery was on the near bank of the river and contained ten heavy guns," he scrawled in his diary, "the next was a bomb-battery of three large mortars; and so on through the whole line; the whole number, American and French, was ninety-two cannon, mortars and howitzers."[39]

For three days the French-American forces, Lafayette's troops, and three thousand of de Grasse's men—some twenty thousand altogether—battered Cornwallis's outnumbered army. Meanwhile, at Mount Vernon, Lucy regressed to her earlier peeves over Henry's silence. On October 8, she sourly wrote that she was "led to conclude that you could not spare time for the perusal of such an epistle. Never was I so anxious as at this moment nor ever less able to bear it. . . . Let me know when there is a ray of hope that I may see you and why you do not write by the post."[40]

That day, Knox's artillerists began pounding the British in an assault leading to the climax of the siege, from October 10 to 12. "A tremendous and incessant firing from the American and French batteries is kept up," Dr. Thacher scribbled in his journal. "The enemy return the fire, but with little effect."[41] Their lackluster efforts, Chastellux believed, resulted from Knox's "military genius . . . [his] artillery was always very well served, the general incessantly directing it and often himself pointing the mortars; seldom did he leave the batteries."[42] At one point during the battle, Washington, Knox, and General Benjamin Lincoln watched the action in an exposed area. When an aide pointed out their danger, the commander in chief curtly replied, "If you are afraid, you have liberty to step back."[43]

While protected from those details, Lucy's anxieties, nevertheless, increased. Another week passed before two letters arrived. Neither was from Knox. "Mrs. Washington and Mrs. Custis [Eleanor "Nelly" Calvert Custis, wife of John Parke "Jacky" Custis] have just been made happy by the receipt of long letters; from their husbands, while I poor unhappy girl, am not worthy of a line," Lucy penned. "It is not possible for any person to be more low spirited, than I have been for more than a week past. Heavens, that I should be neglected at such a time." Pointedly, she added, "Mrs. Washington and her daughter-in-law planned to travel to the army camp at Williamsburg." She, meanwhile, "shall remain here . . . probably ignorant of what is passing at the place where my all is at stake."[44]

Knox had not forgotten her. The same day Lucy wrote to him, in fact, he had dashed off a note from the "Trenches before York" that read, "My love I have only one moment to write by an express . . . to inform the best beloved of my soul that I am well & have been perfectly so. The [night before] last we stormed the enemies' two advanced works with very little loss. . . . I hope in ten or twelve days, we shall with the blessing of heaven terminate it. I shall take care of your Harry for your sake."[45]

Three days later, Wednesday, October 17, his predictions were realized. Euphorically, he wrote Lucy, "I might be the first to communicate good news to the charmer of my soul. A glorious moment for America! This day Lord Cornwallis and his army marches out and piles their arms in the face of our victorious Army."[46]

Thrilled, Lucy replied, "If this should prove true and my Harry is safe how grateful ought I to be to heaven."[47] A week later, Knox assured her, "I hope to have the sweet felicity of embracing you in ten days from today and perhaps sooner." In a jovial reference to his infant son, Hal, he added, "Cannot you impress his memory [so] powerfully with the taking of Lord Cornwallis as to make the little fellow tell it to his children?"[48]

Hopes for a son's tales about Yorktown for another generation of the Washingtons were crushed when George and Martha's son, Jackie, died on November 5 from "putrid fever." Struck by the juxtaposition of that tragedy with the triumph at Yorktown, Knox wrote General Biddle that the Washingtons "amidst flattering public prospects have received the most fatal blow to their domestic felicity."[49]

A week after Jackie's death, the Washingtons returned to Mount Vernon. Obliged to appear before Congress, but grieving nearly as deeply as Martha, Washington consequently brought his wife to Philadelphia on November 20. Before long the Knoxes would join them, for, as Henry explained to General Benjamin Lincoln, he intended to remain with Lucy "until the moment of her difficulty shall be over."[50] Proudly, he wrote General Greene on December 12 that Lucy had "presented me with another son," whom they named Camillus Marcus.[51] Washington was to be his godfather.

Four days earlier, a fleet of 150 ships of the Royal Navy had sailed at dusk from Philadelphia to Sandy Hook, bound for England. Hidden within the thicket of white sails also sped the *Robuste* with Charles Cornwallis and General Arnold aboard. Nearby, a packet ship carried Arnold's wife, Peggy, and her newborn son, James, and toddler, Neddy.

The couple had deliberately separated for the transatlantic crossing. Peggy's decision to travel in an expensive packet ship, Rebecca Shoemaker had gossiped to her daughter, was "more agreeable for her than a man of war, yet not safe for him [Arnold]. They give for the cabin 300 guineas and then took what company they chose, chiefly military, I believe. I do not hear of any females but her maids."[52]

9

"Yet We Wade On"

IF PEGGY'S PERSONAL STAR was on the rise, Arnold's was in freefall as their respective ships headed into the high seas. The *Rebel*, an American privateer, suddenly loomed into view behind the *Robuste*, attempting to capture Arnold. During that chase, high winds and driving rains from an Atlantic storm battered the *Robuste*, impelling Arnold's move to the *Edward*, a transport ship. Ultimately the *Rebel* captured the *Robuste*, but, as London's *Public Advertiser* of January 24 surmised, the sailors were doubtless "chagrined at their disappointment in missing their expected prey."[1]

By January 21, the *Edward* anchored at the Scilly Isles on Britain's west coast, where fishing boats ferried the passengers to shore. Only Arnold remained aboard the *Edward*, determined to wait there until, the London Chronicle reported, "a vessel of force appeared . . . to warrant his safety" and deliver him to Portsmouth.[2] Peggy's trip went more smoothly. Despite a similarly stormy crossing, the packet ship carrying her and her children arrived in Falmouth, England, without incident.

By Tuesday, January 22, the newly reunited Arnolds rode into windswept London in "a good deal of small rain."[3] That day the *Daily Advertiser* announced, "They have taken a house and set up a carriage and will, I suppose, be a good deal visited."[4] The Arnolds' new residence was a handsome five-story townhouse, the tallest in fashionable Portman Square. Other American Loyalists lived nearby, among them William Fitch and his young sisters, Ann and Sarah, who soon befriended the Arnolds.

Margaret Shippen Arnold

Soon after Peggy's arrival with "the General," as she called Arnold, she renewed acquaintance with her American-born cousin, Dorothy Willing Stirling, whose husband, Sir Walter Stirling, introduced Arnold to George III at court. Subsequently, Arnold had a private audience with the king, followed by a stroll through St. James Park with the king and the Prince of Wales.

Afterwards, Arnold boasted to his New York Loyalist friend William Smith that "his Majesty wished me to return to America" and "promised me that I could be promoted."[5] By February 4, the London *Daily Advertiser* reported General Arnold would "shortly to return back to America, and to have the command of the Loyalists."[6]

Peggy, too, was initially swamped with attention. Colonel Banastre Tarleton and other officers who remembered the former belle from Philadelphia now declared Peggy "the most beautiful women in England."[7] One of the women who fussed over her was Elizabeth Lady Amherst, the lovely, fair-skinned wife of Sir Jeffrey Amherst, who introduced Peggy at court on February 10. Immediately she was lionized. George's wife, Queen Charlotte, it was said, became "so interested in favor of Mrs. Arnold as to desire the ladies of the court to pay much attention to her."[8] Contrary to her usual austerity, the plain, good-hearted queen lavished an annuity of a hundred pounds a year upon Peggy for the maintenance of her children, as well as for those not yet born.

On March 19, George III also issued a royal warrant to his paymaster of pensions on Peggy's behalf. "Our will and pleasure is and we do hereby direct, authorize and command, that an annuity or yearly pension of £500 be established and paid by you unto Margaret Arnold, wife of our trusty and well-beloved Brigadier General Benedict Arnold, to commence from the day of the date hereof and continue during our pleasure."[9] After commissions and fees, as General Clinton noted in a memorandum of 1792, Peggy received £350 from the King "obtained for her services, which were meritorious."[10] Revealed when Clinton's papers were publicized in the early twentieth century, the memorandum convinced subsequent historians that Peggy had participated in Arnold's treason.

Superficially, the Arnold's social success in London society in 1782 seemed ensured. Though not fabulously wealthy, the Arnolds lived luxuriously. Their townhouse was outfitted with fine mahogany furniture; their table handsomely appointed with fine silver, crystal, and Wedgwood; their personal needs attended by a staff of servants, with a private coach and four ready to drive them through London. Still, appearances meant far less in England than a man's character, and its lapse inevitably produced a cloud of suspicion as thick and impenetrable as a London fog. Instead of the admiration Arnold anticipated he would receive from the British, he inspired contempt.

Sir Walter Stirling's reaction typified this reaction. Mrs. Arnold, he opined, "was an amiable woman, and was her husband dead, she would be much noticed."[11] By February 16, a satiric "Ode Addressed to General Arnold" by "Lady Craven" appeared in the *Whitehall Evening Post*. The first of its twelve withering stanzas read:

"WELCOME one Arnold to our shore! / Thy deeds on Fame's strong pinions bore/spread loyalty and reason: O! had success thy projects crown'd / Proud Washington had bit the ground / And Arnold punish'd treason."[12]

Political resistance to a continuation of the American war intensified contempt for Arnold. In the lofty halls of Parliament's House of Lords, Thomas, Lord Walsingham, descried the "case of one Arnold, who, coming to this kingdom, with his hand treacherously and traitorously reeking in the blood of his countrymen, closeted with the King, to be received at Court, to be smiled upon, to be caressed, to be rewarded in contamination and to the disgrace of the British army . . . the instrument of that delusion to this country, which . . . have so successful for themselves . . . though so ruinously for this nation, promoted and obtained?"[13]

Another protest came from Anglo-Irish statesman, Edmund Burke. To consider Arnold for a military leadership role was reprehensible, the influential Burke proclaimed in the Commons, "lest the sentiments of true honor, which every British officer [holds] dearer than life, should be afflicted."[14] In a heated March 6 meeting of the House of Commons, Lord Surrey opposed the idea of "placing at the King's elbow a man perhaps the most obnoxious to the feelings of the Americans of any in the King's dominions."[15]

Simultaneously, the Tory government, headed by Lords North and Germain, was crumbling. Leading the Whig opposition to continuation of the American Revolution was the golden-tongued parliamentarian, William Pitt the Younger. "A long and obstinate perseverance in a fatal system of war has brought this country to the brink of ruin," the twenty-two year old declared. "What then is to be done? We can no longer appeal to the reason or feelings of ministers; their conduct [in support of the war] has been in the teeth of reason and feelings. . . . What hath all this purchased for us?— the dismemberment of half the empire and perhaps the extinction of more than half our commerce."[16]

To counter those protests, Arnold met with William Petty-FitzMaurice, Earl of Shelburne, to propose a forty-gun frigate with which to battle the Americans. After weeks of silence from Shelburne, Arnold's proposal was tabled. Public resentment towards Arnold steadily increased. "It is thought that Mr. (commonly called General) Benedict Arnold as soon as the new Ministers are sworn into office, will have it hinted to him that if . . . he does not support his *loyal figure* so often as he has lately done in the Royal presence," sneered the *Morning Herald and Daily Advertiser* on March 28."[17] Before long, Arnold and Peggy were hissed at when they appeared at the theater and in the streets.

Many American Loyalists also reviled Arnold. One of them, a graying attorney, Peter Van Schaack, recorded his personal aversion to the man whom he encountered during a visit to Westminster Abbey. As he passed a marble memorial inscribed with the words, "Sacred to the Memory of Major John André," Van Schaack noticed a nearby couple. "It was General Arnold, and the lady was doubtless Mrs. Arnold. They passed to the cenotaph of Major André, where they stood and conversed together. What a spectacle! The traitor, Arnold, in Westminster Abbey, at the tomb of André, deliberately perusing the monumental inscription which will transmit to future ages the tale of his own infamy."[18]

Whatever discomfort the couple felt about Andre's death was carefully concealed from their British and Loyalist friends. Peggy hid hers beneath a veneer of charm, merriment, and wit as Arnold continued efforts to raise his financial prospects. At the likely suggestion of his friend, Cornwallis, he applied for a post with the East India Company. The application was not only rejected but coldly returned by a disgusted American Loyalist.

The year 1783 held other disappointments. Peggy delivered a daughter named Margaret in January, but in August the baby died. By then she was pregnant again. For all her earlier fragility and nervous energy, Arnold's wife was developing a resilience and fortitude that would have astounded the Shippens. An ornament of London's aristocratic galas, the twenty-two-year-old blonde spent that spring in social engagements to which she invited her visiting friend, Becky Franks, the bride of Colonel Henry Johnston.

From her home at Killarney Castle, Ireland, the following February, Becky described Peggy to another former Philadelphia belle, Williamina Bond Cadwalader. "I can tell you very little of your American acquaintances as I left the place last August & indeed . . . knew very little of them except Mrs. Arnold," Becky explained. Peggy had "always behaved more like an affectionate sister than a common friend, she still continues the same. I hear every week or fortnight from her." In London, as in Philadelphia and New York, Peggy had become immensely popular, "more noticed and more liked than any American that ever came over. She is visited by people of the first rank & invited to all their houses."[19]

Friendships and royal pensions were rapidly becoming Peggy's defense against personal disappointments. Behind closed doors at 18 Portman Square, other sorrows abounded. In March 1784, her fourth child, George, died shortly after his birth. Simultaneously, Arnold, brooding over his half-pay as a retired brigadier general, petitioned the British government for more money. As a former American, Arnold had a right to do so, for in July 1783, Parliament voted into law the Loyalist Claims Commission to recompense those who fled the Revolution. Among Arnold's claims for reimbursement were expenses he had incurred to outfit his American Legion. Another lost sum of money was the £5,000 he had paid for Mount Pleasant as a wedding gift to Peggy, which Pennsylvania seized after his defection. Shrewdly, Arnold failed to mention that his father-in-law, Judge Shippen, had repurchased the house at auction at his own expense. Slippery too was Arnold's claim that, because of his agreement with Clinton, he had refused General Washington's offer for his "command of the American army in South Carolina . . . afterwards given to Greene . . . with the sum of 20,000 pounds."[20] All told, he claimed, the British government owed him £16,125 beyond the £6, 365 Clinton had initially paid.

By late April, the Treasury Office had still not responded. Clinton's payment, Arnold seethed, was "not a full compensation for the loss of my real estate, for risks and services rendered." Given the additional expense of living in London to reclaim that debt and the "loss of time and difficulty attending it," Arnold finally withdrew his claim.[21] Instead the angry forty-four year old vowed to rely only upon himself. He would do so by establishing an international trading enterprise.

Peggy could not have approved: separations from her husband were as anguishing as transatlantic crossings were dangerous. And she was again pregnant. Moreover, though surrounded by social acquaintances, she had few close friends. Nevertheless, by the summer of 1754, "the General" was busily completing the final touches on a new brig, the Lord Middlebrook, for his voyage to New Brunswick. There he intended to sell imports to the influx of Loyalists emigrating there from England and America.

Peggy's description of her situation must have their worried the Shippens, for by early summer, brother-in-law Edward Burd had arrived in London. Accounts of his visit are brief, only mentioning a shopping trip with Peggy to purchase a china set for his wife. All the while, Burd undoubtedly assessed his sister-in-law. Regardless of the Shippens' disgust with Arnold (whom Burd had dubbed that "infernal villain"), to Burd, Peggy seemed reasonably content. Not only did she continue to trust Arnold but did so even at the risk of her future security.[22] On July 13, with utter disregard for her father's costly repurchase of Mount Pleasant at auction, Peggy wrote Judge Shippen that "G. Arnold desires you will be so good as to sell it [Mount Pleasant] for as much as you can," since Arnold was no longer willing "to risk any more money in America."[23]

Two weeks later, Peggy bore a frail baby girl, named Sophia. Once assured that mother and child were stable, Burd returned to Philadelphia.

The following October, Arnold sailed to the British North American colonies. For months Peggy waited for his letter. By March 6, 1786, wracked with suspense about him, she poured her heart out to Judge Shippen. "I assure you, my dear papa, I find it necessary to summon all my philosophy to my aid, to support myself under my present situation. Separated from and anxious for the fate, of the best of husbands, torn from almost everybody that is dear to me, harassed with a troublesome and expensive lawsuit, having all the General's business to transact, and feeling that I am in a strange country, without a creature near me that is really interested in my fate, you will not wonder if I am unhappy."[24]

For the first time, Peggy admitted the sacrifices she had made as Arnold's wife and her sense of utter aloneness. Ironically that was the same message her mirror opposite, Lucy Flucker Knox, had once sounded across the Atlantic during the long years of the Revolution.

Events surrounding the proposed peace with Britain meant new challenges for Lucy and Henry Knox. In March 1782, Washington appointed Knox and Gouverneur Morris, the assistant treasurer of the Revolution, as commissioners for a prisoner exchange in Elizabethtown, New Jersey. Only reluctantly had Henry complied, for he and Lucy were then watching anxiously over their newborn son, Marcus. In late winter the infant had contracted smallpox and was only slowly recovering. From Elizabethtown, on March 22, Henry anxiously assured Lucy, "Every time I am absent from you I am convinced more & more of the utter improbability of living without you. I hope you and our dear little pledges of love and joy [are well] and that Marcus has entirely recovered of the small pox."[25]

That same day Congress approved Washington's recommendation for Knox's appointment as a major general, making him, at thirty-three, the youngest man of that rank in the army. Even that promotion did little to cheer Lucy, whose letters dwelt upon her "unspeakable mortification [disappointment]" at Henry's absence.[26]

By mid-April, the prisoner exchange at Elizabethtown had attracted national attention when a British officer hanged the American prisoner, Captain Joshua Huddy, during his transfer from New York City. The resultant public clamor for American revenge renewed tensions with the British. Washington, consequently, reestablished army headquarters on the Hudson and appointed Knox the new commander of West Point.

By mid-May, Lucy had left the Biddles' home, where she and her children had been living, and accompanied Henry to Newburgh, ten miles north of West Point. To her delight, their new home was a handsome fieldstone house once owned by miller John Ellison. Beneath its high-pitched roof and tall chimneys stood a central hall with wood-paneled rooms, providing her and Henry with a gracious location for the dinners and social gatherings they soon hosted.

Like others who had once enjoyed an elite lifestyle, Lucy craved its return and, whenever opportunity arrived, attempted to recreate it. Washington's orders for a May 31 celebration of the birth of the French dauphin, Louis-Joseph Xavier François, soon provided that opportunity. As he had at Pluckemin, Henry, with Lucy's guidance, organized the festivities. In preparation for the arrival of hundreds of guests, Knox ordered the construction of a 600-foot colonnade artfully festooned with evergreens, fleur-de-lis, muskets, and bayonets. At noon after a morning of prayers, parades, military displays, and gun salutes, the Washingtons, Governor George Clinton and his Sarah, the Knoxes, and other officers arrived by barge and passed through the Grand Colonnade. A banquet for five hundred guests followed and celebration with "13 toasts, particularly adapted to the festival, were drank, under a discharge of 13 canon," reported a local paper.[27]

After "a few bumpers of wine . . . Gen. Washington, who appeared in unusually good spirits, said to his officers, 'Let us have a dance!' reported Captain Edwin Eben. Then "the great commander led the dance, in a "*gender hop*" or "*stag dance*" [italics in original] . . . to the favorite old tune 'Soldier's Joy.'"[28] Another newspaper reported that "Washington attended the ball . . . and with a dignified and graceful air, having Mrs. Knox for his partner, carried down a dance of twenty couple in the arbor on the green grass."[29] By then no one questioned Lucy's role as the reigning hostess of celebrations, a role she continued to hold in public celebrations during the early Federal period.

← →

When, however, officers of the Continental army began to complain about Congressional failure to deliver back pay, memories of that celebration quickly faded. Even the army's beloved drillmaster, Baron Von Steuben, felt the financial strain. "It is been owing to him that a substantial discipline has been established in the American Army," Knox sharply reminded Congressman Samuel Osgood. Lacking a salary, the dedicated Van Steuben had spent so much of his own savings that he "can no longer live without pay."[30]

By August, the Knoxes faced a new personal crisis. From Philadelphia where their eight-year-old daughter Lucy attended boarding school, the Biddles reported that the child's health was rapidly declining. Without further delay Lucy and Henry had her brought to Newburgh, whose fresh Hudson River air they thought would be beneficial. As the girl's condition improved, however, their infant son, Marcus, grew fussy. Initially Lucy and Henry attributed his symptoms to teething, but soon the baby became seriously ill. By August 25, Knox gloomily wrote his brother William that he would probably "never have the pleasure to see him. A few days, perhaps a few hours may decide his fate."[31]

On September 8, Marcus died. "I have the unhappiness, my dear General to inform you of the departure of my precious infant, your god son," Knox wrote Washington two days later. "In the deep mystery in which all human events are involved, the Supreme Being has been pleased to prevent his expanding innocence from ripening."[32]

For nearly a month, Knox stopped writing others. On September 24 he finally conceded to William Alexander (known as Lord Stirling, from his Scottish inheritance) that he had no choice but to accept the child's death: "The misery inflicted upon us poor mortals appears frequently to be too great to be borne. Yet we wade on."[33] Two weeks later Henry wrote Gouverneur Morris that he had suffered "private affliction, in the loss of a fine child, and the [sickness of] the rest of my family."[34]

Lucy was profoundly depressed. Having lost two infants in the space of three years, her dreams of a large, happy family had vanished, as seemingly elusive as the reflected light from a candle sconce. He still hoped, Knox wrote Washington, that Mrs. Knox, by leaning upon the "great principles of reason and religion will be enabled . . . to support this repeated shock to her tender affections."[35] For weeks, he sat by Lucy's side, reasoning with her and assuring her in time all would be well. Death, he confided to his friend, Benjamin Lincoln, "had with a strong and unrelenting hand seized the youngest of my little flock. My utmost attention and philosophy were necessarily exerted to calm the agitated mind of its wretched mother."[36]

Time only slowly mended Lucy and, for that matter, Knox. The following February, while congratulating Nathanael Greene on the British evacuation of the southern states, Knox alluded to the late Marcus as a "little angel."[37] Left unsaid was the exciting but potentially worrisome news: Lucy was once again pregnant.

Concerns over Knox's military "family" simultaneously loomed. In December, when officers met to persuade Congress for reimbursements, they appointed Henry their chairman. By the twenty-ninth, representatives of that committee had presented a draft of Knox's request for a lump sum pension, asserting, "We are in an unhappy predicament indeed, not to know who are responsible to us for a settlement of accounts."[38] Congress soon insisted they were not responsible: the Articles of Confederation did not mandate that they pay military salaries. That infuriated Knox. He thundered to his friend Gouverneur Morris, a Congressional delegate, that if "the present Constitution is so defective, why do not you great men call the people together and tell them so; that is, to have a convention of the States to form a better Constitution?"[39]

By March 10, officers at Washington's headquarters at Newburgh were so frustrated that they circulated a letter calling for a strike. Known as the Newburgh Address, the letter assailed Congress for its neglect. It also urged the soldiers to refuse to defend America, urging them instead to "retire to some yet unsettled country, smile in your turn and mock when their [America's] fear cometh on."[40]

Horrified, Washington called a meeting for Saturday, March 15, at his headquarters. Suspecting that the fractious Horatio Gates had instigated the protest, Washington named him the meeting's chairman. At noon, the officers glumly filed into the meeting hall. After arriving at the podium, Washington paused and then reached into his pocket to pull out a pair of glasses. "Gentlemen," the commander in chief began, "you will permit me to put on my spectacles, for I have not only grown gray, but almost blind, in the service of my country."[41]

A gasp went through the audience. The men listened with rapt attention. The letter, Washington suggested in cool, reasoned tones, must have originated with a Loyalist or someone plotting to destroy the link between the army and government. "Let me entreat you, Gentlemen, not to take any measures, which, viewed in the calm light of reason, will lessen the dignity, and sully the glory you have hitherto maintained; let me request you rely upon the faith of your Country, and place a full confidence in the purity of the intentions of Congress."[42] Washington's heartfelt appeal touched his listeners. Ultimately, as he hoped, the officers rejected the anonymous letter calling for mutiny. Soon afterwards, Congress agreed to grant the officers five years' pay compounded by six percent interest.

To Knox that was still not enough: the pay did not wholly compensate for the sacrifices made by the officers of the Revolution. To remedy that, he drafted a plan for a hereditary organization called the Society of Cincinnati. Besides honoring veterans and their descendants, its mission was to help any members fallen on hard times. Immediately, social libertarians like Thomas Jefferson, Elbridge Gerry, and Samuel and John Adams objected, insisting that the Cincinnati smacked of a new aristocracy. To the outspoken author Mercy Otis Warren, Knox's society mocked the "primeval principles of the late revolution."[43]

In its defense Knox claimed the Cincinnati was an organization "whose intention is pure and uncorrupted by any sinister design." Its state chapters must "erect some lonely . . . shelter for the unfortunate against the storms and tempest of poverty."[44] Even Washington, who was a lifelong Mason, agreed that the Cincinnati was an important organization. On May 14, 1783, he became its first president.

During the eight years of the Revolution, the "tempests of poverty" had swept over the Knoxes. After the British evacuation of Boston in 1776, Henry had depended upon his brother William to restore his book business, monitor his privateering investments, and oversee his finances. Failing to achieve that, William had sailed to Europe in search of more lucrative prospects. While visiting London in 1783, he located Lucy's family—her mother; sister Hannah Flucker Urquart; her brother, Captain Thomas Flucker; and his wife, Sarah. When they met, William was shocked to find the Fluckers in mourning clothes, the consequence, they explained, of the recent and sudden death of Lucy's father, Thomas. When William reported the news to Lucy, it must have released a flood of emotions in her—relief that William had reconnected with her family and grief over her father's death.

On May 14, Knox wrote to Captain Flucker to convey his and Lucy's condolences and inviting them to reconcile. "The war being over we may hope for a revival of intercourse and mutual goodwill between friends who have been separated. Suffer me to press you to write often and to confide in me in the light of a real brother."[45] In a separate letter Knox also sent his sympathies to Lucy's mother.

Practical matters as well as propriety had inspired Knox to write. The Commonwealth of Massachusetts had already seized Loyalist Thomas Flucker's personal estate but not the inheritance of the Waldo Patent, vast tracts of land in the district of Maine extending from the Kennebec to the Penobscot rivers. An ancient inheritance from Lucy's maternal grandfather, General Samuel Waldo, the Patent still belonged to the Fluckers. Once an American-British peace treaty was signed, Lucy and her family could inherit their shares.

Two days after Knox's letter to the Fluckers, Lucy delivered another son the couple again named Marcus Camillus. Henry anxiously announced the birth to William, adding that the newborn seemed in "poor health."[46] For Lucy, the baby's uncertain start was all too familiar, a haunting reminder of earlier difficulties.

Eleven weeks after the September 8, 1783, Treaty of Paris, the British prepared to evacuate New York. By the late morning of November 26, Knox and eight hundred soldiers marched from Harlem through McGowan's Pass (now Central Park), halting at the Bowery and present-day Third Avenue.

At 1 p.m., cannon fire signaled the march of the British to the East River, where they boarded rowboats to reach the royal fleet bobbing in the harbor. In a final sneer, the redcoats had greased the flagpole over Fort George (the site of today's U.S. Customs House) and left the Union Jack waving in the breeze. Within moments, sailor John Arsdale attached cleats to his shoes, climbed the pole, removed the British flag and raised the Stars and Stripes. Simultaneously, American troops, led by Knox, Washington, Governor Clinton, members of the Common Council, and civilians proceeded down Broadway to the Battery to cheering crowds. That historic moment made a lasting impression on one Manhattan woman:

> We had been accustomed for a long time to military display in all the finish and finery of [British] garrison life. The troops just leaving us were as if equipped for a show and with their scarlet uniforms and burnished arms made a brilliant display. The troops that marched in, on the contrary, were ill-clad and weather-beaten and made a forlorn appearance. But then, they were *our* troops and as I looked at them and thought upon all they had done and suffered for us, my heart and my eyes were full.[47]

For ten days, city residents celebrated with parades, parties, balls, toasts, and dinners, culminating with Washington's departure on December 4. By midday, the Continental officers had gathered in a low-ceilinged room at the Fraunces Tavern on the Battery as Washington reviewed the previous eight years. "With a heart full of love and gratitude I now take my leave of you," he said. "I most devoutly wish that your latter days may be as prosperous and happy as your former ones have been glorious and honorable." As the men raised their glasses for a toast, Washington asked them one by one to "come and take me by the hand." Henry Knox, "being nearest to him," took Washington's hand, his eyes filling with tears, and was followed by the other officers.[48]

Later, from a barge in the harbor, Washington waved a final farewell. "Our much loved friend the General has gone from this city to Congress and from thence to Mount Vernon," Knox subsequently wrote Lafayette.[49]

By December 30, only five hundred soldiers remained at West Point with another two hundred scattered throughout other key posts. Knox had been charged with the heart-breaking task of dismissing the men, many of whom lacked the funds to return home. "This business has been painful on account of discharging the officers and soldiers at this [severe] season without pay, and in many instances the men are miserably clad," he unhappily wrote Congressman Osgood that day.[50] Six weeks later, Knox returned to his hometown, Boston.

Awaiting him in a rented farmhouse in the Dorchester neighborhood of the city were Lucy and the children. Owned by the Welles banking family, their two-story saltbox sat at the corner of contemporary Welles Avenue and Washington Street. To Lucy, the long-delayed dream for a normal life had become a reality—a home of her own, a brood of children, and her husband by her side.

With the termination of the war, the prediction of "her Harry" had at last come true, a time "when my Lucy and I shall be no more separated, when we shall set down free from the hurry, bustle, and impertinence of the World, in some sequestered Vale where the Education of our children and the preparation on our own parts for a pure & more happy region shall employ the principal part of our time."[51]

10

"My Regret at This Cruel, Dreadful Separation"

PROBLEMS AS CHILLING AS the snowdrifts around the Dorchester farmhouse preoccupied the Knoxes during the winter of 1784. The first were the couple's precarious finances; the second, their stalled reconciliation with the Fluckers. Both, the couple realized, could be resolved if Henry could settle the late Thomas Flucker's estate and inheritances of the Waldo Patent.

By April 10, Henry had proposed those ideas to Lucy's brother, Captain Thomas Flucker, adding that he hoped to "secure as much as possible" for the family.[1] Thomas had responded warmly but warned that both estates were fraught with legal complexities. Under the Confiscation Act of 1778, Massachusetts had seized his late father's estate, but some of those assets still belonged to his mother, Hannah. Moreover, the Waldo Patent had other claimants, including the Fluckers' cousins, the Winslows.

Gamely, Henry agreed to tackle both estates. To his fifty-eight-year-old mother-in-law, Hannah, he wrote on August 3, "You may rest fully assured that nothing shall be left undone on my part."[2] In a second letter Henry asked his brother-in-law, Thomas, to convey any new information he had on the Waldo estate.

Unmentioned was Henry's personal knowledge of the Maine properties, for that summer he traveled through part of the Waldo Patent's 576,000 acres. The tour had been deliberate, a consequence of his cronyism with friends at the state legislature who had appointed him a commissioner to settle land disputes with the Penobscots of Maine. By autumn,

Thomas Flucker had expressed his family's approval of Henry's offer, assuring him that "your ideas respecting what should be done with my mother's property will have the greatest weight."[3] A week later, Lucy's mother, Hannah, also wrote, thanking Knox for his efforts to "secure as much as possible of my late husband's estate for the benefit of my family." After describing the debts surrounding that estate, she added a sentence that must have brought Lucy to tears: "I hope for the pleasure of hearing from you soon that you, my dear daughter & children are well and happy." Still further down was another, even more poignant line. "I intend writing my daughter soon … she will excuse me now, as I have been lately very ill with the bilious cholic"—a vague medical term related to pains and swelling in the abdomen.[4]

That November, Lucy gave birth to a daughter, Julia, named after the infant who had died at the Pluckemin Artillery Cantonment. By December 8, the Knoxes had also moved to a newly rented home on Boston's then-rural Beacon Hill. The "mansion" or "farm," as its owner, portrait painter John Singleton Copley, called it, was a sprawling, hip-roofed farmhouse overlooking Boston Common and bordered by a dirt path called Beacon Street, two acres west of Governor Hancock's granite mansion. Behind the farmhouse stood a terraced garden, a fruit orchard, and pastures extending beyond contemporary Charles Street to the tidal flats of Charles River Bay.

Soon after the Knoxes' move, a letter arrived from Lafayette explaining that Henry's brother, William, had suffered a mental collapse in Europe. "It grieves me to think I am going to wound your good heart," the Frenchman wrote, "yet find it my duty as a friend rather to give you a pain . . . [or] leave you in the cruelest anxiety." During his emotional crisis, William had crossed the channel to England to live with his friend, London merchant James Webber. Somewhat later, Lafayette received a letter from a Dr. Bancroft reporting that Knox's brother had improved enough to soon "be able to go out." To speed his recovery, the Marquis offered to pay Dr. Bancroft "to see that Billy is well attended with physicians."[5]

Another, happier life-changing event for Knox followed when on March 8, 1785, Congress appointed him secretary at war, forerunner of the later and more familiar title, secretary of war. Having longed for that post, Henry proudly wrote Washington on March 24, "I have accepted the appointment and shall expect to be in New York about the 15th of next month."[6] Still, the new position presented challenges, the most immediate being its modest annual salary of $2,450 a year. From earlier financial reversals, Knox knew he had no flair for business. "From the habits imbibed during the war, and from the opinion of my friends that I should make but an indifferent trader, I thought it was well to accept it, although the salary would be but a slender support," he ruefully admitted to Washington in his March letter.[7]

Underscoring Knox's "indifference" as a trader was the arrival in Boston that April of the British vessel *Hero*. Its cargo included trunkloads of books William had purchased to restore his brother's Boston bookstore. The ship had arrived at an unfortunate moment, just after a merchants' meeting at Faneuil Hall to boycott British goods. Lucy, who was still in Boston, was consequently saddled with crate loads of unsalable books—and Henry with more unpaid bills. The *Hero* had brought still more bad news—a letter from the Fluckers announcing that Lucy's brother, Thomas, had died.

Heightening those tensions was Knox's letter from New York, announcing he had leased a new home in a rural section of the city. The confluence of bad news was too much for Lucy. On May 4, she wrote her husband that his rental "of a house out of town . . . almost makes me shudder." She had, after all, been raised in Boston and had only recently begun to enjoy urban life again, meeting with old friends, playing cards and chess, and even hiring a French milliner. Could not Congress find their new secretary at war a more convenient home in the center of the city? Then, apparently realizing her shrill tone, Lucy caught herself. Self-piteously, she closed by explaining that she would soon retire to her "lonely bed." . . . Life, she wrote, "is such a blank without you. . . . Witness my tears upon this paper.[8]

Henry replied in anger, prompting Lucy's subsequent apology for having "given him pain." To placate her usually patient husband, she stiffly replied, "I am pleased with the house you have taken as a summer residence. Perhaps I may like it in the winter. At any rate I will not find fault with it." Then, more tenderly: "Believe me my love, to be with you and to see you happy, constitutes the sum total of my earthly felicity."[9] Gradually, the twenty-nine-year-old Lucy was evolving from a self-involved drama queen into a more sensitive adult.

That summer Lucy dutifully moved with Henry and their children into the former Bowery home of celebrated English beauty Lady Anne Poellnitz. As she suspected, the "Bouwerie," as the Dutch once called it, was a country road surrounded by grain fields, gardens, and wildflowers. A retreat for well-heeled New Yorkers in the summer, the Bowery was far less populated in the winters. Intensifying Lucy's sense of isolation on the Bowery that winter was a letter from the Fluckers in January 1786 announcing the death of her mother the previous December. More than a decade had passed since Lucy had seen or even heard directly from her mother. Now it was too late for the hoped-for reconciliation.

Though Henry felt for his wife, Hannah Flucker's death meant Lucy would inherit one-fifth of the Waldo Patent; the rest would be divided with her sister, Hannah Flucker Urquart, and the sons of her late brother, Thomas. In 1786, acting as the American overseer of the Fluckers' properties, Henry consequently obtained a quit-claim title on the Waldo properties. Afterwards, he and Lucy began dreaming of the day they would establish a grand home on their share of the Maine lands.

After that year in the Bowery, Knox finally moved the family to a house on Broadway in lower Manhattan. There, in late September 1786, Lucy delivered a baby girl named Caroline. Anxiously, as usual, Henry announced the birth to his Boston friend Henry Jackson, who predicted "the child will do well, although appearances may at present be against it."[10]

Simultaneously, appearances also mitigated against a resolution of a civil uprising in western Massachusetts that seemed a mockery of the democratic ideals of the Revolution. Organized by Revolutionary War veteran Daniel Shays, and thus called Shays's Rebellion, the protest had attracted poor farmers and former soldiers who owed funds to the debt-heavy Commonwealth of Massachusetts. Residents were required to pay their taxes and debts in specie—gold and silver coins difficult to obtain in rural western Massachusetts. When residents failed to do so, the commonwealth had seized their homes and farms, placed the men in debtor prisons, and left their families homeless. By September 28, Knox's friend Henry Jackson reported that seven thousand armed rebels had appeared in Springfield near the national arsenal intending to close down the state supreme court. "What will be the result of this, time must determine," Jackson observed.[11]

Immediately Knox rushed from New York to Massachusetts, assigned men to protect the Springfield arsenal, and collaborated with Governor James Bowdoin to crush the rebellion. In October Knox wrote Washington that the turmoil emanated from America's awkward "political machine, composed of thirteen independent sovereignties . . . perpetually operating against each other and against the federal head ever since the peace." High taxes and the demand for payment in specie were only its superficial spark; at its core, Shays's Rebellion was a power struggle between the haves and have-nots. The latter, Knox wrote, "see the weakness of government; they feel at once their own poverty compared with the opulent." Their protests are a "formidable rebellion against reason, the principle of all government and against the very name of liberty." To remedy it, Knox suggested, "Our government must be braced, changed, or altered to secure our lives and property, even though the early leaders of the nation believed they could govern by benign consent." Instead, he went on, "we find that we are men— actual men, possessing all the turbulent passions belonging to that animal, and that we must have a government proper and adequate for him."[12]

Ironically, those same turbulent passions had also prompted Benedict Arnold to commit treason. A mere three weeks before Shays's Rebellion, the *New Haven Gazette and Connecticut Magazine* reported that the American traitor had "paid a visit, in company with an English officer, to the eastern flank of this Commonwealth, and in a very friendly manner waited on Col. Allan at Dudley-Island [Maine]." Nevertheless, Arnold had "tarried only a few hours, judging it more expedient to sojourn in Nova-Scotia, than in a country ever inimical to parricides [traitors]."[13]

As Peggy had implied in her March 1786 letter to Judge Shippen, Arnold's silence from the North American British colonies meant trouble. Towards the end of that voyage, the former American general had suffered another attack of gout, becoming so ill in Halifax that he hired a pilot and captain to complete his journey across the Bay of Fundy to the seaport city of Saint John, New Brunswick. But crossing the tidal flats of the harbor on December 2, 1785, the *Lord Middlebrook* ran aground. For days afterwards, as the vessel sat listing on the St. John River, scavengers stole "considerable quantities of flour, beef, butter and pork," reported the *Saint John Gazette*, dashing all hopes of profits from sale of those goods.[14]

Nevertheless, other profits were waiting to be made from the thousands of Loyalists who had arrived in Saint John between 1783 and 1785, swelling its population to twelve thousand. To capitalize upon rising land values, Arnold had snatched up hundreds of acres of forest, waterfront property, and town lots. In addition he had purchased a wharf, a warehouse, a general store, a lumberyard, and a residence in Saint John, thus enhancing his rise as one of its most prominent citizens. Filled with ambition, Arnold finally wrote Peggy that he intended to postpone his return to England and would do so only after establishing trade contacts in the West Indies.

On Thursday, June 1, Saint John residents gazed at Arnold's launch of the 300-ton white-oak *Lord Sheffield*. "The General's laudable efforts to promote the interests on this infant colony, had been very productive of its commercial advantage and as such desire the praise of every well-wisher to its prosperity," gushed the *Royal Gazette*.[15]

In anticipation of his long months at sea, Arnold needed trusty assistants in Saint John. His three sons from his first marriage—Benedict Jr., Richard, and Henry—were nearly grown, prompting Arnold's invitation for them to leave Connecticut, where they had returned after his defection, to settle with their aunt Hannah, Arnold's sister, in New Brunswick. The oldest, eighteen-year-old Benedict Jr. joined his father and Connecticut Loyalist Munson Hayt in an enterprise called Arnold, Hayt, and Arnold. By August, young Benedict was managing the general store as his father sailed first to the West Indies and then to London. The family, Arnold announced to his lonely wife, Peggy, must emigrate to Canada the following spring.

Whatever doubts she had about still another relocation were silenced by a new pregnancy. Another incentive for agreement was Arnold's promise that once the family was established in Saint John, Peggy could visit the Shippens in Philadelphia. By June 1787, Peggy, Arnold, their children, and their American Loyalists friends the Jonathan Sewalls, sailed aboard the general's newest ship, the *Peggy*, to Saint John.

Connubial duty, loyalties, desperation, or perhaps a blend of all three steeled Peggy, then in the last weeks of pregnancy, to the Atlantic crossing. Six weeks after their arrival in Saint John, on September 5, 1787, she delivered a son, George, named for England's reigning monarch.

The Arnolds' clapboard home on the corner of King and Cross (now Canterbury) streets was less stately than their London townhouse but, by Saint John standards, still impressive. Two and a half stories high with a gambrel roof, it symbolized Arnold's status as a town father. Within it stood the family's London furnishings, blue-damask sofas, matching curtains, mahogany chairs, cabinets and chests, Wedgwood dishes, giltware, and a globe. Initially, as it had in England, life went well. Surrounded by Loyalist refugees from America and England, Peggy hosted dinners, attended galas, and enjoyed riding horses into the countryside with her friend Elizabeth Hazen Chipman.

Nevertheless, Saint John had evolved from its boom days of Arnold's first arrival. During his absence, the North American British colonies, like those of the United States, had slipped into recession, leaving local residents with little cash or ability to pay their debts. Renters failed to meet their payments; suppliers howled for cash for the goods Arnold bought on credit. Shortfalls appeared in his ledger books. Tenaciously, the former general pressed for payment and, when that failed, initiated lawsuits—some nineteen by spring 1791—against his debtors. Added to that crisis were debts of £2,555 that had been accrued by Arnold's partner, Hayt, straining the partnership nearly to the breaking point. In search of new profits, Arnold reverted to the seas, shuttling between the British North American colonies and the West Indies.

As she had been in London, Peggy was again alone, left to raise her growing brood of youngsters with her sister-in-law, Hannah. Out of necessity, the nearly thirty-year-old mother of four became increasingly independent.

But in contrast to her patriotic shadow, Lucy Flucker Knox, Peggy continued to endure separations from her husband without complaint.

Nor would financial shortfalls deter Peggy from a planned trip to Philadelphia to visit her family. "I am much gratified by your earnest solicitation for me to pay you a visit, and hope to accomplish so desirable an event in the fall," she wrote her sister Betsy (Elizabeth) in early 1789. "Independent of the happiness it will afford me, I feel it a duty to . . . comply with the wishes of parents for whom I feel the highest respect and tenderest affection."[16]

Within her letter Peggy confessed she and Arnold were so disappointed in Saint John that they planned to return to England. "When I leave you, I shall probably bid you adieu forever. While his Majesty's bounty is continued to me," she explained, "it is necessary I should reside in his dominions."[17] Discreetly, Peggy avoided describing the details of those disappointments. Among the most harrowing had been the night of July 11, 1788, when Arnold's warehouse went up in flames. His youngest son, Henry, and his brother, Richard, both of whom slept in the office as guards, had been badly burned and both had barely escaped with their lives. In the wake of those fires, Arnold assured Peggy, he would recoup his losses through his insurance policies with the Sun Assurance Company. Then his now-estranged partner, Hayt, accused Arnold of perpetuating a fraud. The former general, he insisted, set those fires himself to collect the £5,000 value from an over-inflated insurance policy. The two men argued bitterly until finally, as the *Saint John Gazette* announced, "the co-partnership of Arnold, Hayt being dissolved by mutual consent, all persons being indebted to said firm are requested to settle accounts with Munson Hayt."[18] After accusing Hayt of slander, Arnold hired his attorney friends Ward Chipman (then New Brunswick's attorney general and solicitor general) and Jonathan Bliss to represent him. "It is not in my power to blacken your character, for it is as black as it can be," Hayt publicly announced.[19] Predictably the accusation disquieted the Sun Assurance Company, whose agents insisted that Arnold's policy would not be paid off until the origin of the fire was resolved.

In August 1789, as the controversy simmered, Peggy prepared to sail to Philadelphia. "I feel great regret at the idea of leaving the General alone . . .

but as he strongly argues a measure that will be productive of so much happiness to me, I think there can be no impropriety in taking the step," she wrote Elizabeth in apparent guilt. Intensifying Peggy's decision to return home was news that her mother had suffered a stroke. Though hoping to avoid putting "Mamma to the least additional trouble on my account," she added that she could not "conveniently go without one maid and a child."[20] On December 3, 1789, Peggy, little George and an African American slave finally arrived in Philadelphia.

Once there, family members rushed to meet her. Within a few days, Peggy was immersed in a whirl of teas, dinners, and receptions. To her sister Betsy, Peggy gossiped as if she were still a frivolous belle, "The little anecdotes of my friends and acquaintances afford me great amusement, and I feel interested in all their little love scenes. I am convinced that Mrs. A. will never think seriously of Mr. Marsden, though she may carry on a little flirtation with him."[21] Behind Peggy's back, though, some Philadelphians regarded her with contempt. One account revealed that the twenty-nine-year-old matron was treated with "so much coldness and neglect that her feelings were continually wounded."[22] Another observed, "The common opinion was, that, as her presence placed her friends in a painful position, she would have shown more feeling by staying away."[23]

By April 16, 1790, Peggy had returned to Saint John. "How difficult is it to know what will contribute to our happiness in this life," she wrote Betsy the following August. "I had hoped that by paying my beloved friends a last visit, I should insure to myself some portion of it, but I find it far otherwise. The affectionate attention of my friends has greatly increased my love for them, and of course, my regret at this cruel, dreadful separation."[24]

Most wrenching of all was Peggy's departure from the Burds. "I shall never forget, my dear, my beloved Sister, your tender and affectionate behavior to me, and that of my . . . brother[-in-law], Mr. Burd, who has endeared himself extremely to me." The time she spent with their children, Peggy added, evoked "an affection almost parental."[25] Especially touching to her was her niece, a little girl the Burds had named Peggy. Poignantly, the former Philadelphian must have compared her sister's family's harmonious lives to the troubled one she led in Saint John as Arnold's wife.

On May 11, 1790, just after Peggy's return to Saint John, Hayt called Arnold a "scoundrel," publicly announcing, "You burnt your own store, and I will prove it."[26] To clear his name and obtain justice, Arnold postponed the family's return to England. Peggy's spirits drooped. "There has been a succession of disappointments and mortifications in collecting our debts ever since my return home—but I will not begin to relate grievances," she confessed to Betsy, "but endeavor to shake off that gloom that has taken possession of me."[27]

It would not be for another eighteen months, on September 7, 1791, that the case, described by Arnold's defense attorney Ward Chipman as "one of the most hellish plots that ever was laid for the destruction of a man," was tried in the Supreme Court at Fredericton.[28] Two days later, the justices who presided over the case, Joshua Upham and Isaac Allen, found Hayt guilty of willful slander. They also ascertained a value on Arnold's claim for damages to his reputation. But instead of the £5,000 he had anticipated, the justices awarded Arnold a contemptuous twenty shillings. Gleeful announcements appeared in the newspapers on both sides of the Atlantic.

Ultimately, the Sun Assurance Company paid Arnold the full £5,000, but Hayt's accusations, the traitor's past, and his debtors' resentments sank Arnold's reputation in Saint John. One night, soon after the trial, late-nineteenth-century historians claimed that a mob appeared before Arnold's King Street home. According to that undocumented tale, the men smashed windows and doors, then paraded through the house with an effigy tagged with the word "traitor" as a terrified Peggy and her children watched. A street riot followed, becoming so violent that soldiers supposedly appeared from nearby Fort Howe.[29]

Whether true or apocryphal, in December 1791 Arnold and his family returned to Great Britain, leaving Hannah and his three oldest sons to manage his remaining enterprises in the British North American colonies. From London, on February 26, 1792, Arnold wrote Jonathan Bliss, "I cannot help viewing your great city as a shipwreck from which I have escaped."[30]

In truth, the recession had contributed to that shipwreck, but Arnold had piloted the ship and ultimately run it aground. A decade after her marriage,

Peggy realized that her friends were her only anchor, her compass on the tumultuous seas of her husband's oceanic ambitions.

In late January 1787, Knox's friend Benjamin Lincoln and a militia funded by Boston's wealthy businessman crushed Shays's Rebellion in Springfield. "The storm in Massachusetts is over," a relieved Knox wrote Washington.[31] Yet, as Knox confided to Boston shipmaster Stephen Higginson, "some measures will be necessary to prevent a repetition" for "the poor, poor federal government is sick almost to death."[32] Ultimately, those same concerns would lead to the creation of the Constitutional Convention, whose delegates would meet behind closed doors from May through September in Carpenter Hall in steamy Philadelphia. Subsequent to the ratification of the U.S. Constitution, in June 1788, the document became a model of government for other nations.

Contrary to Knox's support for the democratic ideals embodied in the Constitution, he and Lucy aspired to an aristocratic lifestyle. Disdaining his modest salary, he and Lucy routinely lived beyond their means, entertaining grandly in spite of mounting debts, sustained perhaps by the promise of Lucy's Maine inheritance. Deprived of luxuries since her marriage, Lucy now felt them her due, both in compensation for the homeless years of the Revolution and her role as wife of America's first secretary at war. To Henry, high living was "proof" that he had, at last, overcome his humble beginnings and the Fluckers' initial scorn. Everyone knew them: Henry, the Revolution's affable artillery genius; Lucy, the widely acknowledged social authority, the Emily Post of her day.

Within another generation the Knoxes would become iconic figures of the Revolution. "Mrs. Knox," as Rufus Griswold wrote in his 1855 *The Republican Court, or, American Society in the Days of Washington*, "had been one of the heroines of the Revolution, nearly as well known in the camps as her husband . . . both were favorites, he for really brilliant conversation and unfailing good humor and she as a lively and meddlesome but amiable leader of society."[33]

According to Griswold's account, Lucy's elite background often intimidated others into believing that without her cooperation "nothing could be properly done in the drawing room or the ball-room, or any place indeed where fashionable men and women sought enjoyment." As a result, he added, "The house of the Secretary . . . in Broadway . . . was the scene of a liberal and genial hospitality."[34]

A description by army chaplain Manasseh Cutler, who attended one of the Knoxes' dinners, confirmed their lavish entertainments. "Dined with General Knox, introduced to his lady and a French nobleman . . . Several other gentlemen dined with us. Our dinner was served in high style, much in the French taste," read his diary entry of Saturday, July 7, 1786. "Mrs. Knox is very gross [fat] but her manners are easy and agreeable."[35]

Disapproving of the feminine fashions of the day, Cutler noted that Lucy "is sociable, and would be agreeable, were it not for her affected singularity in dressing her hair. She seems to mimic the military style, which to me is very disgusting in a female. Her hair in front is craped at least a foot high, much the form of a church bottom upward, and topped off with a wire skeleton in the same form, covered with black gauze, which hands in streamers down to her back. Her hair behind is a large braid, and confined with a monstrous crooked comb."[36]

Two weeks later Henry and Lucy hosted a second dinner for forty-five veteran officers. So opulent were the food and drink and so brilliant the conversation that one visitor recalled, "General Knox gave us an entertainment in the style of a prince."[37]

But fine food and wines, high fashion and friends would not forestall the tragedies that relentlessly beset the Knoxes. That August, their eleven-month-old daughter, Caroline, died from an infection. That was only partly mitigated by Lucy's November 27 delivery of a "fine black-haired, black-eyed boy," whom the Knoxes named George Washington Knox out of "respect and affection" for the former commander in chief.[38]

The combination of repeated pregnancies, nursing, and fine food had swelled Lucy to gargantuan proportions. She and Knox, Griswold later wrote, "were, perhaps, the largest couple in the city."[39] While visiting New York in 1788, "Nabby," Abigail Adams Smith, also mentioned Lucy's size. "General and Mrs. Knox have been very polite and attentive to us," John Adams's daughter wrote, but she was stupefied by Lucy's girth.[40]

"Mrs. Knox is much altered from the character [appearance] she used to have. She is neat in her dress, attentive to her family and very fond of her children. But her size is enormous: I am frightened when I look at her.; I verily believe that her waist is as large as three of yours at least."[41] One of Knox's business partners, William Duer, was far less kind. Lucy, he carped, "was eccentric in character and concentric in figure."[42]

Obesity also plagued thirty-seven-year-old Henry, whose doctors, noting his leg and foot problems, had ordered him to diet. That may have accounted for Nabby's second comment, "The general is not half so fat as he was."[43]

To celebrate Washington's inauguration, on April 30, 1791, as the first president of the United States, lower Manhattan was illuminated that evening by a sky booming with fireworks. Lucy and Henry, appointed America's first secretary of war, hosted a dinner in Washington's honor. The following Thursday, May 7, guests gathered in the Assembly Rooms on the east side of Broadway for the nation's first inaugural ball. Sixty-five years later Griswold based his account of that event upon a report that, according to Thomas Jefferson, illustrated "the frenzy which prevailed in New York on the opening of the new government."[44]

That night Washington was seated in the Assembly Rooms upon a sofa placed on a rise before whom guests were expected to bow before and after each dance. According to Jefferson's tale, retold in Griswold's *Republican Court*, "Mrs. Knox contrived to come with the President, and to follow him and Mrs. Washington to their destination, and she had the design of forcing from the President an invitation to a seat on the soft. She mounted up the stairs after them, unbidden, but unfortunately the wicked sofa was too short, that, when the President and Mrs. Washington were seated, there was not room for a third person. . . . She was obliged, therefore, to descend, in the face of the company, and to sit where she could."[45]

That story and its subsequent reprinting, Griswold noted in his book, are "all utterly untrue." [46] Indeed Martha Washington had neither attended her husband's inauguration nor had yet arrived in New York. Nevertheless, Griswold's account of that malicious tale in *The Republican Court* reflected Jefferson's—and perhaps others'—resentments of the self-important Lucy.

←→

On June 28, six weeks after the inauguration, the Knoxes' infant son, George Washington Knox, contracted dysentery. Hoping salt air and sunshine would hasten his recovery, Lucy and Henry took the baby on daily boat excursions to Sandy Hook, New Jersey. Inevitably Henry was summoned back to the Department of War to settle land disputes in Georgia with the Creeks. Speaking before the Senate on Saturday, August 22, Knox reiterated his position towards the Native Americans: "Indian tribes possess the right of . . . all lands within their limits respectively . . . in consequence of fair and bona fide purchases, made under the authority, or with the express approbation of the United States."[47]

A few streets away in the nursery of the Knox's Broadway home, Lucy hovered over her listless infant, vainly attempting to restore him to health. In spite of her efforts, little George Washington Knox died.

Still Lucy and Henry hoped to bestow a personal honor upon America's first president. That opportunity arrived on February 7, 1790, with Lucy's delivery of another son whom she and Henry again named George Washington. This time, surely, the child would survive.

PART III

Shadow Sisters

11

"Illusive Bubbles"

DETERMINATION, THE BENIGN COUSIN of defiance, drove Lucy to continue enlarging her family to compensate for her lost children. Sixteen months after birthing the second George Washington Knox, Lucy delivered a daughter, again named Caroline. "Please to inform Lady Kitty that Mrs. Knox on the 8th instant presented me with . . . another child . . . her tenth," Henry wrote New York speculator William Duer in July 1791. "This little stranger is a daughter, and the most lovely we have been blessed with."[1]

By then, Henry and Lucy had relocated to the nation's temporary capital, Philadelphia and lived two miles from its center at Bush Hill. Designed by Andrew Hamilton, the architect of Independence Hall, the sleek mansion's former resident was John Adams who was renting it to Knox. One advantage of the house was its distance from the oppressive heat that smothered Philadelphians in summer. "While the inhabitants of this city are gasping for breath like a hunted hare, we experience in the hall at Bush Hill a delightful . . . breeze," Knox gratefully wrote Adams.[2] By autumn though, he, Lucy, and their growing brood moved into a more convenient location near the War Office at Chestnut and Fifth.

Philadelphia had already regained its pre-Revolutionary elegance, its burnt buildings had been replaced by brick townhouses and shops, its streets were now paved with pebbles and shaded with trees. The city's cultural life had also rebounded. "Great alterations have taken place since I was last here. It is all gayety and from what I can observe, every lady and gentleman endeavors to outdo the other in splendor and show," wrote one officer.

"You cannot conceive anything more elegant than the present taste."³ To Abigail Adams, who had visited the French and English courts, Philadelphia society was friendly and agreeable, its dancing assemblies very good, and the company of the best kind."⁴

Among the city's legendary hosts was Secretary of State Thomas Jefferson, who invited fellow cabinet member Knox to dine soon after Caroline's birth. "I have received your friendly note of this morning for which I sincerely thank you," Henry replied. "I shall frequently avail myself of your kindness, and I should have done so this day . . . had I not previously engaged to Mrs. Knox that I would dine with her being the first time since [the delivery] of her daughter."⁵

As secretary of war, Knox's hours were long. No sooner had he quelled Southern hostilities between Native Americans and white settlers than skirmishes broke out in the northwest corner of what is today Ohio. Reluctantly, Henry dispatched troops to the borders of the Ohio Territory, insisting as he had in the south that the United States supported a policy of "humanity and justice" to produce a "noble, illiberal and disinterested administration of Indian affairs."⁶

Simultaneously, Knox attempted to obtain the two-fifths shares of the Waldo Patent, once owned by the expatriated Fluckers. As his late brother-in-law, Captain Thomas Flucker, had warned, the patent was mired in legalities, some of it claimed by members of the Fluckers' extended family, others by squatters. To untangle those claims, Henry again traveled to New York, where the old claims were apparently filed. Coincidentally, on July 15, Lucy's widowed sister-in-law, Sarah Lyons Flucker, arrived in New York from her native home, the British colony of Antigua, to visit relatives and claim her sons' share of the patent. Impressed with the young widow's pluck, Henry wrote Lucy, "You will be charmed with and proud of her."⁷ Years later the Knoxes' eldest daughter, young Lucy, described Sarah as plain looking but evinced a "peculiar fascination in her manners, which attracted all with whom she came in contact."⁸

Just before Lucy was to meet Sarah, Lucy's seventeen-month-old son, George Washington, became "violently ill," forcing Lucy to postpone the sisters-in-law's rendezvous. After the child's recovery, the two women at last met and became fond friends. Quite unexpectedly, later that summer, tragedy struck. First came a letter from the headmaster of the Princeton, New Jersey, school that Marcus Camillus II, the Knoxes' eight-year old son, attended. The boy had tumbled down a flight of stairs and badly injured his cheek, the headmaster announced. A second letter followed with news that the boy had died the next day, having apparently suffered a fatal concussion.

Shock and disbelief swept over the Knoxes. The loss of young children was common enough in eighteenth century America; about 15 percent never reached maturity. But Marcus, the Knoxes' most promising son, was the fifth of their ten children to die. Privately, Lucy and Henry questioned why they were the victims of so many tragedies.

From Mount Vernon, Washington conveyed his and Martha's sympathies. "I have heard of the death of your promising son with great concern and sincerely condole you and Mrs. Knox on this melancholy occasion." In reply, the president wrote that he hoped the "consolations of religion or philosophy" would heal them in time.[9] Heartbroken, Knox admitted that "neither philosophy nor reason have their proper office."[10] Five months later, he wrote a friend that Lucy was still "inconsolable."[11] A portrait of Marcus, a handsome lad seated at his writing desk, remained on the walls of the Knoxes' homes for decades.

By January 1792 Lucy, pregnant for the eleventh time, was again able to attend the plays, balls, and dinners of Philadelphia with members of prominent families, including the Binghams, Morrises, Chews, and Ingersolls. Nearby, too, lived her old friends Martha and George Washington in the Masters-Penn House, which Washington had recently had remodeled.

The results were so stunning that, after attending Martha Washington's first "levee," or public reception, New Yorker Sally McKean gushed to a friend, "You could never have such a drawing-room; it was brilliant beyond anything you can imagine; and though there was a great deal of extravagance, there was so much of Philadelphia taste in everything that [it] must be confessed the most delightful occasion ... ever known in this country."[12]

As the prominent wife of America's first secretary of war, Lucy also hosted levees, offering her guests tea, coffee, and lemonade, as well an opportunity to play cards or chess. Two years earlier, when still in New York

City, Abigail Adams had scoffed at Lucy's concept of entertaining. Though other prominent women opened their homes for levees, Abigail wrote her oldest sister, Mary Cranch, "one only . . . introduces cards and she is frequently put to difficulty to make up a table at whist."[13]

That unnamed hostess was undoubtedly Lucy. History has not revealed why she was so passionate about games. Cards had long been accepted as a social amusement in New York, as Becky Franks once complained, but Lucy's zeal transcended that. Apparently she enjoyed the competition or found it a way to wall off grief, but whatever the cause, it was matched by the vehemence of Henry's disapproval. "Remember me, my love with all the tenderness I deserve—respect my prejudices as they relate to vile cards," he pleaded, "and for God's sake and mine, renounce them altogether."[14]

In her defense, the Knoxes' eldest daughter, Lucy, later insisted to Elizabeth Ellet, author of the 1848 *Women of the American Revolution*, that her mother's love for her family remained her overriding concern. Not only did the elder Lucy have strong "domestic attachments . . . devotion to household and children," but she "was ready in the noon of life, to give up the delights of society in the metropolis."[15] By that, the younger Lucy referred to her mother's desire to leave Philadelphia to establish a grand home on her grandfather's lands in Maine.

During each summer's outbreak of yellow fever in Philadelphia Lucy and the children fled. Even before their move to the City of Brotherly Love, the Knoxes' Boston friend Henry Jackson had warned Lucy about "the unhealthy climate of that city in the hot season."[16] To avoid contagion Jackson suggested she and the children spend the summers in his spacious home in Dorchester, Massachusetts. By May 1792, Lucy, who was again pregnant, accepted his invitation and brought her sister-in-law, Sarah Lyons Flucker, and both their children.

In Dorchester Lucy again pined for "her Harry," imagining him enjoying himself at dinners and galas in her absence. "My evenings cannot possibly be any cause of jealousy. They are stupid indeed," Henry assured her. "If I dine out which is pretty often, I drink tea . . . come home read the evening paper and about . . . nine go to a solitary and . . . a painful bed, painful from the reflection that the companion of my soul is at a distance—and that I am deprived of the blessed solace of her arms."[17]

He longed to join Lucy in Massachusetts but, as America's new secretary of war was obliged to remain in Philadelphia. "I am upon my probation," he reminded her in late July. "A single lapse of public duty at this moment sinks me, never again to rise."[18] Lured by the prospect of retiring to Maine, he again rode to New York to examine legal papers on the Waldo Patent. "I know not how long it will take to bring the cursed affair here to a close," he wrote. "But I know that I shall not be able to stay here more than three or at most four days. I must be back here [in Philadelphia], Friday or Saturday."[19]

Adding to his worries was Lucy's approaching due date, causing him to "check every post . . . until I shall be informed of your having been safely delivered."[20] The "perils of child-bearing" was only one of Lucy's challenges.[21] Another was the rambunctious behavior of her eldest son, Henry Jackson Knox.

The Knoxes' earlier indulgence of the boy was at least partially to blame for his behavior. While visiting a friend in Boston, Lucy brought young Henry Jackson with her. As the two women chatted, the boy "disarranged" the books in the hostess's library. "Henry must not be restrained, we never think of thwarting *him* in anything," Lucy insisted. Appalled, her friend replied, "But I cannot have my books spoiled, as my husband is not a bookbinder." Enraged, Lucy stormed out of the house with her son.[22]

By the time young Henry was twelve, even Lucy and Henry were worried about him. In an effort to improve his behavior, Lucy toured a school in Hingham, Massachusetts, which prepared young men for Harvard. Though the school's name was not mentioned in Lucy's letters, it was the Derby School (today's Derby Academy), then the town's only secondary educational institution. After learning about it, Knox was impressed. Losing his father when he was twelve had forced Henry to leave Boston Latin School, thus blocking all hopes of attending Harvard. Knox wanted better for his son, and the Derby School seemed to provide that, combining moral training with high educational standards. Without a sound background in both, Knox wrote Lucy, young Henry "will grope through the world, and with bad morals. I love him as I do my life, but I am desirous to devote him to the proper rank of a man by discharging my duty to him."[23]

Though her sister, Sarah, who had also toured the Derby School, decided to enroll her own children there, Lucy, in contrast, balked at the idea, feeling guilty about sending her son away from home. On September 16, in the midst of the dilemma, Lucy bore an eleventh child, a girl she named Augusta Henrietta. "I received on Saturday last my beloved Lucy's letter," Henry joyously wrote from Philadelphia. "I am delighted . . . what heaven in its mercy grant."[24]

As she recovered, Lucy continued to brood about young Henry. "As to our son please to observe finally that I regard your happiness as my supreme object," Knox tenderly assured her. "At the very least, the youth's attendance at boarding school would relieve her of attempting to shape their difficult son. "If he can be made a better man and receive an education at a distance," Knox observed, ". . . it's our duty to afford it to him."[25]

Coincidental with those expressed sentiments was the forty-year-old secretary of war's own questions about time spent away from home. That same September he confided to his fifteen-year-old daughter, Lucy, that he longed to leave his cabinet position. "All my life hitherto, I have been pursuing illusive bubbles which burst on being grasped . . . 'tis high time I should quit public life and attend to the solid interests of my family so that they may not be left dependent on the cold hand of charity." Nevertheless, he intended to retire "with reputation." As secretary of war he could not neglect "for a moment, the services belonging to my station," but he understood that for the sake of his family, he had to "make some exertions for pecuniary objects."[26]

Among those "exertions" were Knox's ventures in land speculation. With his partner, the slimy New York speculator William Duer, Knox naively purchased 2 million acres of Maine land at ten cents an acre from the Commonwealth of Massachusetts. No sooner had the two partners paid back the $10,000 than Duer was apprehended for other debts and thrown into prison. Fortunately, Senator William Bingham, Philadelphia's wealthiest citizen, rescued Knox by purchasing Duer's shares, advancing a loan, and promising the secretary of war one-third of the profits.

At the same time, Henry continued to struggle with rights to the Waldo Patent. On July 4, 1785, the Massachusetts legislature had confirmed Knox's stewardship of its 576,000 acres and three adjoining coastal islands. Technically, Massachusetts still owned two-fifths of the patent's shares from the estate of Lucy's mother. Since back taxes were owed on the property, Henry realized the lowered value of those shares presented a unique opportunity. In June 1791, he met at the Bunch of Grapes tavern with Boston merchant Joseph Peirce, who managed—and here the details remain murky—to auction off the two-fifths' shares of the Flucker portion at the bargain rate of $3,000. The winning bidder was Dr. Oliver Smith, a friend of Knox's brother, William. Six months later, Smith sold the shares to Knox's agent, Henry Jackson. By late 1793 Jackson quietly signed them over to Henry. Somehow (and again the records are unclear), Henry also purchased the remaining one-fifth of the Waldo Patent from the other Flucker heirs.

Slippery as was Knox's land grab of the entire Waldo Patent, nepotism and patronage were common in those days. Even the Knoxes' literary friend, Mercy Otis Warren, whose work praised the "virtue" of the American character, expected Knox to grant favors to her sons. "Though not used to make applications for office," Mercy explained she had "such a confidence in your friendship as justifies . . . the appointment of collection of customs for the port of Plymouth and Duxbury" for her son, Henry. Could Knox also grant a commission or "arrangement of the military department" for her other son, Winslow? Intent upon maintaining his public image, Knox coolly referred her to Washington.[27]

By then Henry longed as much as did Lucy for a country estate like those owned by Jefferson and the Washingtons. After achieving full title to the Waldo Patent, he consequently hired housewright Ebenezer Dunton to construct a mansion in the Maine coastal town of Thomaston. Set on a rise above the St. George River, the house was to be surrounded by gardens, a large farm, and a number of industries Knox intended to found to foster "development of the District of Maine."[28] One obstacle to the mansion's rapid completion was the region's long winters. Another was Knox's duties as secretary of war, which required constant attention to national problems.

Among these were ongoing tribal disputes in Ohio. No less alarming were hostilities between France and Britain over American shipping, resulting in the unlawful capture of American sailors and ships.

In August 1793, yellow fever again swept through Philadelphia, producing the worst epidemic in the city's history. Mosquito- borne, its victims spiked high fevers, hemorrhaged from various orifices, became jaundiced, and often died. "Many are taken off with it . . . they have burned tar in the streets and taken many other precautions, many families have left the city," Elizabeth Drinker penned in her diary.[29] Deaths were so frequent that mourners no longer held traditional funerals. Instead, Drinker noted, "many are buried after night, and taken in carts to their graves."[30] By August 10, Alexander Hamilton had fallen ill, and after sixteen government workers died, Washington and Martha left the city for Mount Vernon.

Only one member of the president's remained: America's secretary of war, who served as Washington's proxy in his absence. As the death toll climbed in excess of a hundred a day, Philadelphia grew silent. "The streets are lonely to a melancholy degree. The merchants generally have fled . . . the stroke is as heavy as if an army of enemies had possessed the city without plundering it," Knox wrote Washington.[31]

From New York, Lucy warned Henry to avoid the center of Philadelphia and stay in nearby Schuylkill Falls. "You [are] not to . . . visit to Philadelphia you cannot go even should the evil abate from this time," she lectured Henry.[32] A full month later, she still fretted about Knox, admitting to him that her days were "clouded by the possibility of your being exposed."[33] Implied in this was Lucy's continued frustration over Henry's dedication to the United States at still another risk to his life.

As usual Knox reassured his wife. With the arrival of November's cooler temperatures, the epidemic had abated and affairs were returning to normal. "There is hope Congress will meet in Philadelphia," he wrote. The current international tensions made it "of no small national importance, that it should be known abroad that the government is administered and the legislature is sitting in the very place of which such dreadful reports have been . . . circulated."[34] To do otherwise would present a weak face to the warring French and British.

By mid-December, newspapers announced that the French had captured, imprisoned, and sold a hundred American sailors into slavery in Algiers. A hue and cry arose across the land, resulting in a March 12, 1794, Congressional appropriation of nearly $700,000 to establish a navy. As secretary of war, Knox was ordered to supervise construction of six high-performance frigates—the USS *United States*, USS *President*, USS *Congress*, USS *Chesapeake*, USS *Constellation*, and USS *Constitution*, or "Old Ironsides."

By May, Henry felt so hemmed in with duties that he complained to his friend Henry Jackson, "I cannot leave my situation in this critical state of affairs."[35] In July another crisis, an armed protest by the farmers of western Pennsylvania over an excise tax on whiskey, compounded those frustrations.

After the September 24 birth of Lucy's twelfth child, Marcus Bingham, Henry finally resolved to retire at the end of the year. "I have never attended to my private affairs, and I have a growing family," he explained to General Wayne that December of 1794. "I must be more attentive, or an unpleasant old age will be stealing up on me."[36] One can almost hear Lucy's pleas behind those words, murmuring about their intended bucolic retirement to Maine.

There, he and Lucy would raise their children without distraction. There too, they might perhaps reform their difficult son, Henry. The Knoxes were not the only ones concerned about the boy. From Hingham in March 1793 Sarah Flucker had written to Lucy that the teenager's proposed trip to Boston during a school vacation should be discouraged, for there he would likely be "exposed to the temptation of the town which may set aside his present habits of regularity."[37]

Whatever "habits of regularity" young Henry might have acquired at the Derby School did not stick. A year later, he wrote to his father that he had no intention of continuing his education but would make his living as a merchant. Higher education served no purpose, the teenager insisted, other than to understand "mathematics & arithmetic perfectly, which can be obtained without going to college." "If, sir, I must go," young Henry threatened, "it will be against my desire."[38]

Although neither knew it, the Knoxes' unstable finances paralleled the Arnolds' own. From London on June 26, 1792, the increasingly practical Peggy had shared her concerns with Judge Shippen: "I am extremely anxious to place the little money that we have reserved for my children . . . to give them a good education which in this country [England] is attended with great expense. Will you, my dear sir, give me your advice and assistance to effect this desirable end?"[39] Belying Peggy's ignorance was her suggestion that her father invest the money she saved from Queen Charlotte's pension in an annuity. "If I recollect when I was in Philada, your bank produced at least seven percent; and you thought the money perfectly secure," she wrote to Judge Shippen. Since "bills are now at Par, *should they continue so, or rise,* and you think it eligible for me to place money in Philadelphia, I beg you will have the goodness to draw upon me for £2,000 Sterling."[40] This was no vapid former Philadelphia belle but a shrewd thinker. Having witnessed a series of Arnold's financial disasters, she had decided she would now invest on her own.

Nevertheless, Peggy continued to defend Arnold. In the next paragraphs of that letter, written several weeks later, she warned Judge Shippen to ignore newspaper reports of Arnold's death in a duel as merely rumors. The surrounding circumstances behind the rumors, though, had caused her "a great deal of pain." The trouble began when a certain Lord Lauderdale "had cast some reflections on his [Arnold's] political character, in the House of Lords." Although Peggy had advised Arnold to ignore the insult, "this is a subject upon which of course, he is, to me silent," she glumly admitted. "All that I can obtain from him, are assurances that he will do nothing rashly."[41]

As a result she summoned "all my fortitude to my aid, to prevent . . . sinking under it, which would unman him and prevent his acting himself." After Arnold demanded an apology, Lauderdale conceded. The former American general had drafted a formal note for him to sign, but when the noble refused, Arnold challenged him to duel. Arnold's second was a Lord Hawke, whom Peggy described as "our particular friend."[42] Lauderdale's second was the colorful Charles James Fox, former British prime minister and head of the Rockingham Whigs.

At 7 a.m. on Sunday, July 6, 1792, Arnold and Lauderdale stood back to back in a field at Kilbourne Wells, Hampstead, as Peggy cowered in a bed in central London. At a signal, the duelers paced off and turned. Arnold fired and missed, provoking a trembling Lauderdale to insist "he had no enmity to General Arnold." But still refusing to apologize, the aristocrat invited Arnold to shoot again. Arnold proudly refused, and Peggy explained that Lauderdale had claimed "he did not mean to asperse his character or wound his feelings . . . was sorry for what he had said."[43]

A report in the June 29 *Evening Mail* confirmed Peggy's account and chortled over the Lauderdale side for its amateurish preparations for the duel. "Mr. Fox apologized to Lord Lauderdale for his inexpertise in charging his pistols" and even admitted, "I never fired but once in my life.'"[44]

Nevertheless, the duel and its potentially grim consequences had ripped through Peggy as brutally as a bullet. In the days before it, she had remained silent. "What I suffered for a week is not to be described; the suppression of my feelings, lest I should unman the general almost . . . proved too much for me; and for some hours, my reason was despaired of," she wrote Judge Shippen a few days later. By the time of her July 6 letter though, she had recovered.[45]

The intrigue had galvanized London society. To Arnold's astonishment, other nobles and highly placed men congratulated him for his courage in the face of public insult. Their approval, Peggy boasted to her father, had been "expressed, universally, and particularly by a number of the first characters in the kingdom." Nor, she added, "am I displeased at the great commendations bestowed on my own conduct upon this trying occasion."[46]

Three weeks later, William Pitt the Younger, by then the prime minister and chancellor of the Exchequer, asked the Treasury Department to review General Clinton's compensation for Arnold's losses in America. Again Arnold insisted that his half-pay pension was "far from being able to provide for and educate a numerous family of children"[47] After a personal meeting with Pitt, the former general wrote Clinton that the prime minister "appeared very much surprised at the small sum I received and asked for 'a little time to consider the matter.'" The "little time" turned into weeks, then months, though ultimately nothing changed.[48]

Still, Arnold, by then fifty-three, would not give up. Gamely, he applied for another military post, but after its rejection, he again decided to strike out on his own. He would do so, he told Peggy, by selling two New Brunswick vessels to fund a privateer with which to attack the French. Filled with enthusiasm, he also wrote his Canadian friend Jonathan Bliss about his plans to sail to the Caribbean for "five or six months" to resume his trade connections[49] Wide-eyed, Peggy, who was again pregnant, listened to her husband's plans. Nothing she could do or say, she knew, could change them.

Only the stormy weather of March 1794 stalled Arnold's departure from Falmouth. Nearby, another ship, carrying exiles from the French Reign of Terror, was similarly delayed in the harbor. Among its passengers was the controversial Prince Talleyrand, Charles Maurice de Talleyrand-Perigord, who, learning that an American general was staying in the same inn while waiting for the weather to clear, begged an introduction. Reluctantly Arnold met him but, the Frenchman recalled, "dared not tell me his name." When Talleyrand asked for letters of introduction in America, Arnold morosely confessed, "I am perhaps the only American who cannot give you letters for his own country. All the relations I had there are now broken. I must never return." Later, Talleyrand realized his acquaintance was Benedict Arnold. "I must confess that I felt much pity for him, for I witnessed his agony."[50]

Later that spring Arnold successfully traded English goods in St. Kitts and on June 4, 1794, headed into the harbor of Pointe-a-Pitre on the Guadeloupe island of Grand-Terre. That same day the French occupied the island, captured Arnold, and cast him onto a prison ship.

In London three weeks later, Peggy delivered a fifth child, William Fitch, named after their American Loyalist friend and neighbor. By August she had learned about Arnold's capture. "I am now in a state of most extreme misery, from the report of your father's being a prisoner to the French at Point-a Peter, Guad[e]loupe," she wrote her stepson Richard in Saint John. "It is contradicted by some gentlemen lately from St. Kitt's but your father's last letter to me, being of the first of June, wherein he says he shall set-off the next day for Point-a-Peter, makes it but too probable."[51]

On August 29, after bribing his guards, Arnold made a daring escape. After squeezing through a cabin window of the prison ship, he shimmied down a rope onto a raft and paddled through shark-infested waters to a small boat, which he rowed to the *Boyne*, a British man-of-war. Soon afterwards he met General Sir Charles "No Flint" Grey, who, oddly enough, had been John André's commanding officer. In spite of his remembrance of the circumstances surrounding André's death, Grey was impressed with Arnold. Ultimately, he rewarded Arnold with two posts: volunteer quartermaster for the British fleet and agent for Guadeloupe's British planters.

With rising hopes for a permanent military position, Arnold lingered in Guadeloupe for a year but finally returned to London in July 1795. To his surprise, Peggy—by then thirty-five years old—had become "very much an invalid" in his absence.[52] He attributed her condition to nerves brought on by his long absence, financial worries, and reports of her mother's death in Philadelphia. Desperate to restore Peggy to health, Arnold brought her to the baths at Cheltenham and to the ocean near Surrey, but she failed to make a full recovery. In December, while congratulating the Blisses on the birth of another child, Peggy wrote, "For my own part, I am determined to have no more little plagues, as it is so difficult to provide for them in this country."[53] By spring, she was suffering from edema. The mere act of walking, Peggy complained in a letter to Judge Shippen on May 2, 1796, produced pains in her leg and caused her body to swell, though her appetite was normal and she appeared in "florid health." As a remedy, her doctors suggested that she consume half portions of food and drink and "never [to] fatigue myself with exercise."[54]

Only one event had brightened her life—receipt of Judge Shippen's portrait. "You could not have bestowed upon me a more valued gift. Repining is useless, but it is surely a hard lot to be so separated from all my relations," Peggy wrote. "Do not suffer absence to weaken your affection for me," she pleaded, "though fate has deprived me of the happiness of contributing to the comfort of your latter days, I could sacrifice almost my life to render them easy, and free from care and pain."[55]

Disappointments, public and private, had marred Peggy's defiant marriage. Suddenly, for the first time since her April 8, 1779, wedding to Arnold, the former Philadelphia belle admitted that her union with Arnold had bankrupted her vitality and spirit.

"An Irresistible but Invisible Force"

ON JUNE 22, 1795, taut sails and a brisk wind carried Lucy, Henry, and their six youngsters on a sloop through Maine's Penobscot Bay onto the St. George River. As the vessel neared shore, a mansion came into view. This was Montpelier, the Knoxes' new home, perched above the river like a great white bird, its nine outbuildings outstretched like welcoming wings.

Lucy was overcome. Here was the palatial house she and Henry had dreamed about for decades, one as imposing as the Washingtons' Mount Vernon and Jefferson's Monticello. The setting was equally stately. To the northeast stood deep pine forests; in the distance shimmered an outline of the Camden Mountains, and, slightly west, stood the sleepy town of Thomaston. As the Knoxes disembarked onto the lawn, a committee of local residents rushed forward to welcome them. Behind a gate embellished with an American eagle of the Order of the Cincinnati, loomed the family's new home, topped by a domed cupola.

In 1794, Knox had instructed his housewright to "build the house plain without carving or other expensive ornament."[1] After Lucy conversed with her Philadelphia friend Anne Willing Bingham, who had once lived in France, though, she added several ideas to the plan. Lucy also decided to name the estate Montpelier after another house owned by a French family that she and Knox once visited.

The mansion was massive. Within its four stories—each three-thousand square feet—were nineteen rooms and twenty-four fireplaces, making Montpelier larger "than any other private house from Philadelphia to

Passamaquoddy," as Knox's awed attorney Henry Jackson later observed.[2] Reminiscent of Philadelphian and Georgian architecture, its colossal dimensions also reflected Lucy and Henry's personal bulk, aristocratic tastes, and fondness for entertainment.

Every aspect of Montpelier was symmetrical. From the front stairs, guests entered the high-ceilinged, lemon-yellow Oval Room. Above its double fireplaces hung portraits of Washington and Knox, beneath which stood a handsome Sheraton card table and a polished wood bureau, or travel case, a gift from Lafayette. Two globes—one terrestrial, the other celestial—flanked the front door. Twin side chambers housed drawing rooms, a dining room, and Henry's library of over 1,500 volumes, one-third of them in French. A central door at the back of the Oval Room opened onto a hall with double flying staircases that led to the bedrooms. One early visitor to Montpelier described it as "a handsome, though not a magnificent structure; neatly, if not sumptuously furnished; sufficiently spacious for the accommodation of a numerous family, with additional lodging for . . . seven or eight friends, or even more."[3]

To celebrate, the Knoxes invited residents of Thomaston to a housewarming. "On July Fourth, we had a small company of upwards of 500 people," Henry drolly wrote Henry Jackson.[4] To feed their guests, Montpelier's chef roasted an ox and, throughout the day harpsichord music, played by the Knox's nineteen-year-old daughter, Lucy, enhanced the elegance of the affair.

By dawn some guests had already arrived. "Men, women and children poured in until the house was completely filled, and babies without number were placed on different beds. . . . It was altogether an amusing scene," young Lucy recalled. "The house was so much larger than anything they had seen before . . . the subject of wonder, every object, having the attraction of novelty."[5] There was only one sour note: the theft that day of Henry's gold watch and two of Lucy's silver cups.

Added to the colorful mix of visitors were members of the Tarrantines, American natives of the Penobscot tribe, who camped upon Montpelier's lawn." For days after the party, the Tarrantines remained on the grounds, eating at Montpelier's expense until even Knox grew impatient. "Now we have had a good visit, and you had better go home," he finally declared.[6]

Their long stay and the thefts of July 4 set Lucy on edge. Although a kind, generous mistress to her servants, Knox's wife quickly acquired a reputation for haughtiness towards locals. One often-told story involved an outing during which Lucy's carriage broke down. As she awaited help from Montpelier, a kindly neighbor invited her to rest in her home. Stiffly, Lucy replied that she preferred to wait outside. Then she stood proudly in the mud until her servants arrived.

Henry, in contrast, endeared himself to Thomaston's residents. Yet it was often known that the former American general would "plan more in a day than could be executed in a year," and Maine proved no exception.[7] Among his dizzying number of enterprises was a new wharf on the St. George, a lime works, brick manufacture, livestock farm, saw mills, lumbering businesses, and a shipyard. Dozens of workers—carpenters, coopers, joiners, blacksmiths, masons, ship builders, and lumberjacks—consequently swarmed over Montpelier with questions and requests for cash and supplies.

"When this great and good man left the Federal cabinet, he became victim to anticipation," his younger Massachusetts colleague, Senator Harrison Gray Otis, later observed. "His own palace raised in the woods was a beau ideal only of the 'castles in the air' which floated in his ardent imagination." The scope and size of his project, Otis reflected, "were worthy of Peter the Great, and would have required no inconsiderable portion of Peter's resources to be carried out."[8]

In lieu of those resources, Knox invited others to invest in his enterprises, hoping especially to interest his wealthy business partner and friend, William Bingham. If he and his beautiful wife, Anne, visited Montpelier that summer, Knox promised they would find Lucy beaming "in her retirement," as hostess of a magnificent estate.[9] Bingham declined the invitation. Saddled with more Maine lands than he could sell, he instead offered Knox's investment plans to Sir Francis Baring in London.

Lucy, disappointed that her friend Anne would not visit and longing for urbane company that first summer, was consequently thrilled when the

Duke de la Rochefoucauld-Liancourt arrived for a visit in early autumn. After contributing to the American Revolution, he had returned to France and served briefly as president of the French National Assembly. During the subsequent Reign of Terror, Rochefoucauld had fled so quickly he had no time to pack. "I have three dukedoms on my head, and not a whole coat on my back," the threadbare noble muttered while at Montpelier.[10] Knox, accordingly, outfitted the duke in new clothes. Recalling that and other kindnesses from Lucy, Rochefoucauld wrote that the Knoxes had treated him with "the same kind concern as if I had been a *near* relation."[11]

In his journal, later published as *Travels through the United States of North America*, he described Knox's wife as "a lady of whom you conceive a still higher opinion the longer you are acquainted with her. Seeing her in Philadelphia, you think of her only as a fortunate player of whist; in her house in the country, you discover she possesses sprightliness, knowledge, a good heart, and an excellent understanding."[12]

Regardless of that "excellent understanding," Lucy's brashness often offended others. Among them was Sir Baring's twenty-one-year-old son, Alexander, the future Baron Ashburton, who, at his father's insistence, sailed from England to Massachusetts in late 1795 to investigate Bingham's description of Knox's investment opportunity. Soon after his arrival, Lucy, who then happened to be in Boston, demanded an introduction. "General Knox is in Philadelphia but I have been introduced to his wife at *her* desire by Mr. Codman," the young man tartly reported to one of his London business partners.[13]

Soon after Knox's return from Philadelphia for the funeral of his long-ailing brother, William, Alexander met the former secretary of war. Immediately, the young Englishman liked him. Knox contributed so much to Maine that, once it became a state, Alexander believed the citizens "will certainly elect him governor. I hope he will affix himself there [Maine], but fear he is too much the man of the world for so retired a life."[14] Ultimately Alexander agreed to purchase two and a half million acres of land and, the following August, joined William and Anne Bingham for a visit to Montpelier.

As usual, Lucy and Henry welcomed their guests with open arms. During that visit, the Reverend Paul Coffin also stopped by Montpelier, just after Knox, Bingham, and Baring had left for a tour of the Waldo Patent. Lucy, her children, and her guest Anne, her daughters and sister had remained at the estate. For weeks a punishing heat wave had plagued Maine, but according to Rev. Coffin, Montpelier's "ventilators" were so efficient that he was "almost frozen for three hours." During a "merry" dinner with wine, "the little misses talking French in a gay mood, Mrs. Bingham was sensible, had been in France, could talk of European politics and give the history of the family of the late king of France."[15]

Beneath that gaiety lay grief. Five months earlier on April 21, 1796, the Knoxes' three-year-old Augusta Henrietta and eighteen-month-old Marcus William Bingham, became ill with "putrid sore throat," today called diphtheria. Soon afterwards six-year-old George Washington Knox also sickened. On Saturday, April 23, the two youngest children died. "Seven healthy, blooming children have been torn almost as suddenly from the same fond parents, who, with lacerated hearts, hang over the bed of another child, laboring under the same disease," reported the *Columbian Centinel.*[16] Miraculously, little George managed to survive.

Six months later, the Knoxes were tested again. Rumors attributed the establishment of their winter residence in Boston to Lucy's need for company, but that may not have been entirely true. "I hope the time is not far distant when you will cease these peregrinations. Mrs. Knox, I know, would be glad to reside at Montpelier," General Daniel Cobb teased Henry, "but your attachment to the social pleasures of the city are not so easily overcome. . . . I fear we shall never see you fixed till you have grown so old as to be useless to yourself and friends."[17]

Ultimately the couple did remain "fixed" in Boston that winter, but not as Cobb imagined. Instead, they were bowed with grief over a second illness and, finally, the death of George Washington Knox. "We find ourselves afflicted by an irresistible but invisible force to whom we must submit," an anguished Henry wrote President Washington. In contrast to Knox's abiding faith in God, Lucy found no comfort in religion. The loss,

Henry haltingly observed, "is almost too great for the inconsolable mother who will go mourning to her grave."[18]

Afterwards, Lucy shunned all reminders of death, including a certain cemetery that lay within sight of Montpelier containing graves of Maine's early settlers. Years earlier Knox had attempted to locate the site of the mansion far from the graveyard, but that would have placed it in a marsh. After George's death, Lucy could no longer bear to look at it. Tearfully, she pleaded with Knox to have the gravestones of the cemetery removed. Vehemently, Henry protested. One day while he traveled, Lucy, nevertheless, ordered servants to take away the headstones and cover all traces of the graves.

Denial and distraction became Lucy's painkillers, aided by devotion to her children, dedication as a hostess, and dependence upon "her Henry" for love and solace.

During the spring and summer, guests from Boston, New York, and Philadelphia filled Montpelier's nineteen rooms. "A hundred beds were made, and ox and twenty sheep often slaughtered in a week and twenty saddle horses and corresponding carriages kept to accommodate guests and sojourners," recalled local historian Cyrus Eaton.[19] To outsiders, the Knoxes' generosity and extravagance soon became legendary. Years later, their eldest daughter, Lucy, attributed her father's largesse to his desire to please others. "His heart," as she put it, "was always much larger than his purse."[20] Reports of the Knoxes' extravagant entertainments soon drifted back to Boston, prompting Henry's horrified attorney, Henry Jackson, to reprimand him for living "in the style of an Eastern Nabob," or governor of an Indian province.[21]

Guests, nevertheless, were obliged to pay a price for their surroundings by indulging Lucy at the card and chess tables. Contrary to Henry's earlier request, she had continued with those games, accompanied by bets with petty cash. Years later, daughter Lucy recalled a typical evening at Montpelier. Her mother nightly "spread tables of cards and other games and partook of them willingly herself." In contrast, Henry was "scarcely a looker on; preferring to converse with those who were not engaged at play; and thus on foot walking from one circle to the other with his cheerful smile and affable speech did he make his guest happy, and himself beloved."[22]

In early 1804, the twenty-three-year-old newlywed Anna Cutts confirmed Lucy's obsession with games. That April, to her sister, Dolley Madison, Anna reported from Boston that "Madame Knox, although very haughty, I find pleasant and sensible. Chess is now her mania, which she plays extremely well, only too often for my fancy . . . every morning after breakfast, there is a summons from her ladyship, which, if I attend, pins me to her apron-string until time to dress for dinner, after which she retires, again inviting me to battle. Out of twenty-one games, in only two, and a drawn game, has she shown me any mercy; she is certainly the most successful player I have ever encountered."[23]

Today Lucy would probably be considered a victim of an obsessive-compulsive behavior disorder, a psychological means of reducing anxieties through the numbing repetition of an activity.

In contrast was Knox's geniality. A familiar and popular figure in Thomaston, Knox often walked through town dressed in black, a gold-headed cane in one hand, the other wrapped in a silk handkerchief to conceal his finger-stub scars from his youthful gun accident. According to historian Eaton, the former secretary of war "loved to see everyone happy, and could sympathize with people of every class and condition, rejoice in their prosperity, and aid them in adversity."[24] Eaton's praise was probably excessive, colored by Knox's many gifts to Thomaston, among them a church, its glass, and a bell that he ordered from Boston's Paul Revere.

Simultaneously, the former secretary of war's enterprises were flagging. Lime from his works proved inferior; the salmon fishery had foundered; livestock sickened with diseases; and Maine's harsh winters had battered his wharves and shipping enterprises. By 1798 Knox's debts so overwhelmed his assets that neither Bingham nor Baring nor even Jackson dared advance him more loans. To raise more cash, Knox sold some of his vast acreage. Finally, he even mortgaged Montpelier.

Beneath Knox's genial image was an increasingly grasping man, one as insistent upon a show of wealth as he was desperate for funds. Theories abound as to why. Perhaps his larger-than-life displays were compensation for the poverty of his youth, the scars of the Fluckers' original snobbery, or Lucy's insistence upon an elite lifestyle. Possibly too, the Revolution and its sacrifices had sparked a sense of entitlement, epitomized by his creation of the Order of the Cincinnati and land grab of the Waldo Patent.

In spite of Knox's earlier efforts, the disposition of the Waldo lands remained a matter of public controversy in Maine. Among those with counter-claims were eight hundred settlers who had lived for years on the Waldo Patent's coastal lands. To placate the settlers and raise funds, Knox had offered low-cost mortgages for them to purchase their plots. Simultaneously he tightened his grip upon those living in the patent's backcountry—squatters, he called them—in reality, poor men and former veterans who, either intentionally or innocently, through the Waldo Patent's tangled web of century-old claims, had cleared land and built farms and homes. In protest, the backwoodsmen argued that Knox's possession of those lands was illegal. Between the late 1790s and first years of the nineteenth century, their hostilities increased. Soon after the Knoxes settled at Montpelier, the "squatters" threatened to burn it; several years later they fired at Knox's surveyors. Their vilifying pamphlet, *The Unmasked Nabob of Hancock Country*, claimed that the Massachusetts legislature had, "by their train of provisos, said it belongs to . . . such a numerous train of heirs, that they could not confirm the patent."[25]

To protect his benevolent public image, Knox shrewdly distanced himself from the struggle. Covertly he hired men to prowl the backcountry as independent land agents and report on the "banditti of the wilderness" or initiate lawsuits against the squatters.[26]

"Nature never deceives us; it is always we who deceive ourselves," the French Enlightenment author Jean-Jacques Rousseau observed in *Of the Social Contract*. The same might have been said about Lucy and Henry at Montpelier. Subsequent to the 1796 triple deaths of their youngsters, the Knoxes settled into a superficially serene existence. At night Henry played chess with Lucy, as their trio of remaining daughters, Lucy, Caroline, and Julia, sat nearby reading or busying themselves with needlework. Two years earlier, Knox's friend Henry Jackson had reported that their difficult son, Henry, was making "cards, wine & women his continual pursuit, at taverns and bad houses," but by the late 1790s, the young man seemed to have matured.[27] In the late 1790s, Knox's namesake served as a Navy midshipman on the U.S.S. *Constitution*.

Then came another blow. In January 1797 the Knoxes' fourteen-year-old daughter, Julia, fell ill from "rapid consumption" and died. Lucy, by then forty-one, was again pregnant but in September delivered a stillborn.

Ten of Lucy's pregnancies and births had come to naught. The here and now—her beloved Henry, her remaining children, young Lucy, Caroline, and Henry Jackson, and her role as gracious hostess—were all that mattered, all that made sense to the devastated matron.

As Lucy attempted to recover from the loss of four children, Peggy Arnold scrambled to secure funds to educate her five. The years following Arnold's return from Guadeloupe had remained economically disastrous. Initially, the Standing Committee of the West India Planters and Merchants had recommended that Arnold receive a military appointment. The "ministry," as Peggy unhappily wrote Jonathan Bliss on December 5, 1795, was "extremely anxious for him to go" but worried about "putting him over the heads of so many old general officers."[28]

In lieu of that appointment the Duke of Portland, Britain's secretary of state, informed the Canadian president that, in recognition of Arnold's "very gallant and meritorious service" at Guadeloupe the Crown had waved a residency requirement and awarded Arnold 13,400 acres of land from the Waste Lands of the Crown in Upper Canada. This included 5,000 acres for Arnold and 1,200 acres for Peggy, their five children, his sons from his first marriage, and sister, Hannah.[29] The land, as its title implied, was remote and undeveloped. Bitterly, Peggy wrote Jonathan Bliss that Arnold's "trip to the West [Indies] gained more credit than money."[30]

Like his former friend and fellow patriot Knox, Arnold continued to live like a wealthy man. Dismissing the steep interest paid on a £10,000 loan to feed the British army in Guadeloupe, which Arnold expected the Treasury Board to reimburse, he moved his family into a splendid townhouse in Gloucester Place. Though surrounded by the trappings of luxury, Peggy worried in silence, suffering from migraines that she described to Judge Shippen as a "violent attack in my head."[31]

Disquieting, too, was the arrival of news in February 1796 that Arnold's eldest son, Benedict, a captain in the British army, had died. For years, relations between father and son had been strained. During a battle in northern Jamaica one of the young officer's legs was shattered. Like his father, young Benedict refused amputation but, less fortunately, had died from gangrene. Guilt, sorrow, and rage flooded over Arnold. "His death is much regretted . . . and a heavy stroke on me," he wrote Jonathan Bliss.[32]

Worries over finances also led Arnold to propose several lucrative schemes to his colleagues. The first, presented to his friend and former military colleague Cornwallis, was Arnold's leadership of five thousand men to liberate the Spanish West Indies. The second, pitched to Lord Spencer, First Lord of the Admiralty, placed Arnold at the head of a five-ship fleet in the English Channel during the Napoleonic War. Ultimately, both proposals were rejected. In despair, Arnold turned to the one area where he previously achieved success: investment in privateers.

Peggy panicked. Aware of Arnold's mounting debts, England's inflationary spiral, and the need for funds to support her children's educations, she wrote Judge Shippen on July 29: "I shall be obliged to you for another remittance, as soon as it is convenient to you, as I assure you that we find it difficult to bring the year about, at the present extravagant rates of every article of life. ... Everything has risen in proportion to bread and meat; all schools have increased their price accordingly, and in short a thousand a year is not equal to six hundred a little time ago."[33]

Having lived luxuriously under the Shippen and Arnold roofs, Peggy suddenly felt financially pinched. "I am almost sick of the struggle to keep up an appearance, which, however is absolutely necessary, in this country, to bring forward a young family," she admitted. With pride she referred to her infant William and older children, George, Sophie, James, and Edward. Hesitant to admit disillusionment with Arnold, Peggy's reaction to news of her younger sister's wedding spoke volumes. "I should be sorry that my dear sister Lea should ever alter her state, as I think her society a great acquisition to you, and matrimony is but a lottery."[34]

Eleven months passed without a word from Judge Shippen. Just why has never been explained, although some historians attributed his silence to disgust with Arnold or perhaps with both him and Peggy. During those months, the Arnolds' frail daughter, Sophia, suffered a nervous disorder that left her legs temporarily paralyzed.

Puzzled by her father's silence, Peggy finally wrote to him the following May, "I cannot believe that I have given you any cause of displeasure, and fear that illness or misfortune have occasioned your silence." Alluding again to Arnold's dire finances, she confessed, "My spirits are much broken and I think I could be contented in a very humble retired situation; but to see my children's rising prospects blasted, would fill me with the keenest anguish."[35] Just before sending that letter, a packet of April 6 arrived with Judge Shippen's bank draft of £140.

Peggy intuitively sensed she would be solely responsible for her children's futures. Her two eldest sons, Edward, eighteen, and James, seventeen, had nearly completed their educations and were slated to join the British army. Sophia, George, and William, however, still had years of schooling ahead. To look to "the General" for financial security was foolhardy, for Arnold had raised Peggy's hopes once too often. The latest disappointment involved the Treasury Board's approval for partial reimbursement for the Guadeloupe loan, which it then retracted. The explanation? The funds were more urgently needed for Britain's anti-Napoleonic pact with Austria.

Nor did Arnold's privateering ventures improve the family's finances. One ship had been captured at sea and another seized by Arnold's creditors. A third, as Peggy had repeatedly warned Arnold, had a captain known for "too free indulgence in his bottle," who lost £2,500 in profits after its capture.[36] On the fourth, a Swedish captain threatened litigation for Arnold's failure to pay for the cargo. Exacerbating those losses was Arnold's purchase of the *Lord Spencer*, whose refitting costs turned out to be exorbitant.

Nevertheless, Peggy continued to sympathize with Arnold's plight. To her eldest, Edward, she confided that his father was in "the most wretched state of mind that I have ever seen him. Disappointed in his highly-raised expectations, harassed by the sailors who are loudly demanding their prize-money . . . without the health or power of acting, he knows not which way to turn himself."[37] Once again Arnold had appealed to William Pitt for a military commission, but somehow, perhaps intentionally, the prime minister lost his papers.

During the last months of 1800 and into the spring of 1801, Arnold's health suddenly flagged. Their father, as Peggy later wrote her stepsons, "never lay two hours of a night in his bed and he had every dreadful nervous symptom, attended with great difficulty of breathing." Still she thought his illness temporary, convinced that "a favorable change in his circumstances . . . would restore peace to his mind . . . [and] reinstate his health."[38] On May 23, she and Arnold consequently rode to Galleywood, near Chelmsford, to stay at the country house of their friends Ann and Sarah Fitch. Eight days later, just as Arnold's health began to improve, an urgent notice arrived about the wayward captain of the *Lord Spencer*. Without further delay Arnold and Peggy returned to London.

Avoiding details, Peggy later wrote her stepsons that her hopes for Arnold's returning health "never took place" because of "heavy demands upon him from different quarters."[39] Once the immediate problems were resolved, Peggy expected she and Arnold would return to the country. But before they left, his throat began to swell. By June 8, Arnold collapsed in bed.

According to the doctor, the former general was suffering from the effects of "repeated gout . . . a general dropsy and a disease in the lungs." Still, he assured the distraught Peggy there was "no cause for apprehension."[40] Arnold's condition deteriorated. Before long he could no longer speak or swallow. On June 10, he slipped into a coma. Only occasionally did Arnold awaken and then only to apologize for his failures. "The distressed situation of his family preyed greatly on his mind and he was imploring blessings upon them," Peggy recalled. At 6:30 a.m. on Sunday, June 14, 1801, as she sat by his bed, Arnold died "without a groan."[41]

"My sister and myself were with Mrs. Arnold when her husband expired,— that we shall not be separated from her for some time," Ann Fitch assured Judge Shippen on June 29. "She evinces, upon this occasion, as you know she had done upon many trying ones, that fortitude and resignation which a superior and well-regulated mind only is capable of exerting."[42]

On June 21, seven mourning coaches and four state carriages rode solemnly through the streets from Gloucester Place across the Battersea Bridge to the ancient brick- and copper-spired church of St. Mary's, a favorite burial place for American Loyalists. There Arnold was laid to rest in a crypt adjacent to his expatriate friends, Samuel Fitch, William Vassal, and Nathaniel Middleton.

The *London Times*, *Gentleman's Magazine*, and *Morning Post* published brief reports of Arnold's death. Subsequently, the *Post* sneered, "Poor General Arnold has departed this world without notice; a sorry reflection this for the Pitts and the Portlands and other turncoats."[43]

As loyal to Arnold in death as she had been in life, Peggy vowed to redeem his reputation as an honorable man.

13

"I Do Not Suffer My Spirits to Overcome Me"

THE TIES OF LOVE and loss bound the Knoxes ever closer during the Montpelier years. Though occasionally separated by Henry's travels or Lucy's visits to Boston, their letters radiated devotion as keenly as when they were newlyweds.

"I long for the moment when I shall be reunited to you, what I hope be before the 10ᵗʰ of next month," Henry penned in August 1797 from Penobscot Bay.[1] Another from 1801 read, "I received, my best beloved, your affectionate cordial of the 16ᵗʰ yesterday. It was indeed a comfort to me."[2] In a third to Lucy in Boston, Knox wrote, "Our affection is the most valued object of my existence."[3]

Lucy's letters from that period reflected concerns about her husband's well-being. One, written in November 1800, refers to Knox's resolve to restrain his temper while he and his difficult son traveled together. "You left us, my dear Harry, so very suddenly on Sunday that one half of your provision remained behind," Lucy observed. "This is an addition to my other anxieties respecting your companion, [young Henry]. I am afraid you will lose sight of the line of conduct you had marked for yourself which . . . even before your departure was a little altered."[4] On another trip during bad weather Lucy wrote, "My dearest friend: Last night received your kind note from Portland—where you had just arrived . . . thank you for this mark of attention. . . . I am led to hope the roads are better than our fears painted them."[5]

Sealing their bond were their lost youngsters. After the death of fourteen-year-old Julia, Knox wrote their Philadelphia friend Clement Biddle, in March 3, 1798, "We have only three children out of 13. . . . My wife's happiness is impaired while she continues on this globe."[6]

Over the years, compassion for Lucy's ten ill-fated births increased Henry's tolerance for his affectionate but prickly wife. One public example occurred as Knox ordered horses prepared for an outing with guests. As they gathered, a groom led Lucy's horse to the door. Enraged that her horse was saddled when she had no intention of riding, Lucy turned to Knox before their guests and demanded an explanation. When he explained that one of their guests was going to borrow her horse, Lucy protested. At that, the red-faced former general turned to the groom and bellowed, "John, put Mrs. Knox's horse in the stable and do not take it out again until God Almighty or Mrs. Knox tells you to!"[7]

Another incident pointed to the couple's religious differences. One Sunday Knox invited the Reverend Thurston Whiting for dinner, but upon his arrival at Montpelier, Lucy rudely forged ahead and seated herself at the dining table. "Rise, my dear, and the parson will ask a blessing," Henry asked. Lucy would not budge. Again, Henry repeated his request, but there a smiling Lucy sat. Finally in his most stentorian tones, Henry insisted, "Rise, my dear, the parson is going to ask the blessing!" A third time Lucy refused. Ultimately, the perplexed minister gave his blessing.[8]

Such scenes, recalled Harrison Gray Otis, who visited Montpelier, rarely fazed him or other guests, for they knew the Knoxes' "mutual attachment never waned. It was . . . well-known that they frequently differed in opinion upon the current trifles of the day," but they always reconciled. In large part that was due to Henry, Otis believed, who "showed his generalship by a skillful retreat."[9]

Another memorable incident occurred after a large dinner. As Montpelier's servants removed the soiled tablecloths, Knox asked them to also take the undercloths that protected the table. Lucy, "in an audible voice," protested. The guests fell silent. Turning to them, Henry drolly announced, "This subject of the undercloth is the only one on which Mrs. Knox and

I have differed since our marriage." What followed was "a general merriment" among the guests.[10]

Henry's debts were not as easily resolved. By 1799, his interest payments on loans were so steep that he declared the family could no longer afford to spend winters in Boston. Even so, Montpelier's hearty patriarch refused to dwell on unhappiness. Even in March 1800, while mourning the December 14 death of his beloved commander, George Washington, he scolded his friend General David Cobb for moroseness. "You mention that your spirits are not good. For God's sake, bear up against the devil of gloom. Put yourself in motion. Visit even me if you can find nothing better," Knox urged. "Get Willich, a new author on diet and regimen, but above all, get— on horseback." Dismissing his own troubles, Knox insisted, "I shall have bright days yet."[11]

Being convinced that his life would improve meant that Knox saw no need to limit his hospitality. Even in late autumn, Montpelier hosted guests, "generally . . . eight or ten per day and commonly from five to ten at night," as Henry noted in November 1801.[12] Indeed by then, he had new reasons for optimism. By the 13th of that month, he had reached agreements with those settled on the Waldo Patent's coastal lands who had either paid mortgages or provided collateral in lieu of cash. "It confirms my judgment of the measures I have pursued," Knox crowed to his wife. "This you will call vanity. I own it and rejoice therein. . . . The heart . . . has a well founded claim to dance a little. But this [is] between ourselves."[13]

Another psychological boost was Knox's election that fall to the Massachusetts General Court. The only disadvantage of the election was the cost of supporting a temporary residence in Boston. A townhouse rental, he warned Lucy, who was again visiting friends in the city, was too expensive. "A lodging [boarding] house will be execrable, and yet feelings must give way to judgment. In either case, we must be economists."[14]

Simultaneously the U.S. Navy had rendered a negative judgment on the Knoxes' son, whose dissipated behavior ruined his chances for a commission as a lieutenant. At twenty-one, young Henry Jackson Knox continued to behave as wildly as when in his teens—squandering money, drinking excessively, and evading responsibilities. The young man was an embarrassment, a scar upon Knox's impeccable public image. Denied promotion in the military and ill-suited for business, young Henry would have to depend upon his parents for support. "My mind can find no other employment for him than to make him our companion," Knox confided to Lucy. "If he gets a wife . . . let him manage a farm . . . with such assistance as his affairs or necessity may require and we can afford."[15]

Eighteen months later, on May 17, 1803, young Henry married Eliza Taylor Reed, the eldest daughter of Josiah Reed, Thomaston's town clerk. Personable and intelligent, Eliza was later described as "faithful in the discharge of her domestic duties and a constant attachment to the moral virtues."[16] Those characteristics may not have been so during the first years of her marriage, though. An innkeeper's bill of March 1805, from the young couple's three-week trip to Boston, revealed days of heavy drinking. Upon their return to Maine, the Knox's son announced that life at Montpelier was too quiet for the young couple. "The sudden change from a retired life to one continual round of dissipation affected our nerves . . . we are both surprised that you bear it so well thro' the whole winter." Disdaining the fact that his parents still paid his bills, Lucy's son sneered, "What completely unfits us, you thrive upon."[17] Within a few years Henry Jackson's marriage would dissolve.

In contrast to their disappointments over their son was the Knoxes' pride in the engagement of their eldest daughter, Lucy. On January 6, 1804, banns were posted for the pretty twenty-three year old's wedding to Ebenezer Thatcher, a Harvard graduate and attorney. Adding to their joy was the establishment of the newlyweds' home in nearby Warren, Maine—and soon afterwards, a granddaughter, Julia, named after the Knoxes' lost daughters. By late 1805 the couple had had a second child, Henry Knox Thatcher.

During those same years, Knox's fortunes also improved. On June 2, 1804, he was appointed to Governor Caleb Strong's council. A month later, Knox's sale of land in Hancock and Lincoln counties for over $200,000 enabled him to pay off one of his mortgages. By 1806 Knox had also paid his debts to friends William Bingham and Francis Baring. His earlier prediction to General Cobb, "I shall yet have bright days," was beginning to come true.

Even so, at fifty-five years of age, Knox contemplated his mortality. To wealthy Boston merchant Samuel Breck he wrote, in January 1806, "Years roll away, and soon we shall be numbered among those who have been atoms upon this atom of a globe, and very soon after, it will be forgotten that we had here any existences." Still, the relentlessly upbeat Knox insisted, "But this ought not in the least degree to cloud any of our present enjoyments."[18]

One of those "enjoyments" was his grandchildren. During a dinner in October, his eldest daughter watched Knox "amusing himself with the playful little Julia—who had entwined herself about his heart." Watching him tease the baby, young Lucy exclaimed, "Oh Father I believe you never will be *old*."[19]

Nor would he be. Several days earlier, Henry had swallowed a chicken bone. At that time he immediately left the table and sequestered himself in a nearby china pantry to clear his throat. When he returned, he assured his worried wife and daughters that he was fine. But by October 20 Henry felt so ill that he wrote merchant Walter Beale in an uncharacteristically weak hand that he had to postpone their appointment because of "a disposition which will probably prevent my setting out this week."[20] On October 23 Henry was complaining of intense pain—the first time, his eldest daughter recalled, that he had mentioned any discomfort. Alarmed, his wife Lucy summoned a doctor who vainly tended him for two days. On Thursday, October 25, at 8 a.m., in agony and "in full possession of his mind," Henry died.[21]

A subsequent medical report revealed that the swallowed chicken bone had traveled through Knox's intestines and created internal wounds that had become infected.

Lucy and her children were stunned. "My best of fathers is no more," mourned his son. "Everything that could be was tried, but all in vain. He is gone, I trust, to a happier and better place."[22]

Knox's flabbergasted widow could not be consoled. The loss of "her Harry," the beloved anchor of her life, set Lucy adrift.

← →

The following Tuesday, October 28, 1806, on a day as sunny as Knox's disposition had been, crowds gathered at Montpelier for his military funeral. Following a service in the mansion, the local militia, an artillery company, cavalry, and infantry marched to a beating drum across the front lawn to Knox's favorite oak tree. Nearby, on the St. George River, ship flags flew at half-mast. In Thomaston, Paul Revere's bell tolled from the church Knox had founded. After a military salute from a minute gun, the Revolutionary War general's coffin was lowered into the ground, followed by a dramatic blaze of musketry.

"The great and good General Knox departed this life yesterday," reported the *Columbian Centinel*. Added to "his merits as a military chief and public man were joined those qualities which conciliate affection and engage esteem . . . which made him the delight of his family and the promoter of social happiness." The *Centinel* added ironically, "The affairs of his fortune which for some years had been perplexed and difficult, had taken a course offering him pleasant anticipations."[23]

Similar expressions of praise resounded through newspapers, letters, and the memories of those who fought alongside him in the Revolution. Among the most famous was Dr. James Thacher's tribute in his diary, later published as *Military Journal of the American Revolution*: "Long will he be remembered as the ornament of every circle in which he moved, as the amiable and enlightened companion, the generous friend, the man of feeling and benevolence."[24]

Knox's will had bequeathed half of his estate to Lucy, its value, exclusive of his lands, worth $100,000. But without Henry, Lucy was lost. One reflection of her profound grief appears in a poem she penciled into the flyleaf of an account book, "'Tis hard to think you cannot come / Your presence like the fading of a flower / Now lingers upon me, and I listen for your step." The poem continue, "I miss my husband, when morning breaks forth / and the birds carol in the trees." Other stanzas referred to those times "her Harry" had comforted her: "Where, where was the arm that could pillow my head," while "other hands did caress me ... no [care] . . . like thine."[25]

After Knox's death, Montpelier's legendary entertainments ceased. Some evenings Lucy invited guests to Montpelier to play cards or chess. One letter from her married daughter suggests that Lucy enjoyed her grand-children; others, that she turned her attention to insuring that her younger daughter Caroline, fifteen at the time of Knox's death, would eventually marry well. The girl, though less handsome than her older sister, was also gregarious and popular. A clergyman visiting Thomaston some years later described her as "the lovely Caroline." When Nathaniel Hawthorne visited Montpelier in 1837, he recalled Caroline, by then fifty-six, as a "mild and amiable woman."[26]

To find the young Caroline a suitable husband, Lucy escorted her to Boston in the winter months and sometimes left her there with affluent friends. Then, on May 21, 1808, after staying with Caroline in Boston, Lucy proposed that they and a friend take a "little excursion into the country for a week for the benefit of my [Caroline's] health."[27] During the trip they met one of Caroline's male acquaintances and his friend, James Swan, the curly-haired son of a wealthy Boston family whom Lucy knew. The attrac-tion was immediate.

For five days, Lucy, her daughter, and her friend traveled along the Con-necticut River Valley with the young men. "Surely never were people more supremely happy, than two [in] the party were." Caroline, nearly eighteen, wrote her older sister on June 17. With Lucy's blessings, she, Swan, and their friends took a ferry across the Hudson one day and were married by a Belleville, New Jersey, minister. "Tell me, my sister, can you conceive of more perfect happiness than that I now enjoyed married to the man of my heart loving and beloved," the bride coyly wrote.[28]

Lucy's triumph was redoubled when the newlyweds, probably at Caro-line's urging, decided to reside with her at Montpelier. "I always lived with my mother until her death and I never have known the same delightful home feeling since this place has been my own as when she was here to meet me with a welcome and caress," Caroline reminisced years later.[29]

Yet the joy that Caroline's marriage evoked was soon shattered by news that the Knox's spendthrift son had been placed in a Boston debtor's prison. After his release, young Henry enrolled in the Medical School of

Dartmouth College, graduated in 1811, and served as a surgeon's mate on the privateer *America*. Soon though—and here, again, the details are hazy—his earnings were seized by creditors. By 1818 he had returned to Montpelier and served as his mother's clerk.

Records about the widowed Lucy's life became increasingly vague. Determined to maintain her residence at Montpelier but plagued by debts, Lucy subsisted by selling off parcels of Montpelier's acreage. In September 1817, Lucy, invited the Massachusetts governor, John Brooks, to stay at Montpelier during his visit to Thomaston. Brooks accepted at the last minute, creating a flurry of activity among the servants at the deteriorating estate. By 1822 as Caroline warned a friend who planned to visit, "The days of show and profusion are all gone and we are a plain, retired country family."[30]

In late May 1824, Lucy fell ill with an infection that intensified with each passing week. At 3 a.m. on June 20, 1824, she died. Lucy was sixty-eight years of age. During her last moments, Lucy imagined she was again young and attending a ball with "her Harry"—the greatest joy she had ever known.

Six months before his own passing, Henry had written Lucy from Boston, "It would have afforded me great and sincere satisfaction, were we together."[31]

Perhaps, at last, they were.

Although Knox's death shattered Lucy's zest for life, widowhood had prompted Peggy Arnold to rally. The former Philadelphia belle's evolution from the fragile, compliant bride of the American traitor to a restrained wife was remarkable enough, but what followed was even more surprising: a revelation of strengths Peggy long held in reserve.

Her transition was born of necessity. Less than two weeks after Arnold's death, Peggy's friend Ann Fitch wrote Judge Shippen about her courage, praising the new widow for her "fortitude and resignation."[32] Peggy, nevertheless, resented that her late husband had left his financial affairs entirely in her hands. She wished, as she wrote her stepsons Richard and Henry, that "your dear Father did not join some male friend of respectability in the executorship."[33] With help and advice from family friend Daniel Coxe, Peggy soon learned the truth: Arnold's debts outweighed his assets. Horrified, Peggy immediately reduced her expensive lifestyle.

Essentially, she had been dealt a double blow. In addition to the "loss of a husband whose affection for me was unbounded," as she wrote her brother-in-law, Edward Burd, she was "left in very embarrassed circumstances with a little dependent family." The creditors could readily seize her annual pension of £500 and the £110 awarded each of her five children. Reminding Burd that her own brother, Neddy, had lost part of her investment years earlier, she hoped to draw on whatever remained. "I cannot suppose but that my present unhappy situation will be taken into consideration upon this occasion," Peggy observed. "Have the goodness, my dear Mr. Burd, to tell me candidly what dependence I may reasonably place upon this resource." Never, she admitted, had she "felt myself so helpless."[34]

Left unsaid was a provision in Arnold's will that also rocked Peggy to the core—the request for a certain John Sage of New Brunswick, to receive land, an income, and education. The fourteen year old was subsequently assumed to be Arnold's illegitimate son, sired during his first trip to Saint John with an unnamed Native American of that community. Recently, historian Barry Wilson observed that the date of Sage's birth mitigates against that since Arnold's arrival in Saint John in December 1785 was only four months before Sage's birth on April 14, 1786. Other theories abound. Among them that Sage was the product of Arnold's liaison with a mistress carried aboard his ship from Great Britain, or that he was Arnold's grandson and had been sired by seventeen-year-old Benedict Jr., who brought the child to Connecticut.[35]

Whether true or not, Peggy was shocked by the discovery of his existence and by Arnold's remembrance of Sage in his will. "My sufferings are not of the present only," was Peggy's one oblique comment about it to her brother-in-law Burd. "Years of unhappiness have passed, I had cast my lot, complaints were unavailing and you and my other friends are ignorant of the many causes of uneasiness I have had."[36]

Nor would she specify the nature of those sorrows with Judge Shippen, who, through deft political maneuvering, had risen in 1799 to become

Pennsylvania's chief Supreme Court justice. Instead Peggy's letter focused upon her ongoing symptoms of ill health: a certain "confusion in my head resembling what I can suppose would be the sensations of anybody extremely drunk." Some physicians attributed her indisposition to earlier illnesses, she explained, others to nerves, frayed by a "long loss of rest, anxiety of mind, the irreparable loss of a most tender and affectionate husband, and the total change of my circumstances and mode of living."[37]

Even so, Peggy vowed to fulfill two goals. "I am making every exertion to keep up as much as possible the respectability of the family," she explained to her son Edward, "determined . . . that the fortunes of my children shall not be marred by the change in our situation."[38]

On June 2, 1802, Peggy thanked Judge Shippen for his financial assistance and his invitation for her to return to Philadelphia, but she had decided to postpone any decision "till I see how this business will terminate." In any case, she wrote, she would "take no measures that are not directed by prudence."[39]

By autumn 1802, Peggy had reduced expenses by auctioning off her furniture, silver, and other valuable possessions and by renting the townhouse at Gloucester Place. "I am now living in a very small house in Bryanston Street, using furniture purchased from Carolow; who is now a more independent woman than her mistress," she informed her stepsons.[40] Her two eldest sons, Edward and James, she added, had donated their pensions to help finance their younger brothers' educations.

The following October, after spending the summer in the country with friends, Peggy wrote her father that she had decided against living in rural England. Without the financial means to socialize with the local gentry, life would be "too lonely for either my dear girl [her daughter Sophia] or myself." Nor would life in a country town suit her, for its residents were "chiefly composed of card playing, tattling old maids and people wholly unaccustomed to genteel life." Instead, Peggy would remain in London near friends and those "who know how to manage." There she could "live as cheap, as in almost any other part of England." Admittedly that would mean certain sacrifices, the most painful of which was "the want of a carriage."[41]

In a justified—if uncharacteristically self-congratulatory—letter of November 1802 Peggy wrote her stepsons that she had accomplished "the settlement of the most troublesome business that had ever devolved upon a female." She had paid all of Arnold's "*ascertained* debts within a few hundred pounds" (italics in original) and would soon eliminate the rest.[42] That letter probably surprised Arnold's sons. Having remained ignorant of their father's financial struggles, Peggy continued, they knew "so little his heart, his motives, and his embarrassed circumstances, as to be induced to write him in a style to wound, and distress him."[43]

The "boy who is with you," as she referred to John Sage, "ought to be taught, by his own labor, to procure his own livelihood. He ought never to have been brought up with any other ideas." Nevertheless she would arrange for his receipt of the promised Canadian lands.[44] Chagrined that no one in the family—Arnold's stepsons, his children with Peggy, or herself—"will ever have the value of a guinea from their dear father's property," she still believed that repayment of Arnold's debts would restore his honor.[45] Moreover, she also intended to help support her sister-in-law, Hannah. "I will never suffer the sister of my husband to want," she added, vowing to "supply her from my own little income."[46]

This was a newly empowered Peggy. Nor, she explained, did she have plans to return to Philadelphia. "My anxiety to get your little brothers on in life, will deprive me on this gratification," she explained.[47] Her eldest son, Edward, would serve in the British army in Bengal; her second son, James, an army officer was then stationed in Tinmouth; seventeen-year-old George studied at London's New Royal Military College; eight-year-old William attended a boarding school; and her frail daughter, Sophia, still lived with her at home.

And, indeed, within another year Peggy had paid off the rest of Arnold's debts "and not reserved even a towel or a tea spoon" she wrote Edward. The one remaining problem was her "indifferent"—but actually frightening—state of health.[48] Six months earlier, on July 3, 1803, Peggy confided to Betsy that she had consulted two doctors "in the female line." Their diagnosis was "a complaint of the womb" that obliged her to "keep almost constantly in a recumbent posture.[49] Soon afterwards the physicians refined their diagnosis to "the dreaded evil, a cancer." Lately, she added, "I have . . . been much worse, in consequence of a very large tumor."[50]

That same July day Peggy explained to her father, Judge Shippen, "To prevent another [tumor] is now the great object, but I am not much encouraged to hope for success."[51] Alarmed, her friends brought her to the countryside as she reclined on a seat in the carriage.

By May, Peggy's letter to her sister Betsy was even more piteous: "I have been indeed very near death, my dear sister, and my complaints are such, as to give me but little hope of long continuing an inhabitant of this world." Opium had become her painkiller. "Nevertheless, I do not suffer my spirits to overcome me," Peggy insisted. "I have much to be thankful for—most particularly for the very uncommon attention and kindness that I hourly experience from my numerous friends. . . . I have the best advice that London can afford, and am constantly attended by two of the most eminent physicians."[52]

On July 5, 1804, Daniel Coxe, the friend who advised Peggy on finances after Arnold's death and often visited her at Bryanston Street, wrote Judge Shippen that his once-lovely daughter "now lies on a sick bed, very painful and alarming . . . looking so ill as to shock me. She was not able to write to you or would have [done] it— She begged me to say for her all duty & affection to you and her sisters."[53]

Six weeks later, on August 24, Peggy, forty-four, died.

So it was that two defiant brides of the Revolution met death much as they had lived their lives—one clinging to youthful memories of love, the other with the resignation and steely will of a seasoned martyr.

14

The Brides' Legacies

AFTER LUCY'S DEATH, HER daughters hoped to memorialize her as one of the legendary patriot wives of the American Revolution.

The name of General Henry Knox was already honored. In 1791, citizens in Eastern Tennessee's Great Valley had renamed their largest town Knoxville. The 1802 establishment of the U.S. Military Academy at West Point, modeled at least in part upon the Pluckemin Artillery Cantonment, also fulfilled one of their father's earliest dreams. Written accounts of the Revolution had praised Knox for his character as well as for his contributions to the American cause. "To praise him for his military talents alone would be to deprive him of the eulogium he merits; a man of understanding, gay, sincere, and honest—it is impossible to know without esteeming him, or to see without loving him," wrote the Marquis of Chastellux.[1]

Chief Justice John Marshall's five-volume *Life of George Washington* praised Knox for his "past services and an unquestioned integrity . . . sound understanding."[2] By 1834, William Sullivan's *Familiar Letters on Public Characters and Public Events* recalled that Knox's "face had a noble expression, and was capable of displaying the most benignant feeling. . . . This was the true character of his heart. . . . The mind of Knox was powerful, rapid and decisive. . . . He had a brilliant imagination, and no less brilliant modes of expression."[3]

Yet, it would not be until 1848 that a remembrance of Lucy Flucker Knox finally appeared as a chapter in Elizabeth Ellett's *Women of the American Revolution*. The author, unable to locate the Knox children, had based her portrait upon information from Maine congressman Lorenzo Sabine, editor of the *Eastport Sentinel* and author of the 1847 book *The American Loyalists*. Ellett's chapter on Lucy Knox was a "brief & somewhat inaccurate account" of their mother, complained daughter Lucy to her sister Caroline in February 1849.[4] Although Ellett had extolled their mother's intellect for its "high order," she also wrote that Mrs. Knox had said that if she had to live her life over, she would have been "more of a wife, more of a mother, more of a woman."[5] That admission infuriated the Knoxes' eldest daughter. "Now whatever may have been her fondness in former days for the world & its attractions—I am well assured that they never led her to neglect her own family," she wrote to Caroline.[6]

Immediately after the publication of *Women of the American Revolution*, Lucy wrote to Ellett, who immediately "begged" for more information.[7] By then, Lucy's comments had been incorporated into Ellett's *Godey's Lady's Book* article, "Sketch of Mrs. Henry Knox." But once again, Lucy thought that her mother had been unjustly represented. Although Ellett described Mrs. Knox as a "remarkable woman,"[8] Lucy wrote her sister, she "said some things which I never thought of saying, such as the influence of my mother . . . over the minds of General & Mrs. Washington, which I certainly never asserted."[9]

Privately, Lucy Knox Thatcher blamed herself for not knowing more about her mother's life. "When our dear mother was yet with us, I did not take the pains, I . . . ought to have done to inform myself of a thousand particulars of her eventual life," she admitted to her sister. "Anecdotes I have none. Do you recall any?"[10]

Apparently Caroline had none or, if she did, they never appeared in print. By then, she had been twice widowed. Ultimately Caroline's marriage to James Swan had been unhappy, terminating with his 1834 death. Two years later, she married Senator John Holmes, with whom she lived happily, if all too briefly, until he died, in 1843.

In contrast to his sisters, the Knoxes' son, Henry Jackson, had led a checkered life. After squandering his small inheritance, he appealed to his father's old friends, who, taking pity upon him, appointed him a justice of the peace and notary public. By the 1820s he had turned to religion. "You will be much surprised to hear that your Uncle Knox has lately become a pious man—his conversion is one of the most wonderful [surprising] things I have ever met with," Lucy wrote one of her children.[11] In repentance for years of rebellion, Henry Jackson Knox joined the local First Congregational Church and became a proud citizen of Thomaston. He died on October 9, 1832, at fifty-two years of age.

Following her second widowhood, Caroline lived alone at Montpelier, where she struggled to maintain the mansion. After Nathaniel Hawthorne visited Thomaston on Saturday, August 12, 1837, he described Montpelier as "a large, rusty-looking edifice of wood." The mansion and its environs, he wrote in *American Notebooks*, "may be taken as an illustration of what must be the result of American schemes of aristocracy. It is not forty years, since this house was built, and Knox was in his glory but now the house is all in decay, while, within a stone's throw of it, is a street of neat, smart white edifices . . . occupied chiefly by thriving mechanics." The general's descendants, Hawthorne noted, "are all poor" and their inheritance "merely sufficient to make a dissipated and drunken fellow of the one of the old General's sons."[12]

Subsequent historical scholarship linked Hawthorne's portrayal of the grasping Judge Pyncheon in his 1851 *House of the Seven Gables* to Knox. Both figures, Hawthorne observed, owned vast tracts of Maine lands through an earlier Indian contract with the Massachusetts General Court, an arrangement, coincidentally, that also applied to the mortified author's own ancestors.

On at least one count Hawthorne was right: the expense of maintaining Montpelier was more than Knox's children could afford. By 1849, Lucy had confided that to one of her own daughters. The family homestead was "ever lovely and ever must be to me a sacred spot. . . . [But] I sincerely wish my sister could dispose of it. . . . It is wholly unprofitable ... a great care and bill of expense." By June 29, 1851, she had written to Caroline, urging her to sell it, "however painful the sacrifice."[13]

Four months later, on October 17, Caroline died. Rather than allowing the house to be abandoned, Lucy moved in. There, she too, was confounded by similar "ten thousand associations and reminiscences."[14] Rather than sell Montpelier, she auctioned off some of the surrounding acreage into street lots that she named after family members. Three years almost to the day of Caroline's death, on October 12, 1753, Lucy Knox Thatcher passed away. Montpelier and the remaining property were then divided among her descendants.

By 1855 Lucy's son, Admiral Henry Knox Thatcher, had sold the estate for $4,500. Subsequently, Montpelier fell into disrepair. In 1868 the old mansion was demolished to make room for the Knox and Lincoln Railroad. The tombs of Henry and Lucy Knox and several of their children were consequently removed and re-buried in Thomaston's cemetery.

The residents of Thomaston, nevertheless, continued to honor their famous town father. Each July 25, the Henry Knox Chapter of the Daughters of the American Revolution celebrated the general's birthday. By the 1920s, an offshoot of that chapter, the Knox Memorial Association, began a national fund-raising campaign in cooperation with the Knoxes' great-great grandson, Henry Thatcher Fowler. On July 26, 1929, the Knox Memorial Association broke ground for construction of a replica of the original Montpelier.

Today, a copy of Henry and Lucy Knox's home stands near the original site in Thomaston as a popular Maine museum and a monument to their colorful lives.

No such memorials exist for Benedict and Peggy Arnold. As the former Philadelphia belle's letters to her family of 1801–1804 showed, the children were the sole survivors of her union with Arnold. Through Peggy's sale of her home, furnishings, and valuable possessions, her youngsters completed their educations, mixed in England's highest circles, and led lives of character and accomplishment. In various ways, the Arnolds' four sons and daughter each sought to countermand their father's notoriety.

Their eldest son, Edward, served in the 6th Bengal Cavalry, rising to the position of its paymaster in 1806. Horrified by the devastation of a famine in Northern India, Edward anonymously donated warehouses of food to the starving residents of Muttra.

At eighteen, the second son, James, joined the Corps of Royal Engineers to participate in British campaigns in Malta and the West Indies. Among his heroic deeds was an offer to lead a risky attack in Surinam. "No braver man than my father ever lived, but you know how bitterly he has been condemned for his conduct at West Point," James reminded his commanding officer. "Permit me, I beg you, to do what I can to redeem the same."[15] Appointed a lieutenant-general, James was later knighted by King William IV.

The Arnold's third son, George, joined the 2nd Bengal Cavalry and held the rank of lieutenant-colonel at the time of his early death in November 1818.

Their fourth son, William Fitch, became a captain in the 19th Royal Lancers and later retired as a justice of the peace to a country seat in Buckinghamshire. He left six children.

During the last years of Peggy's life, her sons Edward and James had volunteered their royal pensions (as well as allowances from Judge Shippen) to help their younger siblings complete their educations. So apparently had the Arnold's fifteen-year-old daughter, Sophia. After Judge Shippen's death, Edward wrote the family asking that Sophia be recompensed. "What must now devolve to her . . . should . . . not only compensate for the loss of her allowance from my grand-father, but add also so considerably to her income."[16] By 1813, the pretty, cultured, and religious eighteen-year-old Sophia had married Captain Pownall Phipps of the aristocratic Mulgrave family at Muttra. Frail from childhood, Sophia died fifteen years later.

After Peggy's death, her children informed their Canadian stepbrothers about family events. Among those letters was one of October 25, 1813, announcing Sophia's marriage; another, sent a year later, reported Edward's death and explained that his will left Richard and Henry £1,500 in "affectionate recollection of you both."[17] On July 30, 1823, during the last years of her life, Sophia wrote to her Uncle Burd that her brother William had just purchased an estate in Buckinghamshire, adding, "We are to pay them a visit, when we leave Bath."[18]

Another link between the two sets of children were the Canadian lands awarded by the Crown for Arnold's service to Guadeloupe. Frustrations over their remoteness later led the fifty-six-year-old James Arnold to write his sixty-eight-year-old stepbrother Richard in 1837 that he wished they could "dispose of it to tolerable advantage." Though land prices might rise in the future, he said, "we may not be here to enjoy the benefit of it."[19]

Equally frustrating to the heirs were their efforts to salvage Arnold's reputation. To this day, his name is essentially synonymous with "traitor." Nor is the former Revolutionary War general's name connected with any of the battlefields preserved by America's National Park Service.

Only one oblique reference to Arnold's courage at the Battle of Saratoga exists: the Boot Monument, placed at Saratoga National Historic Park in 1887 by a major general of the New York militia. Behind the statue of a left boot of a Revolutionary War officer an inscription reads, "In memory of the 'most brilliant soldier' of the Continental army who was desperately wounded on this spot the sally port of Borgoynes [sic] Great Western Redoubt, 7th October, 1777 winning for his countrymen the decisive battle of the American Revolution and for himself the rank of Major General."

By the end of nineteenth century, Arnold's descendants could not find the tombs of Peggy and Benedict. An 1828 letter from Colonel Pownall Phipps indicated that his wife, Sophia Arnold Phipps, and her parents had been "deposited in a vault" within St. Mary's Church at Battersea, but by 1875, the crypt contained 424 coffins.[20] As they decayed, some of the coffins burst open, impelling the church to bury them beneath a foot of concrete.

St. Mary's had retained a plan of the coffin rows, but many of their identification plates, or plaques, had faded over time. After 1920, church officials presented some of them to the Battersea Central Public Library. Others were placed upon the church crypt's walls and columns. Yet those of Peggy Arnold, Benedict Arnold, and Sophia Arnold Phipps were missing.

Coffin records at the Battersea Central Public Library under the names "Arnold" and "Phipps" revealed an astonishing lapse. The coffins of Peggy and Sophia had been listed but not the one of Benedict Arnold. Instead, a "Frederick Arnold" had been listed with the death date of June 14, 1801, a mistake or misreading of the former general's name on his coffin plate, or, perhaps, a deliberate omission.

In 1976, St. Mary's added four new stained-glass windows to the ground floor of the church. One, donated by Arnold admirer and apologist Vincent Lindner of New Jersey in honor of Benedict and Peggy Arnold and their daughter, Sophia, hangs in the nave's westernmost south window At its center stands a portrait of Arnold, beneath which are a display of the arms of General Washington. Four flags flank the portrait. On the left are two, the first representing the Union flag of 1777, replaced with thirteen stars, and the second, a contemporary American flag. To the right is the Union flag of 1776 with the British emblem and modern Union Jack. An inscription reconciles Arnold's former political loyalties with the contemporary British-American friendship.

It reads: "Beneath this church lie buried the bodies of Benedict Arnold, sometimes general in the army of George Washington And of his faithful and beloved wife Margaret Arnold of Pennsylvania And of their Beloved daughter Sophia Matilda Phipps. The two nations whom he served / In turn in the years of their enmity / Have united in enduring Friendship."

In 2004 another Arnold admirer, William Stanley of Connecticut, donated a memorial plaque of Peggy and Benedict Arnold to St. Mary's to replace an earlier one. Upon it their names, as well as their birth and death dates, are listed. Placed in the church basement, the plaque remains visible to anyone entering the door of the church's day-care center.

To most Americans, Peggy remains an enigmatic and nearly forgotten figure. Early historians depicted the former Philadelphia belle as a Loyalist whose fondness for British officer John André led her to corrupt Arnold's political views. By the early twentieth century, members of her family attempted to correct that view. Between 1900 and 1902 Shippen descendant Lewis Burd Walker published a series of articles in the influential *Pennsylvania Magazine of Biography and History*, citing family letters and Peggy's postwar correspondence to defend her innocence.

Several writers portrayed Peggy as either an innocent victimized by Arnold's duplicity or as a wily conniver. In 1941, subsequent to collector William L. Clement's gift of General Henry Clinton's wartime papers to the

University of Michigan, Mark Van Doren published *The Secret History of the American Revolution*, which exposed Peggy's royal pension of £500 a year "for her services, which were very meritorious." Thereafter historians widely agreed that Peggy had been an accomplice in Arnold's treason.[21] Later novels and films depicted Peggy as a sexual siren, Arnold's coconspirator, and even as the prime instigator of his treason. Among the most recent such portraits was the 2003 A&E drama *Benedict Arnold: A Man of Honor*, starring Aidan Quinn as Arnold and Flora Montgomery as a seditious Peggy.

As described in the pages above, Arnold had repeatedly voiced his discontent with the leaders of the American Revolution well before his marriage to Peggy Shippen. That the eighteen-year old bride would naturally sympathize with her husband's complaints is obvious to anyone who has been in love.

Less predictable was the fascination with which we still regard the former Philadelphia belle today.

ACKNOWLEDGMENTS

THE CHALLENGE OF TRACING the elusive lives of Peggy Shippen Arnold and Lucy Flucker Knox could never have been achieved without help and interest from historical experts, scholars, librarians, editors, and colleagues. To all of them I express my deepest appreciation. Peter Drummey, the Massachusetts Historical Society's Stephen T. Riley Librarian, suggested several little-known resources at that institution one wintery Saturday morning, including a silhouette of Lucy Flucker Knox, the only known representation of her, as well as the ring Benedict Arnold presented to his Boston sweetheart, Betsy DeBlois. As I continued my research, he provided other suggestions, including information about a Massachusetts militia. Numerous other staff members at the society became indispensable to my research, from head of research services Elaine Grublin to reference librarian Tracy Potter and Anna Cook, who gave permission to reprint Catherine Knox Snow's August 16, 1822, letter to her friend.

The daunting task of reading through over eight thousand letters in the Henry Knox collections was ameliorated by the discovery that the Gilder Lehrman Institute of American History had digitized nearly all of General and Mrs. Knox's correspondence. Special thanks are due to Sandra Trenholm, director of that institute, who tracked down some of the collection's more obscure letters, suggested other sources, and expressed interest in the evolution of this work. With my appreciation also to Alyson Barrett-Ryan, former reference librarian at the Gilder Lehrman Institute, for help accessing the Henry Knox Papers on that site.

In Thomaston, Maine, Ellen S. Dyer, director of the Montpelier Museum, and archivist Sophia Mendoza spent several days helping me identify historical sources, local papers, and books that provided insights and critiques of the Knoxes and their impact upon that region. Following that visit, Ms. Dyer suggested additional sources, background information, and local legends about the Knoxes. Thanks are also due to Norma Jane Langford, communications professor at Northeastern University, who shared her knowledge about the American Loyalists who emigrated to the North American British colonial provinces during the Revolutionary era. An invaluable historical expert on Benedict Arnold was author James Kirby Martin, Distinguished University Professor of History at the University of Houston, who not only provided suggestions for sources and sites in the United States and England but also generously read portions of the manuscript, sent comments, and enthusiastically supported the scope of this project.

Phillip Seitz, Curator of History and Fermentation at Cliveden, a historic mansion in Philadelphia owned by the National Trust for Historic Preservation, graciously cleared his calendar to talk with me and suggested key background materials on eighteenth-century Philadelphia and its residents. Thanks are also due to the staff at the Historical Society of Pennsylvania, especially Cary Majewicz and Dana Dorman, for help with the Shippen Family Papers and online access to early editions of the *Pennsylvania Magazine of History and Biography*. Amanda Fulcher, archivist at the National Society of Daughters of the American Revolution, provided invaluable information about the Henry Knox Papers and the reminiscences of his daughter Lucy Knox Thatcher.

Several Canadian researchers enhanced research on Benedict Arnold's years in Saint John, New Brunswick, among them Amber McAlpine of the New Brunswick Museum Archives and Research Library for her guidance on the Arnold collections in Canada, and her colleague Jennifer Longon for permission to reprint letters from the Benedict Arnold Fonds. My thanks also to Francesca Holyoke, head of the Archives and Special Collections at the University of New Brunswick Archives Library for her conscientious efforts to send me to the Benedict Arnold-Munson Hayt Fonds. Margaret Conrad, professor emerita of history at the University of New Brunswick, graciously read a draft of the manuscript, made several important suggestions, and alerted me to the historical distortions often associated with Arnold's life in Saint John.

Marla Miller, director of the Public History Program at the University of Massachusetts, took time from her busy schedule to read a draft of the manuscript and provided a thoughtful comment. In London's St. Mary's Church in Battersea, the burial place of Benedict and Peggy Shippen Arnold, Sunny Walker-Kier gave me a tour of the parish church, followed by a discussion with the reverends Peter Wintgren and Adam Boulter about the Arnolds and other prominent individuals buried there. I am especially grateful to the Battersea Parish Church's archivist, Sven Tester, for help with the history of the Arnold tomb, the Benedict Arnold stained-glass window, his comments on a draft of the manuscript, and his outreach to a historical scholar on behalf of this book.

For public opinions on Arnold in England, the British Library's Newspaper Archive at Colindale, North London, provided a wealth of historical articles. With my appreciation also to Dr. Tony Trowles, head of the Abbey Collections and librarian at Westminster Abbey, for access to a photograph of the John André tomb. While researching Peggy Shippen Arnold in England, I also found information at the Bath and North East Somerset Record Office on the lifestyles of affluent eighteenth-century visitors.

Research librarians Lauren Robinson and Colleen Hayes of the Sandwich, Massachusetts, Public Library, cheerfully and tirelessly accessed two centuries of books, articles, and monographs on the Knoxes, the Arnolds, and the American Revolution that were indispensable to this work. Often, Ms. Robinson and Ms. Hayes ensured extensions for those books beyond their renewal dates so that I could complete the research.

With my appreciation to Jude Pfister, chief of cultural resources at the Morristown National Historical Park for information about their archives, and to Moor Park ranger and historian Eric Olsen for references to the "hard winter" of 1779–80. Robin Ray, recreation director of the Township of Bedminster, New Jersey, and Marie Crenshaw at the Clarence Dillon Library provided little-known important information on the Pluckemin Artillery Cantonment. I also thank Dr. Herbert Bischoff, director of historical studies at the Hermitage Museum in Ho-Ho-Kus, New Jersey, for his insightful comments on Theodosia Prevost and Peggy Shippen Arnold.

Author Clare S. Brandt also offered information on her earlier research efforts on Benedict Arnold in England.

Susan Lintelmann, manuscript coordinator at the library of the West Point Military Academy, answered questions and provided suggestions for original Arnold materials. Elaine McConnell, rare books coordinator of that library, provided for references to the West Point birthday celebration for the French dauphin. Thanks also to Richard Hoch of the White Plains Historical Society for background materials on the famous battle and the army camp at White Plains. Nor can I forget a fascinating conversation with Gary Petagine and Sean Grady, impersonators of Benedict Arnold, and their suggestions for additional source materials on Joshua Hett Smith, West Point, and the Hudson.

This list would not be complete without expressing appreciation to the board members of the Women Writing Women's Seminar of the Graduate Center of the City University of New York, who invited me to speak about the challenges of writing a double biography at that university's Leon Levy Biography Center in April 2011. Wallace Exman, former Manhattan editor and vice president of the Cape Cod Writers Center, generously agreed to read a draft of the book and offered a number of important suggestions for the early chapters.

From the book's inception through the research and writing process, Beacon Press executive editor Gayatri Patnaik has been a consistent source of inspiration, encouragement, and support, for which I am deeply grateful. Praise is also due to her assistant, Rachael Marks, for her attention to myriad details and enthusiasm for this work. I also want to thank Beacon Press managing editor Susan Lumenello, who conscientiously copyedited the book and did so with verve and patience.

Writing can be a lonely and isolating process, but that was greatly ameliorated by the forbearance of my dear husband, Bill, the first reader of these pages, whose astute analysis and suggestions helped improve the manuscript. For that and a thousand other kindnesses, I am indebted.

ABBREVIATIONS

Archives

BAP	Benedict Arnold Fonds, New Brunswick Museum
CMHS	Henry Knox Papers, Collections of the Maine Historical Society
CP	Henry Clinton Papers, University of Michigan
GWP	George Washington Papers, Library of Congress
HKP	Henry Knox Papers, Gilder Lehrman Institute of American History
MHS	Henry Knox Papers, Massachusetts Historical Society
NSDAR	Henry Knox Letters, National Society Daughters of the American Revolution, Americana Collection

Individuals

BA	Benedict Arnold
MA	Margaret (Peggy) Shippen Arnold
GW	George Washington
HC	Henry Clinton
HF	Hannah Flucker
HJ	Henry Jackson
HJK	Henry Jackson Knox
HK	Henry Knox
JA	John André
JB	Jonathan Bliss
LK	Lucy Knox
NG	Nathanael Greene
SS	Samuel Shaw
TF	Thomas Flucker
WK	William Knox

PREFACE
1. LK to HK, August 23, 1777, HKP.
2. Walker, "Life of Margaret Shippen," 25: 461.

CHAPTER 1
"The Handsomest Woman in America"
1. Engle, *Women in the American Revolution*, 156.
2. Hatch, *Major John André*, 90.
3. *Adams Family Correspondence*, 2: 169–70.
4. Walker, "Life of Margaret Shippen," 24: 414.
5. *Bland Papers*, "From a Lady in Philadelphia to Mrs. Theodorick Bland, Jr.," 92.
6. Trevelyan, *American Revolution*, 280.
7. Franks, "A Letter," 216.
8. Faris, *Romance of Old Philadelphia*, 116–17.
9. *Extracts from the Journal of Elizabeth Drinker*, 48.
10. *Letters of John Adams*, 1: 194.
11. Duane, *Extracts from the Diary of Christopher Marshall*, 107.
12. Wainwright, "A Diary of Trifling Occurrences," 450.
13. Hatch, *Major John André*, 82.
14. Silverman, *Cultural History*, 336.
15. "From a Late Philadelphia Paper," *Continental Journal and Weekly Advertiser*, July 30, 1778.
16. Wainwright, "A Diary of Trifling Occurrences," 462.
17. Hatch, *Major John André*, 93.
18. André, "Particulars of the Mischianza," 353.
19. Ibid., 354–55.
20. Ibid., 356.
21. Ibid., 354.
22. Walker, "Life of Margaret Shippen," 24: 414.
23. Ibid.
24. Lewis, *Memoir of Edward Shippen*, 16.
25. Walker, "Life of Margaret Shippen," 24: 414.
26. Ibid.
27. Lewis, *Memoir of Edward Shippen*, 16.

28. Smith, *Authentic Narrative*, 45.
29. Callahan, *Peggy*, 25.
30. Todd, *Real Benedict Arnold*, 171.
31. *Extracts from the Journal of Elizabeth Drinker*, 103.
32. Stedman, *History of the Origin*, 385.
33. André, "Particulars of the Mischianza," 356.
34. *Pennsylvania Packet*, May 13, 1778.
35. *Extracts from the Journal of Elizabeth Drinker*, 102.
36. *Sally Wister's Journal*, 180.
37. Armes, *Nancy Shippen*, 64–65.
38. Clinton, *American Rebellion*, 86.
39. Boylan, *Benedict Arnold*, 147–48.
40. *Papers of Nathanael Greene*, 2: 444.

CHAPTER 2
"The Best and Tenderest of Friends"
1. Drake, *Life and Correspondence*, 15.
2. *Diary and Autobiography of John Adams*, 3: 445–46.
3. Chastellux, *Travels in North-America*, 112.
4. HK to LF, March 1774, HKP.
5. Drake, *Life and Correspondence*, 16.
6. Thatcher, "Reminiscences," 3, NSDAR.
7. Ibid.
8. John Murray to HK, August 11, 1774, HKP.
9. Griffiths, *Major General Henry Knox*, 44.
10. Ibid.
11. Thacher, *Military Journal*, 484.
12. LK to HK, April 1776, HKP.
13. HK to LK, January 2, 1776, HKP.
14. HK to LK, July 6, 1775, HKP.
15. HK to LK, July 9, 1775, HKP.
16. Callahan, *Henry Knox*, 39.
17. John Adams to James Warren, July 23, 1775, *Warren-Adams Letters*, 1: 87.
18. Lea, *Hero and a Spy*, 44.
19. HK to LK, November 16, 1775, HKP.
20. HK to LK, November 27, 1775, HKP.
21. HK to LK, January 5, 1777, HKP.
22. *Diary and Autobiography of John Adams*, 2: 227.
23. GW to LK and HK, February 1, 1776, HKP.

24. HK to William Burbeck, February 25, 1776, HKP.

25. Fleming, *1776*, 181.

26. Goldsmith, *She Stoops to Conquer*, 8.

27. LK to HK, April 1776, HKP.

28. Ibid.

29. HK to LK, May 20, 1776, HKP.

30. HK to WK, July 11, 1776, HKP.

31. Ibid.

32. HK to LK, July 8, 1776, HKP.

33. LK to HK, July 1776, HKP.

34. Ibid.

35. HK to LK, July 11, 1776, HKP.

36. LK to HK, July 18, 1776, HKP.

37. WK to LK, July 11, 1776, HKP.

38. LK to HK, July 18, 1776, HKP.

39. LK to HK, July 13, 1776, HKP.

40. HK, to LK, August 1, 1776, HKP.

41. HK to LK, November 1, 1776, HKP.

42. LK to HK, November 6, 1776, HKP.

43. Ibid.

44. Washington, *Writings*, 282.

45. Brooks, *Henry Knox*, 79.

46. HK to LK, January 2, 1777, HKP.

47. Brooks, *Henry Knox*, 60.

48. BA to LK, March 4, 1777, HKP.

49. LK to HK, April 3, 1777, HKP.

50. *Writings of George Washington*, 7: 352–53.

51. HK to LK, April 1, 1777, HKP.

52. David Franks to LK, December 17, 1777, HKP.

53. LK to HK, April 3, 1777, HKP.

54. HK to LK, April 26, 1777, HKP.

55. LK to HK, April 31, 1777, HKP.

56. HK to LK, April 26, 1777, HKP.

57. LK to HK, May 8, 1777, HKP.

58. HK to LK, May 17, 1777, HKP.

59. LK to HK, May 26, 1777, HKP.

60. LK to HK, July 17, 1777, HKP.

61. Martin, *Narrative of a Revolutionary Soldier*, 170.

62. HK to LK, December 2, 1777, HKP.

63. HK to LK, October 29, 1777, HKP.

64. HK to LK, December 22, 1777, HKP.

65. Drake, *Life and Correspondence of Henry Knox*, 56.

66. Arnold, *Life of Benedict Arnold*, 215.

67. Decker, *Benedict Arnold*, 285–86.

CHAPTER 3
"The Delight, and Comfort of Her Adoring General"

1. HK to WK, May 27, 1778, HKP.

2. Ibid.

3. Boyle, *Writings from the Valley Forge Encampment*, 131.

4. *Papers of General Nathanael Greene*, 2: 444.

5. HK to WK, September 23, 1776, HKP.

6. HK to WK, May 27, 1778, HKP.

7. HK to LK, June 29, 1778, HKP.

8. Wainwright, "A Diary of Trifling Occurrences," 463.

9. Walker, "Life of Margaret Shippen," 25: 480.

10. Lea, *Hero and a Spy*, 298.

11. "Benedict Arnold's Oath of Allegiance."

12. *Extracts from the Journal of Elizabeth Drinker*, 106.

13. Arnold, *Proceedings of a General Court Martial*, 21.

14. *Extracts from the Journal of Elizabeth Drinker*, 106.

15. *Sally Wister's Journal*, 62.

16. BA to HJ, June 1778, HKP.

17. HK to WK, June 25, 1778, HKP.

18. Flexner, *Traitor and the Spy*, 223.

19. Decker, *Benedict Arnold*, 302.

20. Lewis, *Memoir of Edward Shippen*, 18.

21. Hazard, *Register of Pennsylvania*, 389.

22. Walker, "Life of Margaret Shippen," 24: 417.

23. Arnold, *Life of Benedict Arnold*, 240.

24. Hart, *Mary White*, n.p.

25. Ibid.

26. Lea, *Hero and a Spy*, 306.

27. Ibid., 305–6.

28. Walker, "Life of Margaret Shippen," 25: 37.

29. Flexner, *Traitor and the Spy*, 241.

30. Walker, "Life of Margaret Shippen," 25: 480.

31. Lea, *Hero and a Spy*, 307.

32. Ibid., 308.

33. Brandt, *Man in the Mirror*, 162.

34. *Letters of Delegates to Congress*, January 27, 1779, 523.

35. *Pennsylvania Packet*, November 14, 1778.

36. Arnold, *Proceedings of a General Court Martial*, 12.

37. Ibid.; Joseph Reed to John Jay, January 25, 1779, 13; Joseph Reed to GW, April 24, 1779, both in Hazard, *Pennsylvania Archives*, 337f.

38. John Cadwalader to NG, December 5, 1778, Lee Papers, 270.

39. Brandt, *Man in the Mirror*, 163.

40. Ibid., 165–66.

41. Flexner, *Traitor and the Spy*, 36.

42. Walker, "Life of Margaret Shippen," 25: 35–36.

43. Ibid., 38.

44. Arnold, *Life of Benedict Arnold*, 230.

45. Walker, "Life of Margaret Shippen," 25: 38.

46. Lewis, *Memoir of Edward Shippen*, 7–8.

47. HK to WK, February 2, 1779, HKP.

48. Lea, *Hero and a Spy*, 317.

49. Ibid., 317–19.

50. Arnold, *Life of Benedict Arnold*, 231.

51. Flexner, *Traitor and the Spy*, 245.

52. Arnold, *Life of Benedict Arnold*, 230.

53. Ibid.

54. HK to WK, February 13, 1779, HKP.

55. Walker, "Life of Margaret Shippen," 25: 39.

56. *Adams Family Papers*, 2: 183.

57. Flexner, *Traitor and the Spy*, 253.

58. Walker, "Life of Margaret Shippen," 25: 40.

CHAPTER 4
"Our Sweetest Hopes Embittered by Disappointment"

1. HK to WK, November 16, 1778, HKP.

2. *Writings of George Washington*, 14: 122.

3. HK to WK, November 15, 1778, HKP.

4. HK to WK, February 28, 1779, HKP.

5. Thacher, *Military Journal*, 159.

6. *Pennsylvania Packet*, March 6, 1779.

7. "Ball at Pluckemin in 1779 Was Big Social Event of the Revolution," *Somerset (NJ) Messenger-Gazette*, May 17, 1939.

8. *Papers of General Nathanael Greene*, 3: 354.

9. *Pennsylvania Packet*, March 6, 1779.

10. Ibid.

11. *New Jersey Journal*, February 23, 1779.

12. HK to WK, February 28, 1779, HKP.

13. HK to WK, April 3, 1779, HKP.

14. HK to WK, April 24, 1779, HKP.

15. HK to WK, May 7, 1779, HKP.

16. HK to WK, May 18, 1779, HKP.

17. Clinton, *American Rebellion*, 125n7.

18. HK to LK, June 14, 1779, HKP.

19. HK to LK, June 29, 1779, HKP.

20. Mellick, *Story of an Old Farm*, 471.

21. *Papers of General Nathanael Greene*, 4: 244.

22. HK to LK, August 8, 1779, HKP.

23. Cadou, *George Washington Collection*, 75.

24. Boswell, *Life of Dr. Samuel Johnson*, 160.

25. Van Doren, *Secret History*, 287.

26. Walker, "Life of Margaret Shippen," 25: 453.

27. Lea, *Hero and a Spy*, 324.

28. Chesterfield, *Letters*, 256–57.

29. Lea, *Hero and a Spy*, 325–26.

30. Ibid., 326.

31. Ibid., 327–28.

32. Ibid., 330.

33. MA to Edward Shippen, July 5, 1801, Shippen Family Papers.

34. Pope, *Poetical Works*, 145.

35. Van Doren, *Secret History*, 196.

36. Ibid., 439–40.

37. Lea, *Hero and a Spy*, 339.

38. Ibid.

39. BA to GW, May 15, 1779, GWP.

40. Lea, *Hero and a Spy*, 339.

41. "Diary of Grace Growden Galloway," 55: 79.

42. Van Doren, *Secret History*, 201–2.

43. Lea, *Hero and a Spy*, 343.

44. Ibid., 345.

45. Ibid., 348.

46. Ibid., 350.

47. Ibid., 351.

48. Ibid., 352.
49. Ibid., 355.

CHAPTER 5
"Fortitude under Stress"
1. "Diary of Grace Growden Galloway," 58: 181–82.
2. Lea, *Hero and a Spy*, 357.
3. Ibid.
4. Ibid., 357–58.
5. *Extracts from the Journal of Elizabeth Drinker*, 122.
6. Lea, *Hero and a Spy*, 361.
7. Ibid., 362.
8. Ibid.
9. Hatch, *Major John André*, 214–15.
10. Martin, *Narrative of a Revolutionary Solder*, 143.
11. Sherman, *Historic Morristown*, 333.
12. Thacher, *Military Journal*, 185.
13. Brandt, *Man in the Mirror*, 186.
14. Lea, *Hero and a Spy*, 366.
15. Ibid., 379–80.
16. Ibid., 380–81.
17. Ibid., 385.
18. *Papers of General Nathanael Greene*, 5: 365.
19. *Writings of George Washington*, 17: 357.
20. Martin, *Narrative of a Revolutionary Solder*, 148.
21. "To the Magistrates of New Jersey," circular, January 8, 1780, GWP.
22. New Jersey State Archives.
23. Lea, *Hero and a Spy*, 381.
24. Ibid., 382.
25. Ibid., 386.
26. Ibid., 387.
27. Ibid., 397.
28. Ibid., 390.
29. Ibid., 395.
30. Ibid., 398.
31. Ibid., 399–400.
32. Ibid., 403.
33. Flexner, *Traitor and the Spy*, 311.
34. Arnold, *Life of Benedict Arnold*, 284–85.
35. Van Doren, *Secret History*, 468.

36. Ibid., 303.
37. *Writings of George Washington*, 19: 309.
38. Van Doren, *Secret History*, 303–4.
39. Ibid., 304.
40. Lea, *Hero and a Spy*, 421.
41. Smith, *Authentic Narrative*, 15–16.
42. Ibid., 17.
43. David Franks to BA, August 28, 1780, GWP.
44. Arnold, *Life of Benedict Arnold*, 234.
45. Ibid.
46. BA, "Travel Instructions," August 1780, GWP.
47. Bischoff, "Resourceful Woman," 94.
48. Pidgin, *Theodosia*, 173.

CHAPTER 6
"As Good and Innocent as an Angel"
1. BA to HK, August 8, 1780, HKP.
2. Hamilton, *History of the United States*, 78.
3. GW to BA, September 13, 1780, GWP.
4. Lea, *Hero and a Spy*, 315.
5. Van Doren, *Secret History*, 285.
6. Ibid., 265.
7. Smith, *Authentic Narrative*, 16.
8. Van Doren, *Secret History*, 315; Hart, *Varick Court of Inquiry*, 124–25, 171–72; Johnston, "Colonel Varick," 336.
9. Van Doren, *Secret History*, 319.
10. Ibid.
11. Ibid., 317.
12. Ibid.
13. Beverly Robinson to BA, September 19, 1780, GWP.
14. Van Doren, *Secret History*, 327.
15. Ibid., 328.
16. Ibid., 474.
17. Hatch, *Major John André*, 235.
18. Van Doren, *Secret History*, 339; Hart, *Varick Court of Inquiry*, 126–27, 178–79.
19. Van Doren, *Secret History*, 342–43.
20. Ibid., 343–44.
21. Ibid., 344.
22. Lea, *Hero and a Spy*, 532.
23. Ibid., 491.
24. Ibid., 493.

25. Ibid.

26. Van Doren, *Secret History*, 345–46.

27. Ibid., 346.

28. Lea, *Hero and a Spy*, 533.

29. Sparks, *Life and Treason*, 108.

30. Hamilton, *Library of American History*, 40.

31. Lea, *Hero and a Spy*, 533.

32. Van Doren, *Secret History*, 348.

33. Lea, *Hero and a Spy*, 533.

34. Sparks, *Life and Treason*, 108.

35. Flexner, *Traitor and the Spy*, 372.

36. BA to GW, September 25, 1780, GWP.

37. Van Doren, *Secret History*, 348–49.

38. Ibid.

39. Lea, *Hero and a Spy*, 510–11.

40. Walker, "Life of Margaret Shippen," 25: 294.

41. Lea, *Hero and a Spy*, 511.

CHAPTER 7
"A Momentary Pang"

1. Hatch, *Major John André*, 251.

2. Koke, *Accomplice in Treason*, 111.

3. Hatch, *Major John André*, 251.

4. Abbatt, *Crisis of the Revolution*, 48.

5. GW to NG, September 25, 1780, GWP.

6. Callahan, *Henry Knox*, 164.

7. Van Doren, *Secret History*, 352–53.

8. Thacher, *Military Journal*, 256.

9. Ibid., 256–57.

10. Smith, *Authentic Narrative*, 44

11. Hatch, *Major John André*, 242.

12. Ibid., 242–43.

13. Ibid., 244.

14. Ibid., 246.

15. Scheer, *Rebels and Redcoats*, 382.

16. JA to GW, September 24, 1780, GWP.

17. Flexner, *Traitor and the Spy*, 377.

18. Van Doren, *Secret History*, 382.

19. Chastellux, *Travels in North-America*, 282.

20. Walker, "Life of Margaret Shippen," 25: 183.

21. Ibid., 156.

22. Ibid., 157.

23. *Pennsylvania Packet*, September 30, 1780.

24. Burd, "Notes and Queries," 380.

25. *Pennsylvania Packet*, October 3, 1780.

26. Burd, "Notes and Queries," 380.

27. Ibid., 381.

28. Ibid.

29. Flexner, *Traitor and the Spy*, 378.

30. Ibid.

31. Walker, "Life of Margaret Shippen," 25: 160.

32. "Minutes of the Supreme Executive Council," 520.

33. Flexner, *Traitor and the Spy*, 380.

34. Walker, "Life of Margaret Shippen," 25: 296.

35. Ibid., 162.

36. Ibid., 161.

37. *Writings of George Washington*, 7: 533–34.

38. Van Doren, *Secret History*, 487.

39. Ibid., 486–87.

40. Ibid., 487.

41. Ibid., 487–88.

42. Ibid., 366–69.

43. Ibid., 488.

44. HC to JA, October 1, 1780, *Bulletin of the Fort Ticonderoga (New York) Museum* 16, no. 3 (2000): 235.

45. Webb, *Reminiscences*, 297.

46. *Papers of Alexander Hamilton*, 448–49.

47. Ibid.

48. Van Doren, *Secret History*, 475.

49. JA to GW, October 1, 1780, GWP.

50. Hatch, *Major John André*, 272.

51. Ibid., 273.

52. Thacher, *Military Journal*, 228.

53. Ibid.

CHAPTER 8
"Haste Happy Time When We Shall Be No More Separate"

1. Chastellux, *Essay on Public Happiness*, ii.

2. Chastellux, *Travels in North-America*, 112.

3. Ibid.

4. HK to WK, October 30, 1780, HKP.

5. SS, "Circular Address to the New England States," October 7, 1780, American Revolution Collection, 1763-1783, Gilder Lehrman Institute of American History, New York.

6. HK to WK, December 2, 1780, HKP.

7. Thacher, *Military Journal*, 246.

8. Washington, *Writings*, 407–8.

9. Brooks, *Henry Knox*, 141.

10. Lea, *Hero and a Spy*, 544–46.

11. Ibid., 559.

12. Van Doren, *Secret History*, 480–81.

13. Benedict Arnold, "Proclamation to Americans," October 20, 1780, GWP.

14. *Writings of George Washington*, 20: 189.

15. Lea, *Hero and a Spy*, 575.

16. Walker, "Life of Margaret Shippen," 25: 162–63.

17. Ibid., 163.

18. Randall, *Benedict Arnold*, 581.

19. Clinton, *American Rebellion*, 210.

20. BA to HC, January 23, 1781, CP.

21. Burnett, *Letters of Members*, 530.

22. BA to HC, January 23, 1781, CP.

23. Wharton, *Through Colonial Doorways*, 213.

24. Walker, "Life of Margaret Shippen," 25: 162–63.

25. Thacher, *Military Journal*, 263–64.

26. HK to WK, July 20, 1781, HKP.

27. LK to HK, July 26, 1781, HKP.

28. HK to LK, July 26, 1781, HKP.

29. LK to HK, August 12, 1781, HKP.

30. NG to HK, August 7, 1781, HKP.

31. Arnold, *Life of Benedict Arnold*, 352.

32. Sparks, *Life and Treason of Benedict Arnold*, 325.

33. Thacher, *Military Journal*, 271–72.

34. HK to WK, September 4, 1781, HKP.

35. HK to WK, September 9, 1781, HKP.

36. Thatcher, "Reminiscences," 3.

37. LK to WK, September 29, 1781, HKP.

38. WK to LK, October 1, 1781, HKP.

39. Martin, *Narrative of a Revolutionary Soldier*, 200.

40. LK to HK, October 8, 1781, HKP.

41. Thacher, *Military Journal*, 283.

42. Chastellux, *Travels in North-America*, 282.

43. Thacher, *Military Journal*, 285.

44. LK to HK, October 16, 1781, HKP.

45. HK to LK, October 16, 1781, HKP.

46. HK to LK, October 17, 1781, HKP.

47. LK to HK, October 23, 1781, HKP.

48. HK to LK, October 31, 1781, HKP.

49. HK to Clement Biddle, November 12, 1781, HKP.

50. HK to Benjamin Lincoln, November 12 1781, HKP.

51. HK to NG, December 12, 1781, HKP.

52. Walker, "Life of Margaret Shippen," 25: 163.

CHAPTER 9
"Yet We Wade On"

1. *Public Advertiser* (London), January 24, 1782.

2. *London Chronicle*, January 22, 1778.

3. "Historic Chronicle," *Gentleman's Magazine*, March 1782.

4. *Morning Herald and Daily Advertiser* (London), January 22, 1782.

5. Flexner, *Traitor and the Spy*, 399.

6. *Morning Herald and Daily Advertiser*, February 4, 1782.

7. Arnold, *Life of Benedict Arnold*, 363.

8. Drake, *Historic Fields*, 258.

9. Arnold, *Life of Benedict Arnold*, 363.

10. Van Doren, *Secret History*, 386.

11. Flexner, *Traitor and the Spy*, 399.

12. "Ode Addressed," *Whitehall Evening Post* (London), February 16, 1782.

13. *Public Advertiser* and *Morning Herald and Daily Advertiser*, March 8, 1782.

14. Lomask, "Benedict Arnold," 86.

15. "Historic Chronicle," *Gentleman's Magazine* 52 (March 1782): 147.

16. "Summary of Proceedings in the Second Session of the Present Parliament," *Gentleman's Magazine* 52 (March 1782): 103.

17. *Morning Herald and Daily Advertiser*, March 28, 1782.

18. Van Schaack, *Life of Peter Van Schaack*, 147–147.

19. Stern, "Dear Mrs. Cad," 18–19.

20. Randall, *Benedict Arnold*, 595.

21. Ibid.

22. Walker, "Life of Margaret Shippen," 25: 160.

23. Arnold, *Life of Benedict Arnold*, 369.

24. Walker, "Life of Margaret Shippen," 25: 167.

25. HK to LK, March 22, 1782, HKP.

26. LK to HK, April 10, 1782, HKP.

27. *Independent Ledger and the American Advertiser* (Boston), June 17, 1782.

28. Simms, *History of Schoharie County*, 535.

29. Brooks, *Henry Knox*, 167.

30. HK to Samuel Osgood, July 9, 1782, HKP.

31. HK to WK, August 25, 1782, HKP.

32. HK to GW, September 10, 1782, HKP.

33. HK to William Alexander, September 24, 1782, HKP.

34. HK to Gouverneur Morris, October 8, 1782, HKP.

35. HK to GW, September 10, 1782, HKP.

36. HK to Benjamin Lincoln, December 20, 1782, HKP.

37. HK to NG, February 2, 1783, HKP.

38. HK to Alexander McDouglas, February 21, 1783, HKP.

39. HK to Gouverneur Morris, February 21, 1783, HKP.

40. *Writings of George Washington*, 26: 211n29.

41. Ibid., 222n38.

42. Washington, *Writings*, 497–99.

43. Mercy Otis Warren, August 2, 1787, Warren Family Letters and Papers.

44. HK to Benjamin Lincoln, May 21, 1783, HKP.

45. HK to TF, May 14, 1783, HKP.

46. HK to WK, August 23, 1783, HKP.

47. Freeman, *George Washington*, 462–63.

48. Drake, *Historic Fields*, 174.

49. HK to Marquis de Lafayette, December 14, 1783, HKP.

50. HK to Samuel Osgood, December 30, 1783, HKP.

51. HK to LK, August 8, 1779, HKP.

CHAPTER 10
"My Regret at This Cruel, Dreadful Separation"

1. HK to TF, April 10, 1784, HKP.

2. HK to HF, August 3, 1784, HKP.

3. TF to HK, September 19, 1784, HKP.

4. HF to HK, September 25, 1784, HKP.

5. Marquis de Lafayette to HK, June 12, 1785, HKP.

6. HK to GW, March 24, 1785, HKP.

7. Ibid.

8. LK to HK, May 4, 1785, HKP.

9. LK to HK, May 9, 1785, NSDAR.

10. HJ to HK, September 28, 1786, HKP.

11. HJ to HK, September 28, 1786, HKP.

12. HK to GW, October 23, 1786, HKP.

13. *New Haven Gazette and Connecticut Magazine*, August 10, 1786.

14. *Saint John (Newfoundland) Gazette*, December 20, 1785.

15. *Royal Gazette* (New York), June 6, 1786.

16. Walker, "Life of Margaret Shippen," 25: 454.

17. Ibid.

18. *Saint John (New Brunswick) Gazette*, October 27, 1789.

19. Quigley, *Benedict Arnold*, 50.

20. Walker, "Life of Margaret Shippen," 25: 455–56.

21. Ibid., 457.

22. Sabine, *Sketches of the Loyalists* 2, 179.

23. Walker, "Life of Margaret Shippen," 25: 168.

24. Walker, "Life of Margaret Shippen," 24: 457.

25. Ibid.

26. Munson Hayt, affidavit, May 8, 1790, Benedict Arnold-Munson Hayt Fonds.

27. Walker, "Life of Margaret Shippen," 25: 457.

28. Quigley, *Benedict Arnold*, 51.

29. Wilson, *Benedict Arnold*, 207–14.

30. BA to JB, February 26, 1792, F1–4, BAF.

31. HK to GW, February 22, 1787, GWP.

32. HK to Stephen Higginson, January 28, 1787, HKP.

33. Griswold, *Republican Court*, 171–72.

34. Ibid., 172.

35. Cutler, *Life and Journals of Manasseh Cutler*, 230–31.

36. Ibid.

37. Drake, *Life and Correspondence*, 102.
38. HK to GW, December 11, 1787, GWP.
39. Griswold, *Republican Court*, 172.
40. *Adams Family Correspondence*, 8: 273.
41. Ibid.
42. Griffiths, *Major General Henry Knox*, 50.
43. *Adams Family Correspondence*, 3: 273.
44. Griffiths, *Major General Henry Knox*, 156.
45. Ibid., 157.
46. Ibid.
47. HK to GW, July 7, 1789, HKP.

CHAPTER 11
"Illusive Bubbles"
1. HK to William Duer, July 10, 1791, HKP.
2. HK to JA, June 20, 1791, HKP.
3. Wharton, *Through Colonial Doorways*, 228–29.
4. Griffiths, *Major General Henry Knox*, 271.
5. HK to Thomas Jefferson, July 19, 1791, HKP.
6. HK to GW, July 7, 1789, HKP.
7. HK to LK, July 25, 1791, HKP.
8. Thatcher, "Reminiscences," 16, NSDAR.
9. GW to HK, September 8, 1791, HKP.
10. HK to GW, September 8, 1791, GWP.
11. HK to John Marsden Pintard, November 14, 1791, HKP.
12. Wharton, *Through Colonial Doorways*, 228
13. Mitchell, *New Letters of Abigail Adams*, 55.
14. Griffiths, *Major General Henry Knox*, 46.
15. Ibid., 49.
16. HJ to LK, November 28, 1790, HKP.
17. HK to LK, July 8, 1792, HKP.
18. HK to LK, July 29, 1792, HKP.
19. HK to LK, August 19, 1792, HKP.
20. HK to LK, September 5, 1792, HKP.
21. HK to LK, September 23, 1792, HKP.
22. Eaton, *History of Thomaston*, 222.
23. HK to LK, September 9, 1791, HKP.
24. HK to LK, September 17, 1791, HKP.
25. HK to LK, September 17, 1792, HKP.
26. Drake, *Life and Correspondence*, 108–9.

27. *Warren-Adams Letters*, 2: 315.
28. Ibid., 316.
29. *Extracts from the Journal of Elizabeth Drinker*, 190.
30. Ibid., 193.
31. HK to GW, September 18, 1793, GWP.
32. LK to HK, October 5, 1793, HKP.
33. LK to HK, November 1, 1793, HKP.
34. HK to LK, November 5, 1793, HKP.
35. HK to HJ, May 10, 1794, HKP.
36. HK to General Anthony Wayne, December 5, 1794, HKP
37. Sarah Lyons Flucker Beaumez to LK, March 17, 1793, HKP.
38. HJK to HK, March 31, 1794, HKP.
39. Walker, "Life of Margaret Shippen," 25: 459.
40. Ibid.
41. Ibid., 460.
42. Ibid., 461.
43. Ibid., 462.
44. *Evening Mail* (London), June 29, 1792.
45. Walker, "Life of Margaret Shippen," 24: 462.
46. Ibid.
47. Randall, *Benedict Arnold*, 606.
48. BA to HC, October 17, 1792, CP.
49. BA to JB, February 10, 1794, F1–13, BAF.
50. Talleyrand, *Memoirs*, 174–75.
51. Walker, "Life of Margaret Shippen," 25: 464.
52. Ibid.
53. Ibid., 465.
54. Ibid.
55. Ibid.

CHAPTER 12
"An Irresistible but Invisible Force"
1. Henry Knox Papers, Collection 166, Box 21/1, CMHS.
2. HJ to HK, May 8, 1794, HKP.
3. La Rochefoucauld, *Travels through the United States*, 1, 421.
4. Callahan, *Henry Knox*, 348.
5. Ibid., 349.

6. Brooks, *Henry Knox*, 240.
7. Callahan, *Henry Knox*, 350.
8. Brooks, *Henry Knox*, 265.
9. Callahan, *Henry Knox*, 351.
10. Brooks, *Henry Knox*, 241.
11. La Rochefoucauld, *Travels through the United States*, 449–50.
12. Ibid., 449.
13. Callahan, *Henry Knox*, 351.
14. Ibid., 352.
15. Eaton, *History of Thomaston*, 231.
16. *Columbian Centinel* (Boston), April 27, 1796.
17. Daniel Cobb to HK, December 13, 1796, HKP.
18. HK to GW, January 13, 1797, HKP.
19. Eaton, *History of Thomaston*, 211.
20. Thatcher, "Reminiscences," 11–12, NSDAR.
21. HJ to HK, August 7, 1795, HKP.
22. Griffiths, *Major General Henry Knox*, 45.
23. Madison, *Memoirs and Letters*, 39–40.
24. Eaton, *History of Thomaston*, 221.
25. Ely, *Unmasked Nabob*, 5.
26. Taylor, *Liberty Men*, 165.
27. HJ to HK, March 22, 1795, HKP.
28. MA to JB, December 5, 1795, F1-21, BAF.
29. Arnold, *Life of Benedict Arnold*, 389.
30. MA to JB, December 5, 1795, F1-4, BAF.
31. Walker, "Life of Margaret Shippen," 25: 467.
32. BA to JB, February 20, 1796, F1–24, BAF.
33. Walker, "Life of Margaret Shippen," 25: 466.
34. Ibid.
35. Ibid., 467–68.
36. Brandt, *Man in the Mirror*, 272.
37. Taylor, *Some New Light*, 26.
38. Goodfriend, "Widowhood of Margaret Shippen Arnold," 229.
39. Ibid.
40. Walker, "Life of Margaret Shippen," 25: 472.
41. Goodfriend, "Widowhood of Margaret Shippen Arnold," 229.
42. Walker, "Life of Margaret Shippen," 25: 472.
43. Taylor, *Some New Light*, 26.

CHAPTER 13
"I Do Not Suffer My Spirits to Overcome Me"

1. HK to LK, August 13, 1797, HKP.
2. HK to LK, November 20, 1801, HKP.
3. HK to LK, May 8, 1802, HKP.
4. LK to HK, November 12, 1800, HKP.
5. LK to HK, April 4, 1804, HKP.
6. HK to Clement Biddle, March 3, 1798, HKP.
7. Brooks, *Henry Knox*, 265.
8. Ibid., 263.
9. Ibid., 264.
10. Ibid.
11. HK to David Cobb, March 22, 1800, HKP.
12. HK to LK, November 20, 1801, HKP.
13. HK to LK, November 13, 1801, HKP.
14. HK to LK, November 20, 1801, HKP.
15. Ibid.
16. Griffiths, *Major General Henry Knox*, 53.
17. HJK to LK, March 28, 1805, HKP.
18. HK to Samuel Breck, January 13, 1806, HKP.
19. Thatcher, "Reminiscences," 5, NSDAR.
20. HK to Wales & Beale, October 20, 1806, HKP.
21. Thatcher, "Reminiscences," 19, NSDAR.
22. Callahan, *Henry Knox*, 380.
23. Ibid., 381; *Columbian Centinel*, October 29, 1806.
24. Thacher, *Military Journal*, 483–84.
25. Flyleaf, Account Book (1796), Henry Knox Papers, 1789–1797, Manuscript Division, Library of Congress.
26. Griffiths, *Major General Henry Knox*, 57.
27. Caroline Knox Swan to LK, June 17, 1808, accession 4098(p), NSDAR.
28. Ibid.
29. Griffiths, *Major General Henry Knox*, 49.
30. Caroline Knox Swan to unnamed friend, August 16, 1822, vol. 2, penned in Knox's letterbook, January 8, 1774–March 1775, MHS.
31. HK to LK, March 17, 1806, HKP.
32. Walker, "Life of Margaret Shippen," 25: 472.

33. Goodfriend, "Widowhood of Margaret Shippen Arnold," 225.

34. Walker, "Life of Margaret Shippen," 25: 473.

35. Wilson, *Benedict Arnold*, 230–32.

36. Ibid.

37. Ibid., 475.

38. Taylor, *Some New Light*, 63.

39. Walker, "Life of Margaret Shippen," 25: 477.

40. Ibid., 482.

41. Ibid., 480.

42. Goodfriend, "Widowhood of Margaret Shippen Arnold," 238.

43. Ibid., 225.

44. Ibid., 239.

45. Walker, "Life of Margaret Shippen," 25: 482.

46. Ibid.

47. Ibid., 483.

48. Taylor, *Some New Light*, 64, 66.

49. Walker, "Life of Margaret Shippen," 25: 486.

50. Ibid., 490.

51. Ibid.

52. Ibid., 491.

53. Walker, "Life of Margaret Shippen," 25: 495.

CHAPTER 14
The Brides' Legacies

1. Chastellux, *Travels in North-America*, 112.

2. Marshall, *Life of George Washington*, 213–14.

3. Sullivan, *Familiar Letters*, 85.

4. Griffiths, *Major General Henry Knox*, 91.

5. Ellett, *Women of the American Revolution*, 87.

6. Griffiths, *Major General Henry Knox*, 87.

7. Ibid., 88.

8. Ellett, "Sketch of Mrs. Henry Knox," 110.

9. Griffiths, *Major General Henry Knox*, 90.

10. Ibid., 87–88.

11. Ibid., 56.

12. Hawthorne, *American Notebooks*, 23.

13. Griffiths, *Major General Henry Knox*, 101.

14. Ibid.

15. Taylor, *Some New Light*, 408.

16. Ibid., 413.

17. Ibid., 415.

18. Ibid., 414.

19. Ibid., 417.

20. Ibid., 48.

21. Van Doren, *Secret History*, 386.

Abbatt, William. *The Crisis of the Revolution: Being the Story of Arnold and André*. New York: William Abbatt, 1897.

Adams, John. *Adams Family Papers*. Volume 2. Boston: Massachusetts Historical Society, 1961–

———. *Diary and Autobiography of John Adams*. Volumes 2, 3, and 4. L. H. Butterfield, Leonard C. Faber, and Wendell D. Garrett, eds. Boston: Massachusetts Historical Society, 1961.

———. *Letters of John Adams, Addressed to His Wife*. Volume 1. Charles Adams, ed. Boston: Charles C. Little and James Brown, 1841.

Adams Family Correspondence. Volumes 1, 2, 3, and 8. L. H. Butterfield, Leonard C. Faber, and Wendell D. Garrett, eds. Boston: Massachusetts Historical Society, 1963–

Amory, Martha Babcock. *The Domestic and Artistic Life of John Singleton Copley, R.A.: With Notices of His Works, and Reminiscences of His Son, Lord Lyndhurst, Lord High Chancellor of Great Britain*. Boston: Houghton Mifflin, 1882.

André, John. "Particulars of the Mischianza." *Gentleman's Magazine* 48 (July 1778): 353–57.

Armes, Ethel, ed. *Nancy Shippen, Her Journal Book: The International Romance of a Young Lady of Fashion of Colonial Philadelphia with Letters to Her and about Her*. New York: Benjamin Blom, 1968 (orig. 1935).

Arnold, Benedict, and Francis Suydam Hoffman. *Proceedings of a General Court Martial for the Trial of Major General Arnold*. New York: Privately printed, 1865.

Arnold, Isaac Newton. *The Life of Benedict Arnold: His Patriotism and His Treason*. Chicago: Jansen, McClurg & Co., 1880.

Atlantic (New Brunswick) Advocate, March 1963.

Benedict Arnold Fonds. New Brunswick Museum, Saint John.

Benedict Arnold-Munson Hayt Papers, Library Archives, University of New Brunswick.

"Benedict Arnold's Oath of Allegiance," May 30, 1778. National Archives, War Department Collection of Revolutionary War Records, 1709–1939. Washington, D.C.

Berkin, Carol. *Revolutionary Mothers: Women in the Struggle for America's Independence*. New York: Alfred A. Knopf, 2005.

Bigelow, John, ed. *The Life of Benjamin Franklin, Written by Himself*. Volume 3. Philadelphia: J. B. Lippincott, 1854.

Bischoff, Henry. "A Resourceful Woman in Revolutionary Bergen County: Theodosia Prevost at the Hermitage." In *The Revolutionary War in Bergen County: The Times that Tried Men's Souls*, Carol Karels, ed. Charleston, SC: History Press, 2007.

The Bland Papers. Volume 1. Charles Campbell, ed. Petersburg, VA: Edmund & Julian C. Ruffin, 1840.

Bobrick, Benson. *Angels in the Whirlwind: The Triumph of the American Revolution.* New York: Simon & Schuster, 1997.

Boswell, James. *The Life of Dr. Samuel Johnson.* Volume 4. New York: John R. Anderson & Co., 1889.

Boylan, Brian Richard. *Benedict Arnold: The Dark Eagle.* New York: W. W. Norton, 1973.

Boyle, Joseph Lee. *Writings from the Valley Forge Encampment of the Continental Army, December 19, 1777–June 19, 1778.* Volume 1. Bowie, MD: Heritage Books, 2000.

Brandt, Clare. *The Man in the Mirror: A Life of Benedict Arnold.* New York: Random House, 1994.

Brooks, Noah. *Henry Knox, a Soldier of the Revolution: Major-General in the Continental Army, Washington's Chief of Artillery, First Secretary of War Under the Constitution, Founder of the Society of the Cincinnati; 1750-1806.* New York: G. P. Putnam's Sons, 1900.

Burd, Edward. "Notes and Queries." *Pennsylvania Magazine of History and Biography* 40 (1916).

Burnett, Edmund C. *Letters of Members of the Continental Congress.* Volume 5. Washington, D.C.: Carnegie Institution of Washington, 1931.

Cadou, Carol Borchert. *The George Washington Collection: Fine and Decorative Arts at Mount Vernon.* Manchester, VT: Hudson Hills Press, 2006.

Callahan, North. *Henry Knox, General Washington's General.* New York: Rinehart & Company, 1958.

———. *Peggy.* New York: Cornwall Books, 1983.

Carbone, Gerald M. *Nathanael Greene: A Biography of the American Revolution.* New York: Palgrave McMillan, 2008.

Chadwick, Bruce. *George Washington's War: The Forging of a Revolutionary Leader and the American Presidency.* Naperville, IL: Sourcebooks, 2004.

Chastellux, Francois Jean, Marquis de. *An Essay on Public Happiness.* Volume 1. London: T. Cadell in the Strand, 1774.

———. *Travels in North-America, in the Years 1780–81–82.* New York: White, Gallaher & White, 1827.

Chesterfield, Lord, and Philip Dormer Stanhope. *Letters, Sentences and Maxims.* New York: G. P. Putnam's Sons, 1888.

Clinton, Henry. *The American Rebellion: Sir Henry Clinton's Narrative of His Campaigns, 1775-1782.* William B. Willcox, ed. New Haven, CT: Yale University Press, 1954.

Cubbison, Douglas R. *Historic Structures Report: The Hudson River Defenses at Fortress West Point, 1778-1783.* West Point, NY: U.S. Military Academy, Directorate of Housing and Public Works, 2005.

Cunningham, John T. *The Uncertain Revolution: Washington & the Continental Army at Morristown.* West Creek, NJ: Down the Shore, 2007.

Cutler, William Parker, and Julia Perkins Cutler. *Life, Journals, and Correspondence of Rev. Manasseh Cutler, LLD.* Volume 1. Cincinnati: Robert Clarke & Co., 1888.

Decker, Malcolm. *Benedict Arnold: Son of the Havens.* New York: Antiquarian Press, 1961.

Drake, Francis S. *Life and Correspondence of Henry Knox: Major-General in the American Revolutionary Army.* Boston: Samuel G. Drake, 1873.

Drake, Samuel Adams. *Historic Fields and Mansions of Middlesex.* Boston: James. R. Osgood and Co., 1874.

Drinker, Elizabeth (Mrs. Henry). *Extracts from the Journal of Elizabeth Drinker.* Henry D. Biddle, ed. Philadelphia: J. B. Lippincott Company, 1889.

Duane, William, ed. *Extracts from the Diary of Christopher Marshall, 1774–1781.* Albany, NY: Joel Munsell, 1877.

Dyer, Ellen. *Montpelier: This Spot So Sacred to a Name So Great.* Thomaston, ME: Friends of Montpelier, 2004.

Eaton, Cyrus. *History of Thomaston, Rockland, and South Thomaston, Maine: From Their First Exploration, A.D. 1605: With Family Genealogies.* Volume 1. Thomaston, ME: Thomaston Historical Society, 1972.

Ellett, Elizabeth Fries. *Women of the American Revolution.* Volume 1. New York: Baker & Scribner, 1848.

————. "Sketch of Mrs. Henry Knox." *Godey's Lady's Book and Magazine* 38 (1849).

Ely, Samuel. *The Unmasked Nabob of Hancock County.* Portsmouth, NH: Charles Peirce, 1796.

Engle, Paul. *Women in the American Revolution.* Chicago: Follett Publishing Company, 1976.

Faris, John T. *The Romance of Old Philadelphia.* Philadelphia: J. B. Lippincott, 1918.

Fleming, Thomas. *1776: Year of Illusions.* New York. W. W. Norton, 1975.

Flexner, James Thomas. *The Traitor and the Spy: Benedict Arnold and John André.* Boston: Little Brown, 1975 (orig. 1953).

Fowler, William M., Jr. *American Crisis: George Washington and the Dangerous Two Years after Yorktown, 1781–1783.* New York: Walker & Company, 2011.

Franks Johnson, Rebecca. "A Letter of Miss Rebecca Franks, 1778." *Pennsylvania Magazine of History and Biography* 16 (July 1892).

Freeman, Douglas Southall. *George Washington.* Volume 5. New York: Scribner, 1952.

Galloway, Grace Growden, and Raymond C. Werner. "Diary of Grace Growden Galloway." *Pennsylvania Magazine of History and Biography* 55, no. 1 (1931), and 58, no. 2 (1934).

George Washington Papers, Library of Congress, Washington, D.C.

Goldsmith, Oliver. *She Stoops to Conquer, or the Mistakes of a Night.* Dudley Miles, ed. Boston: Ginn & Co., 1917.

Goodfriend, Joyce D. "The Widowhood of Margaret Shippen Arnold: Letters from England, 1801–1803." *Pennsylvania Magazine of History and Biography* 115, no. 2 (April 1991).

Greene, Nathanael. *The Papers of General Nathanael Greene.* Volumes 2–5. Richard K. Showman, ed. Chapel Hill: University of North Carolina: 1980, 1983, 1986, 1989.

Griffiths, Thomas Morgan. *Major General Henry Knox and the Last Heirs to Montpelier.* Arthur Morgan Griffiths, ed. Lewiston, ME: Twin City Printery, 1965.

Griswold, Rufus Wilmot. *The Republican Court, or, American Society in the Days of Washington.* New York: D. Appleton & Co., 1855.

Halfpenny, Pat. *Worthy of the Connoisseur's Greatest Care, Pierced Creamware.* London: International Ceramics Fair & Seminar Ltd., 2007.

Hamilton, Alexander. *The Papers of Alexander Hamilton.* Harold C. Syrett and Jacob Cook, eds. New York: Columbia University Press, 1961.

————. *The Works of Alexander Hamilton: Comprising His Most Important Official Reports; an Improved Edition of the Federalist, on the New Constitution, Written in 1788; and Pacificus, on the Proclamation of Neutrality.* 12 volumes. New York: Williams and Whiting, 1810.

Hamilton, John Church. *History of the United States: Life of Alexander Hamilton.* Volume 2. Boston: Houghton, Osgood & Co., 1879.

Hamilton, Sinclair. *Library of American History: Sinclair Hamilton Collection of American Illustrated Books, Containing Biographical Sketches.* Cincinnati: U. P. James, 1855.

Hart, Albert Bushnell, ed. *The Varick Court of Inquiry to Investigate the Implication of Colonel Richard Varick (Arnold's Private Secretary) in the Arnold Treason.* Boston: Bibliophile Society, 1907.

Hart, Charles Henry. *Mary White—Mrs. Robert Morris: An Address Delivered by Request at Sophia's Dairy Near Perrymansville Harford Co Maryland, June 7th 1877, on the Occasion of the Reinterment of the Remains of Colonel Thomas White before a Reunion of His Descendants, Halls—Whites—Morrises.* Philadelphia: Collins, 1878.

Hatch, Robert McConnell. *Major John André: A Gallant in Spy's Clothing.* Boston: Houghton Mifflin, 1986.

Hawthorne, Nathaniel. *The American Notebooks.* New Haven, CT: Yale University Press, 1932 (orig. 1868).

Hazard, Samuel. *Pennsylvania Archives, Selected and Arranged from Original Documents in the Office of the Secretary of the Commonwealth, Conformably to Acts of the General Assembly,* February 15, 1851, and March 1, 1852, Commencing 1778. Volume 7, 337f.

————. *The Register of Pennsylvania, January–July 1829.* Volume 3. Philadelphia: W. P. Geddes, 1829, 389.

Henry Clinton Papers. William L. Clements Library, University of Michigan, Ann Arbor.

Henry Knox Letters. National Society Daughters of the American Revolution, Americana Collection, accession 4098(p), Washington, D.C.

Henry Knox Papers. Collections of the Maine Historical Society, Portland.

Henry Knox Papers. Massachusetts Historical Society, Boston.

Henry Knox Papers (1750–1806), GLC 02437. Gilder Lehrman Institute of American History, New York.

Henry Knox Papers (1789–1797). Library of Congress, Washington, D.C.

Jasanoff, Maya. *Liberty's Exiles: American Loyalists in the Revolutionary World.* New York: Knopf, 2011.

Johnston, Henry P. "Colonel Varick and Arnold's Treason." *Magazine of American History* 8, no. 11 (November 1882): 717–33.

Karels, Carol, ed. *The Revolutionary War in Bergen County: The Times That Tried Men's Souls.* Charleston, SC: History Press, 2007.

Kerber, Linda. *Women of the Republic: Intellect and Ideology in Revolutionary America.* Chapel Hill: Institute of Early American History and Culture, University of North Carolina Press, 1980.

Klein, Randolph Shipley. *Portrait of an Early American Family: The Shippens of Pennsylvania Across Five Generations.* Philadelphia: University of Pennsylvania Press, 1975.

Koke, Richard J. *Accomplice in Treason: Joshua Hett Smith and the Arnold Conspiracy.* New York: New-York Historical Society, 1973.

Lea, Russell M. *A Hero and a Spy: The Revolutionary War Correspondence of Benedict Arnold.* Westminster, MD: Westminster Books, 2008.

Leake, Isaac Q. *Memoir of the Life and Times of General John Lamb: An Officer of the Revolution.* Albany, NY: Joel Munsell, 1850.

The Lee Papers. Collections of the New-York Historical Society, NYHS Publication Fund III, 1778–1782.

Letters of Delegates to Congress, 1774–1789. Volume 11. Paul H. Smith et al., eds. Washington, D.C.: Library of Congress, 1976–2000.

Lewis, Lawrence. *A Memoir of Edward Shippen, Chief Justice of Pennsylvania, Together with Selections from His Correspondence.* Philadelphia: Collins, 1883.

Loane, Nancy K. *Following the Drum: Women at the Valley Forge Encampment.* Washington, D.C.: Potomac Books, 2009.

Lomask, Milton. "Benedict Arnold: The Aftermath of Treason." *American Heritage* 18, no. 6 (October 1967).

Madison, Dolley. *Memoirs and Letters of Mrs. Madison.* L. D. Cutts, ed. Boston: Houghton, Mifflin, 1896.

Marshall, John. *The Life of George Washington, Commander in Chief of the American Forces.* Volume 5. London: Richard Phillips, 1807.

Martin, James Kirby. *Benedict Arnold, Revolutionary Hero: An American Warrior Reconsidered.* New York: New York University Press, 1997.

Martin, Joseph Plumb. *A Narrative of a Revolutionary Soldier.* New York: New American Library, 2001 (published privately 1830 by the author).

Mayo, Lawrence Shaw. *Jeffrey Amherst.* New York: Longmans, Green and Co., 1916.

Mellick, Andrew, Jr. *The Story of an Old Farm, or Life in New Jersey in the Eighteenth Century.* Somerville, NJ: Unionist-Gazette, 1889.

"Minutes of the Supreme Executive Council of Philadelphia." *Colonial Records of Pennsylvania.* Volume 12. Harrisburg, PA: Theo Fenn & Co., 1853.

Mitchell, Stewart, ed. *New Letters of Abigail Adams, 1788–1801.* Boston: Houghton Mifflin, 1947.

Moore, Frank, ed. *Diary of the American Revolution from Newspapers and Original Documents.* 2 volumes. New York: Charles Scribner, 1860.

National Society Daughters of the American Revolution, Americana Collection, Henry Knox Exhibit, Washington, D.C.

New Jersey State Archives, Trenton. Revolutionary War Correspondence, Box 27, File 7.

Pidgin, Charles Felton. *Theodosia: The First Gentlewoman of Her Time.* Boston: C. M. Clark Publishing Company, 1907.

Pope, Alexander. *The Poetical Works of Alexander Pope, Esq.; to Which Is Prefaced the Life of the Author.* Volume 1. Samuel Johnson, ed. Philadelphia: Crissy & Markley, 1853.

Puls, Mark. *Henry Knox: Visionary General of the American Revolution.* New York: Palgrave Macmillan, 2008.

Quigley, Louis. *Benedict Arnold: The Canadian Connection.* New Brunswick: Queue Publishing, 2000.

Randall, Willard Sterne. *Benedict Arnold: Patriot and Traitor.* New York: Dorset Press, 1990.

———. *George Washington: A Life.* New York: Holt, 1998.

Risch, Erna. *Supplying Washington's Army.* Special Studies Series. Washington, D.C.: Center of Military History, U.S. Army, 1981.

Rochefoucauld, Francois de la. *Travels through the United States, the Country of the Iroquois and Upper Canada, in the Years 1795, 1796 and 1797, with an Authentic Account of Lower Canada.* London: R. Phillips; sold by T. Hurst and J. Wallis, 1799.

Sabine, Lorenzo. *Sketches of the Loyalists with an Historical Essay.* 2 volumes. Boston: Little, Brown, 1864.

Sargent, Winthrop. *The Life of Major John André, Adjutant-General of the British Army in America.* New York: D. Appleton and Company, 1871.

Scheer, George F., and Hugh F. Rankin. *Rebels and Redcoats: The American Revolution Through the Eyes of Those Who Fought and Lived It.* New York: Da Capo Press, 1957 (repr. 1987).

Sherman, Andrew M. *Historic Morristown: Story of Its First Century.* Morristown, NJ: Howard Publishing Company, 1905.

Shippen Family Papers, 595C, Folder 2. Historical Society of Pennsylvania, Philadelphia.

Silverman, Kenneth. *A Cultural History of the American Revolution.* New York: Columbia University Press, 1987.

Simms, Jeptha Root. *History of Schoharie County and Border Wars.* Albany, NY: Munsell & Tanner, Printers, 1845.

Smith, Joshua Hett. *An Authentic Narrative of the Causes Which Led to the Death of Major André, Adjutant-General of His Majesty's Forces in North America.* London: Mathews and Leigh, 1808.

Sparks, Jared. *American Biography: Benedict Arnold.* New York: Harper & Brothers, 1902.

———, ed. *Life and Treason of Benedict Arnold.* Boston: Hilliard, Gray and Co., 1835.

———. *The Writings of George Washington: Being His Correspondence, Addresses, Messages, and Other Papers, Official and Private.* Boston: Russell, Odiorne and Metcalf, and Hilliard, Gray and Co., 1835.

Spear, Moncrieff J. *To End the War at White Plains.* Baltimore: American Library Press, 2002.

Stedman, Charles. *The History of the Origin, Progress and Termination of the War.* Volumes 1–2. London: J. Murray, Fleet-Street, J. Debrett, Piccadilly, and J. Kerby, 1794.

Stegeman, John F., and Janet A. Stegeman. *Caty: A Biography of Catharine Littlefield Greene.* Providence: Rhode Island Bicentennial Foundation, 1977.

Stern, Mark A. "Dear Mrs. Cad: A Revolutionary War Letter of Rebecca Franks," *American Jewish Archives Journal* 57 (2005): 15–24.

Stuart, Nancy Rubin. *The Muse of the Revolution: The Secret Pen of Mercy Otis Warren and the Founding of a Nation.* Boston: Beacon Press, 2008.

Sullivan, William. *Familiar Letters on Public Characters and on Public Events from the Peace of 1783 to the Peace of 1815.* Boston: Russell, Odiorne and Metcalf, 1934.

Talleyrand, Charles Maurice de. *Memoirs of the Prince de Talleyrand.* Volume 1. Raphael Ledos de Beaufort, trans. London: Griffith, Farran, Okeden and Welsh, 1891.

Tallmadge, Benjamin. *Memoir of Col. Benjamin Tallmadge.* New York: Thomas Holman, 1858.

Taylor, Alan. *The Divided Ground: Indians, Settlers, and the Northern Borderland of the American Revolution.* New York: Alfred A. Knopf, 2006.

———. *Liberty Men and Great Proprietors: The Revolutionary Settlement on the Maine Frontier, 1760–1820.* Chapel Hill: University of North Carolina Press, 1990.

Taylor, J. G. *Some New Light on the Later Life and Last Resting Place of Benedict Arnold and of his wife, Margaret Shippen.* London: George White, 1931.

Thacher, James, MD. *Military Journal of the American Revolution.* Hartford, CT: Hurlbut, Williams & Company, 1862.

Thatcher, Lucy Knox. "Reminiscences of LFK Thatcher." Henry Knox Exhibit, accession 4098(q), National Society Daughters of the American Revolution, Americana Collection, Washington, D.C.

Todd, Charles Burr. *The Real Benedict Arnold.* New York: A. S. Barnes & Co., 1903.

Trevelyan, George Otto. *The American Revolution.* Volume 4. London: Longmans, Green & Co., 1907.

Van Arsdale, Edward H. "Pluckemin During the Revolution." Unpublished manuscript. Bedminster, NJ: Clarence Dillon Library, April 8, 1976.

Van Doren, Mark. *Secret History of the American Revolution.* Clifton, NJ: Augustus M. Kelley, 1973.

Van Schaack, Henry C. *The Life of Peter Van Schaack.* New York: D. Appleton & Co., 1897.

Wainwright, Nicholas B. "A Diary of Trifling Occurrences, Philadelphia, 1776–1778." *Pennsylvania Magazine of History and Biography* 82 (1958): 411–65.

Walker, Lewis Burd. "Life of Margaret Shippen. Wife of Benedict Arnold," *Pennsylvania Magazine of History and Biography*, volume 24 (1900): 257–66, 401–29; volume 25, no. 4 (1901): 20–46, 145–90, 289–302, 452–97; volume 26 (1902): 71–80, 224–44, 322–34, 464–68.

Warren-Adams Letters: Being Chiefly a Correspondence among John Adams, Samuel Adams, and James Warren, 1778–1814. Volumes 1 and 2. Massachusetts Historical Society, 1925.

Warren Family Letters and Papers: 1763–1814. 2 volumes. Charles Warren, ed. Pilgrim Hall Museum, Plymouth, MA.

Washington, George. *The Papers of George Washington: Colonial Series.* 10 volumes. W. W. Abbott, Dorothy Twohig, and Philander D. Chase, eds. Charlottesville: University Press of Virginia, 1983–1995.

————. *Writings.* John Rhodehamel, ed. New York: New American Library, 1997.

————. *The Writings of George Washington.* Volumes 7, 14, 17, 19, 20, and 26. John C. Fitzpatrick, ed. Washington, D.C.: U.S. Government Printing Office, 1931–1944.

————. "Letters from Headquarters, Feb. 16, 1779." *The Writings of George Washington from the Original Manuscript Sources, 1745–1799.* John C. Fitzpatrick, ed. American Memory Historical Collections, Library of Congress, Washington, D.C.

Webb, Watson J. *Reminiscences of General Samuel B. Webb.* New York: Globe Stationery & Company, 1882.

Weig, Melvin J., and Vera B. Craig. *Morristown National Historical Park, New Jersey: A Military Capital of the American Revolution.* Historical Handbook Series, no. 7. Washington, D.C.: National Park Service, 1950, repr. 1961.

Wharton, Anne Hollingsworth. *Through Colonial Doorways.* Philadelphia: J. B. Lippincott Company, 1893.

Wilson, Barry K. *Benedict Arnold: A Traitor in Our Midst.* Montreal: McGill-Queen's University Press, 2001.

Wister, Sally. *Sally Wister's Journal, a True Narrative: Being a Quaker Maiden's Account of Her Experiences with Officers of the Continental Army, 1777–1778.* Bedford, MA: Applewood Books, 1902, repr. from the original.

Printed in the United States
By Bookmasters